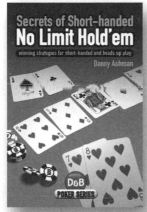
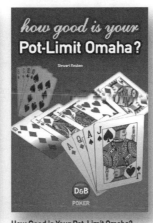

Professional Middle Limit Hold'em

Real Play: Hand by Hand

Tristan Steiger

www.dandbpoker.com

First published in 2009 by D & B Publishing

Copyright © 2009 Tristan Steiger

British Library Cataloguing-in-Publication Data

A catalogue record for this book is available from the British Library.

ISBN: 978 1 904468 47 9

All sales enquiries should be directed to D&B Publishing:
e-mail: info@dandbpoker.com,
Website: www.dandbpoker.com

Cover design by Horatio Monteverde.
Printed and bound in the US.

Contents

Part 2: Theory

Foreword

Since the beginning of the new millennium poker has experienced an unprecedented boom, triggered by the invention of the in-table camera that makes it possible for the TV viewer to see the hole cards. Before the use of the 'mini-cams' poker was only rarely shown on TV.

Poker is a complex game but if you can see everybody's hole cards it becomes mostly trivial. Therefore, after having watched several poker episodes many viewers fall victim to the mistake that they are now experts. Then they flock to the card rooms and a rude awakening awaits them.

I like to watch poker on TV but I regard it as what it is: entertainment. That's why the TV stations air poker. They don't want to improve your poker skills; they want to entertain you. If you watch poker on TV for this reason, that's fine, but you are misguided if you think it will help your game. The truth is, no matter how often you watch these poker shows, it will not make you a top player, and not even a good one.

There are two main reasons why what you see on TV will not help your game. First, playing poker without seeing everyone's hole cards is a completely different game. Second, what is shown on TV is of very little relevance to most people's play.

Most poker shows are from large-tournament play. When the World Series of Poker started in 1970 there were six entrants, all of them top professional poker players. Today the major tournaments have thousands of entrants. Those that make it to the final table are not necessarily the best, but are often the luckiest players. The thousands of hands captured are edited so only the most interesting hands are shown[1]–and, certainly, the hands aren't chosen for their instructive value.

The TV networks now show high-stakes cash games as well. It's definitively interesting to see a player raising $100,000, but there are a couple of things to consider. Only a few players have the wherewithal to play in a $300-$600-$1,200 no-limit hold'em game. Besides the fact that the players are paid to participate, for most of them being in front of the camera is a huge boost both to their ego and to their degree of fame. Thus, their market value goes up and they can negotiate even more lucrative commercial agreements.

The producers of these high-stakes poker shows are not interested in showing how poker is played on an expert level; what they want is a lot of action to attract viewers. So the producers always make sure that there are some loose-aggressive players like Daniel Negreanu, Sammy Farha, Gus Hansen or Mike Matusow at the table. If everyone played like Doyle Brunson or Barry Greenstein, there wouldn't be much of a game. Hence, what you see on TV bears scant resemblance to a real high-stakes game and even less to the poker game at which the average player sits.

One of the attractions of hold'em poker is that, on the surface, it's a very simple game. There are no complex rules or procedures, and anyone who has ever seen a deck of cards can understand how the game is played in about five minutes. Though the rules are simple and the players' options are limited (check, fold, call and raise), poker is not easy to master. It takes time, dedication and the will to learn. If you have the desire to improve your game, then this book can help you. Its purpose is twofold: to show you how winning middle-limit hold'em is really played and to help you to reflect on some concepts and strategies in poker.

The first part of the book shows you every hand I played for one week in a $30-60 limit hold'em game in Las Vegas, Nevada, against a variety of

---

[1] For instance, in 2006 Chip Reese and Andy Bloch battled seven hours heads-up for the inaugural World Series of Poker H.O.R.S.E. title. Only a couple of hands were shown on TV.

players whose skill ranged from negligible to considerable. Nothing has been altered, cut or manipulated. You see the hands as I played them. (The names of most players have been changed to protect their identities.)

The second part discusses some selected theoretical and practical aspects of the game. An important emphasis is on the crucial difference between low- and middle-limit games. Few of us will ever play in the ultra-high-stakes games as seen on TV. However, to move up to middle limits is a realistic goal. Therefore, I outline the characteristics of middle-limit games, and I explain how they differ from the low limits and what it takes to be successful at these games.

This book is not for beginners. It will not explain how the game is played and will not teach you elementary poker principles. It's assumed that the reader has some playing experience and some basic understanding of the game. If you have trouble with the rules, or you don't understand position, outs and pot odds, then you should read one of the many introductory hold'em books first[2].

Two types of readers will profit most from this book. First there are the low-limit players intending to make the transition to middle-limit games, and second are the middle-limit players struggling to beat the game.

Although I had been thinking of writing this book for a while, it was Lewis Lorton (Columbia, Maryland, USA) who finally pushed me towards writing it. This book would not have been possible without the time he spent reading and commenting on its various iterations. His responses helped me to present my thoughts and ideas more clearly and compellingly, for which I am deeply grateful.

---

[2] A good starting point is Byron Jacobs, *Beginner's Guide to Limit Hold'em*, D&B Publishing 2005.

Part 1: Practice

 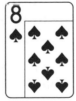

Introduction

When I was playing low-limit hold'em at the Mirage in Las Vegas, I often wondered about the difference between the games I played and middle-limit games[3]; how good are the players in these games, how do they play, what do they know that I don't know? In contrast to high-limit games that are held away from the public gaze (and are mostly mixed games anyway), you can observe the action of the middle-limit games from the rail.

I observed these games fairly often, and usually no one objected. You can learn a lot by watching the action, but you only get reliable information when there is a showdown or when someone shows his hand. However, most hands are folded before the showdown even by loose players, so you don't know what the player had and why he folded.

Before I stepped up to middle-limit play, I often wished for a book that provided a hand-by-hand analysis of real play, and not just some isolated examples, to give me an idea of what constitutes good middle-limit play. I

---

[3] What low-, middle- and high-limit games are is a matter of definition. In this book I define low-limit games to have a small blind less than $10, middle-limit games to have a small blind more than $10 and less then $100, and high-limit games to have a small blind greater than $100. E.g., typical low-limit games are $3-6 or $6-12 and typical middle-limit games are $20-40 or $40-80.

16

wrote this book to fill that gap. For one week I recorded every hand I played in the $30-60 limit hold'em game at the Bellagio in Las Vegas.

You will see every hand I was dealt and how I played it. Nothing (except some player names) has been made up. In the heat of the battle I might have neglected to record a bet or fold in a multiway pot, but besides these inadvertent errors you can view the hands exactly as they were played, with nothing altered.

The rules of limit hold'em are pretty much the same everywhere. However, some procedures differ from one card room to another.

Unlike most low-limit games, the Bellagio $30-60 game is not a raked game but a time-fee game. Every half-hour it costs you $6 to play. A new player must post an amount equal to the big blind or wait for the big blind[4]. He can post in any position except the button. The game is played ten-handed or less. One bet and four raises are allowed on any street, hence it can cost $150 to see the flop. The number of raises is unlimited once the hand becomes heads-up.

I will describe all the hands I played, including those folded before the flop. I will usually not comment on these hands, since it's generally obvious why I folded. I use the following abbreviations to indicate the position in which I folded pre-flop:

BB	Big blind
SB	Small blind
B	Button
CO	Cutoff (the position before the button)
UTG	Under the gun (player to the left of the BB who acts first in pre-flop play)

The abbreviation 'RIF' indicates one or several raises in front of me. That helps you to understand why I folded a hand or didn't get a free play in the big blind. Notice that a full game does not imply eight free hands per

---

[4] The exception is if you come from a broken game or a must-move game.

round. Often players are changing seats, taking a break or sitting out hands. Thus it's possible to be in early position, having previously been in the cutoff seat.

For clarity and reference reasons, the hands are numbered within each session. For example, "1/45" denotes the 45th hand in the first session.

I will relate my thought process for each hand I played. Just take my explanations as a guideline and don't accept them blindly. Often there are several reasonable courses of action, and the fact that you would have played differently doesn't imply that you are wrong and I am right. Make sure that you haven't overlooked anything and that you have a good reason for your decision. I'll tell you why I did what I did, but you may come up with a different play for a better reason.

Chapter 1

Sessions 1-8

Session 1: Bellagio, Monday, September 5, 8:40 p.m.

The Bellagio poker room is busier than usual for a Monday, but not as much as I expected. It's Labor Day, but most tourists have already left town. Four $30-60 tables are in progress and no seat is available. Lemlem, the floorperson, puts my name on the list and I scout the games. All look reasonably good. After 15 minutes my name is called and Lemlem points to table 28. The 2 seat is open, one of my favorite seats[5]. Is this a good omen? I let the button pass and post behind it.

Until recently you had only two options when sitting down at a table. You could wait for the big blind or post immediately to get a hand. Now you have two additional options: you can post between the small blind and the button or you can 'buy' the button, which means you post both blinds and get the button on the next hand. When you only post the big blind, the button passes you the next hand and you are one to the right of the button (which is often called the cutoff seat). Which of these options is the best?

Most players "post between" and want to talk you into doing the same (often assisted by the dealer) by explaining that this way "you get an extra

---

[5] I like the end seats (seats 2, 3, 8 and 9) because they give you the best vantage point from which to observe the other players.

hand". That's true; if you post behind the button you lose one hand. But you're in the worst possible position when you post between, whereas posting behind the button puts you in the second-best position. No one can convince me that the extra hand gives me an advantage over posting in a much more favorable position. Posting behind the button is undoubtedly the best option.

Session 1: Hands 1-2

I post and am dealt **Q-5** in the cutoff seat. Two players in front of me call, I check, and both blinds play, so we see the flop five-handed. The flop comes A-6-J. A player in front of me bets; I fold quickly.

Next hand is **K-7**, an easy fold.

Session 1: Hand 3

Some people are walking, so I'm already in early position. The player in front of me raises. I hold 9♦-9♣.

Pocket nines are tricky to play against a raise. A reraise or a fold may be in order, depending on the raiser. I look over to the 10 seat. I have never seen that player before. I can't fold 9-9 because many players raise with all sorts of hands. Having no idea what this raise means, I reluctantly call. One player behind me calls, the small blind calls, and the big blind folds. Four players, pot $270.

The flop is 6♣-7♦-8♦. This looks good—no overcards and an open-ended straight draw—but it is extremely dangerous. The small blind and the original raiser both check, I bet my overpair, the player behind me reraises, and the small blind makes it three bets. The original raiser folds. What shall I do? It makes no sense to escalate the betting; I'm not sure if I hold the best hand, and neither player will fold to a reraise. On the other hand, my holding is too good to fold. Even if I'm currently behind, I have an open-ended straight draw, although it is not very strong. This is tempered by the fact that there is a flush draw, and if another player holds a 9 or 10-9, I'm drawing at half the pot. I call, as does the player behind me. Three players, pot $540.

The turn card is A♣. The small blind goes all-in for 10 bucks. The ace is a bad card for me, but I don't think it has hit one of the other players. I call, as does the player behind me. Three players, one is all-in, pot $570.

The river is 9♠ (board: 6♣-7♦-8♦-A♣-9♠). Incredible. I hold pocket nines but the last card I want see is another nine! I check and the player behind me bets. In all likelihood I'm beat, but the pot is too big to fold my set. I call; he shows me 5-6 and takes the side pot. The main pot goes to the small blind with 10♣-7♣. Though I still had the best hand on the turn[6], the way the hand developed there was no way I could win. The only possibility might have been to reraise before the flop, but someone who is willing to call two bets might as well call three bets with inferior holdings, something I have seen many times before.

Session 1: Hands 4-5

The next hand I'm already under-the-gun. I fold **Q-7**.

When you have the big blind you usually hope for a free play. You never know; you might flop a big hand and surprise the other player with a "big blind special". But a free play is rare at the $30-60 level, as most pots are raised. This time it's three bets when the action comes to me with **Q-J**. Usually that's not a bad holding in the big blind, and I would call a raise, but not a reraise. Clear fold.

Session 1: Hand 6

I'm dealt **5-3** in the small blind. Two players have limped, as do I. To see why I called with 5-3 offsuit, though it doesn't get much worse than that, you must understand the structure of the $30-60 game. I wouldn't have called in a $20-40 game because the small blind is only half the big blind (small blind $10, big blind $20). In the $30-60 game the small blind is two-thirds of the big blind (small blind $20, big blind $30), so it costs you only $10 to play.

David Sklansky says that if the small blind is two-thirds of the big blind, you should play any two cards if there is no raise[7]. I have no reason to

---

[6] I had not only the best hand on the turn, I was a big favorite to win the hand as well; 9♦-9♣: 59.52%, 10♣-7♣: 28.57%, 6♥-5♦: 11.90%.

[7] See David Sklansky/Mason Malmuth, *Hold'em Poker for Advanced Players*, 1999, p. 45.

doubt Sklansky because his math is sound. It's just too cheap not to play. Even if there is only one caller, you get 8-to-1 odds[8]. No two cards are that much of an underdog, especially in an unraised pot. Amazingly, I even see very good players routinely fold the small blind for just one chip.

Question 1/1:

Calling with a weak hand out of the small blind is mathematically correct, but this doesn't mean that your call is automatic. What other factors must you consider?

Back to the actual hand, we are four players, pot $120. The flop is K-10-5. A king is a dangerous card, a ten more so. I'm definitely not betting into this flop with bottom pair. I might bet a flop of K-5-4 or possibly K-7-5 and proceed cautiously. There is a bet and I give up.

Session 1: Hands 7-12

I fold the next several hands: **4-2** on the button, **3-3** in the cutoff seat, then **A-9**, **7-5s**, **4-4** and **5-2s** under-the-gun.

Session 1: Hand 13

I have the big blind when a new player posts behind the button. A middle-position player calls, the new player in the cutoff seat checks, and the small blind calls, as I do with A♣-4♣.

Four players, pot $120. The flop comes A♠-9♠-6♠. I've flopped top pair but with a weak kicker, and there is a possible flush on board. The small blind checks. How to proceed is far from obvious. I'm almost certainly beat if a player holds an ace, and someone may have made a flush. That speaks against betting. On the other hand, if I'm best, I can't let a player with a small spade draw for free. I bet, both players behind me fold and the small blind calls. Two players, pot $180.

---

[8] There is $80 in the pot ($30 from the caller, $30 from the big blind and $20 from the small blind) and it costs you $10 to play.

The turn is the A♦. The small blind checks. It's time to analyze the small blind's holdings. He is an Asian guy who likes to play a lot of hands and go too far with them. Still, I doubt that he would chase with a nine or six on this board. He either has an ace and is afraid of the possible flush, or he has a flush draw (probably the king or queen of spades). A bet is mandatory now. If he has slowplayed a flush and check-raises me, I still have 10 outs[9] to beat him. I bet, he calls. Two players, pot $300.

The river is the 3♥ (board: A♠-9♠-6♠-A♦-3♥). He checks; I bet; he folds. He doesn't show his hand, but what else but a high spade could he have?

Session 1: Hand 14

I call from the small blind with **K-5** in an unraised pot. Five-handed, the flop comes 6♦-7♥-3♣.

It's tempting to bet the gutshot and hope that everyone will fold. But that's not going to happen. Since the cards are low and close together, you can bet that most of the other players will have either a) a strong hand (like a straight or two pair); b) a draw (like 9-8); or c) overcards. The chance that everyone will fold to my bet is practically zero. If the turn is not a four or a king, I'll wish I hadn't bet. And if there is heavy action after my bet, I'll have to muck my hand, losing one bet. I check. As expected, there is a bet and a raise, so I fold.

Session 1: Hands 15-16

I fold the next two hands, **6-2** on the button and **K-3** in the cutoff seat.

Session 1: Hand 17

It's folded to me. I'm pleased to see Q♦-Q♥ and I raise. The button and both blinds call. Four players, pot $240.

The flop is 6♣-8♥-K♣. Both blinds check. The king on board is awkward but better than an ace (lots of players will stay with A-x, but not K-x). I must bet here because I don't want to give a free card with what may be

---

[9] 1 ace, 3 fours, 3 nines and 3 sixes to make a full house.

the best hand. If someone holds a king, I will sooner or later hear from him. I bet, the button calls, and both blinds fold. Two players, pot $300.

The turn is 9♥. I have no idea what the button could have. I saw him play a lot of weak hands. He could have a king, an eight, a six, a flush draw, an open-ender (9-7) or a gutshot (5-4 or 10-9). All in all, I think I'm still the favorite. I bet; he calls. Two players, pot $420.

The river card is 3♠ (board: 6♣-8♥-K♣-9♥-3♠). The trey at the end changes nothing. If I was in the lead on the turn, I still have the best hand. I bet, he folds.

The bet at the end is crucial. If he has a king you lose that bet anyway. If you don't bet, your opponent will realize that you don't have a king (remember the river is not a threatening card) and will bet behind you. The pot is too big not to call with pocket queens. The difference is when he is chasing you with an eight or six thinking you might only have two high cards such as A-Q or A-J. If you don't bet, he will gladly check behind you and you lose that bet at the end.

Session 1: Hands 18-19

In middle position I fold **K-5**. Then under-the-gun I pick up K♠-K♦ and raise the pot. The player right behind me, two middle-position players and the cutoff call.

We see the flop five-handed (pot $350): 8♥-6♥-J♠. That's good for my kings. However, with a flush draw and two open-ended straight draws (10-9, 7-5) possible, the board is dangerous. Naturally, I would like to eliminate as many players as possible, but being first to act makes this difficult. Since I was the pre-flop raiser, checking to try for a check-raise is a dangerous undertaking. The last thing I want is to give everyone behind me a free card, so I bet; all four opponents call. Still five players, pot $500.

The turn is 5♠. Not a bad card. It gives someone with 7-4 a straight, but it's very unlikely one of my opponents called a raise with that hand. Being confident that I have the best hand, I bet. The player right behind me calls, the two middle-position players fold and then, to my surprise, the cutoff raises. He is a young guy, maybe 25 years old. I haven't played with him before and I have no read on him. I have no idea what he could have, but confronted with a raise, I must quickly determine this.

If someone raises on the turn, the first thing to do is to look at how the turn card could have helped him. The only possible hands that could have profited from the turn are 5-5 and 6-5. Both hands are possible but unlikely. To me it looks like the flop has hit him big and, being in last position, he slowplayed his hand. With two pair on the flop he would have raised, thus I put him on a set of jacks, eights or sixes. A bluff or semi-bluff makes little sense because there is a caller, and the chance that we both would fold to his raise is minuscule. I don't like it but I fold my kings. Two players, pot $800.

The river is 4♦ (board: 8♥-6♥-J♠-5♠-4♦). Both players check. The cutoff shows A-K and takes the pot with ace high! I'm completely shocked to see that hand. I misread the situation and gave the cutoff too much credit. He played the hand horribly and I played it even worse. Of course, if the cutoff knew that the caller had just a draw, I had him beat, and I would lay down my hand to his raise, then he made a world-class play. I doubt that was the case. I outguessed myself, tried to be smart by making a big laydown, and therefore forfeited a pot I should never have lost.

Session 1: Hands 20-40

Nothing happens for the next several hands, giving me time to recover from by bad play: **Q-2** (BB, RIF), **10-3** (SB, RIF), **A-6** (B, RIF), **8-3s** (CO), **Q-3**, **10-7s**, **Q-8**, **Q-2** (UTG), **J-3** (BB, RIF), **10-6** (SB, RIF), **7-3** (B), **K-Q** (CO, RIF), **8-7s** (RIF), **J-9**, **10-8**, **9-6**, **10-8** (UTG), **K-7** (BB, RIF), **J-10** (SB, RIF), **7-6** (B, RIF), **8-6s**.

Session 1: Hand 41

I call with **K♥-10♣** in the hijack seat after the player in front of me limps. The big blind gets a free play. Three players, pot $110.

Flop: 4♥-5♥-6♥. The big blind bets, the middle-position player calls, and I call with the second nut-flush draw. Three players, pot $200.

The turn card is 9♣. The big blind bets and the middle-position player folds. With position and a good draw a semi-bluff is often a good play. But I think the big blind probably has either a made hand or a flush draw. In neither case would he fold to my bet; hence, I call. Two players, pot $320.

The river makes things interesting: 8♥ (board 4♥-5♥-6♥-9♣-8♥). The big blind checks and I check behind. Angry because he didn't draw the last bet out of me, the big blind turns over A♠-7♥ for the straight flush. Though I lost, at least this time I made a good play.

You may ask why I checked behind. Couldn't it be that the big blind had no flush? I guess many players would have bet. The correct play is quite straightforward. I'm behind if my opponent has a straight flush or an ace-high flush. It's possible that he would check both hands: with the straight flush to trap me (from the way I played the hand it was quite obvious that I had a flush draw) or with the ace-high flush because he was afraid of a possible straight flush. Did I know that he had a better flush than me? Of course not! He would have played a set or straight the same. The point is that he likely wouldn't call my bet if he was beat . What hands would I bet if I didn't have a flush? Without a flush I would happily check behind him.

You might object. Couldn't my opponent have had a hand such as J♥-10♥, giving him a flush that got counterfeited on the river, in which case I should bet? The objection is valid. First, betting is tricky. He would definitely call with a jack-high flush (probably with any flush), but if he raised I'd be in an awkward position. The pot was simply too big to comfortably fold the third nuts. Second, I was quite sure he didn't hold a counterfeited flush. When the 8♥ hit the board at the end he checked immediately and showed no signs that he was worried in the least. When an average player like my opponent has a non-nut flush on the turn, he of course knows that he doesn't want to see another flush card. But when that flush card shows up on the river it usually takes him a moment to determine how that affects his hand and what to do about it. If he has the A♥ or the 7♥ he can act immediately. The same is true should he hold a set on the turn. In that case he is hoping that the board will pair at the end. When the fourth flush card shows up it's clear that he can no longer bet, so there is nothing to think about. Hence, I was convinced that my opponent had either a better flush or a set (maybe a straight), and in both cases checking behind is the correct play.

Session 1: Hands 42-48

I fold **9-6** in early position and **5-4s** under the gun.

In the big blind I get a free play with **8-7s**. Five players, flop: Q-A-J. I quickly fold when there is a bet.

Next hand it's four bets to me in the small blind. With **9-7** there is not much to think about. Then I'm dealt **8-4** on the button and **9-5** in the cutoff. On the next hand it's folded to me and I raise with **A-K**. Only the small blind calls. The flop is excellent: K-Q-5. The small blind checks, I bet and he calls. The turn brings another five. My opponent checks; I bet and win the pot.

Session 1: Hands 49-51

I fold the next two hands, **A-9** and **9-2**, then I pick up another **A-K** three spots behind the big blind. The under-the-gun player folds, the next player limps and I raise. Only the limper calls. Two players, pot $170.

The flop is Q-Q-5. The limper checks, I bet and he calls (pot $230). The turn is a 10. My opponent checks again. I don't want to give a free card if I'm ahead. On the other hand, the flop makes calling tough if you don't have anything. So the most likely hands for my opponent are a queen and a pocket pair. I'm drawing close to dead if he has a queen; a free card benefits me if he has a pair. My opponent is not a very sophisticated player, which means he fits exactly into the category of players who always wait for the turn to check-raise if they flop trips. I check. Still two players, pot $230.

Question 1/2

If my opponent has a queen, how much of an underdog am I to win the hand?

The river brings a 7 (board: Q-Q-5-10-7). His bet comes as no surprise. I call and he shows Q♥-J♥. Okay, my call is debatable. The point is this: If you check behind on the turn, many players automatically bet the river. You showed weakness by checking the turn in position, which for these players is an invitation to bet the river no matter what they have. Therefore, you have to call a fair percentage of the time if you can beat a bluff; otherwise your opponent's play shows an immediate profit.

Session 1: Hands 52-56

In early position I fold **5-2**, and then **K-8s** under the gun.

On the next hand there is an early-position raise and everyone folds to me in the big blind. I quickly fold **A-9**. This is not a hand you want to play heads-up and out-of-position against an early-position raiser.

In the small blind I fold **10-6** to a raise.

Next hand I have the button and things get interesting. The UTG player limps, the player behind him raises and the next player calls, as do a middle-position player and the cutoff. I have 6♥-6♦ on the button. Since the original limper will definitely call, there are five players, giving me pot odds of 5-to-1. You are about a 7.5-to-1 underdog to flop a set when you have a pocket pair. But with that many players, I will certainly win another 2.5 big bets should I flop a set, and there are still the two blinds that could increase the pot odds even further. Given the current odds and the implied odds, it would be a crime to fold. I call, both blinds fold and the limper calls. Six players, pot $410.

The flop comes 8♠-6♠-8♦. The limper checks, the original raiser bets, the player behind him raises and the middle- position player and the cutoff both call. There is no question that I hold the best hand. Only 8-8 and 8-6 beat me. I usually don't slowplay big hands on the flop, especially when there is multiway action, but if I escalate the betting we might lose some players that are already drawing dead with straight- and flush- draws, and one of the early-position players may raise again. Hence, I just call. Now, the under-the-gun player who had just checked the flop makes it three bets. The flop bettor and the raiser both fold and the remaining three players, including me, call. We are down to four players, pot $860.

The turn card is 2♦. The under-the-gun player bets, the middle-position player folds, the cutoff calls and I raise. The under-the-gun player reraises and the cutoff calls again. Time to consider what my two remaining opponents may hold. Fortunately, it's not too difficult. The under-the-gun player must have an eight. An overpair is highly unlikely as he only check-called before the flop, and with a paired board he would probably not play that strongly. The cutoff just called all the way, which looks like a draw, most likely a spade-flush draw. What is the best course of action here?

I'm concerned that if I raise again the cutoff will realize that he is drawing dead and fold his hand. This would cost me the opportunity to win one or two additional bets from him if a spade comes on the river and he makes his flush. If we only look at the cutoff seat, calling is probably better than betting. I've put the UTG player on trips but not a full house or quads[10]. If I raise, he'll probably call the turn and check-call the river. If I just call, he will bet the river, giving me the chance to raise. In both cases I win two big bets. The advantage of just calling is that I can take a cheap look at the river, which will enable me to save money if he fills up.

I'm pretty sure I know what he has. There are only three possible holdings that an average player like him would have called with before the flop: A-8s, 9-8s and 8-7s. However, these holdings are not equally likely. If I had to put numbers on it, I would say there is 5% chance that he has 8-7s, 10% for 9-8s and 85% for A-8s. To the average player a hand like A-8s is much more tempting than medium suited connectors from early position. Thus, if an ace would fall on the river my alarm bells would go off. Since calling looks a little better than raising, I call. Three players, pot $1,400.

Unfortunately, the river is 4♥ (board: 8♠-6♠-8♦-2♦-4♥). As expected, the cutoff folds quickly to the under-the-gun player's bet. I raise and the bettor calls. I show my pocket sixes and my opponent mucks his hand. Too bad—now we don't know if he really had A-8s.

Session 1: Hands 57-66

J-7s (CO, RIF), K-2, A-3, A-6 (UTG), A-4s (UTG), 9-4s (BB, RIF), 9-4 (SB, RIF), 10-2 (B), Q-7 (CO).

After two players have limped, I call with Q♦-10♦ in middle position. Four-handed we see the flop: A♣-6♠-A♦. One of the early-position players bets and I fold.

---

[10] If you ask why I don't consider that my opponent may have quads my answer is: It's just too unlikely to worry about it. You can't play successful poker if you constantly fear that your opponent has the nuts. Yes, I have flopped a full house when one of my opponent made quads. If it happens, it happens. Use this as a guideline: If you flop a monster vs. an even better hand and you don't lose a lot of money, there is something wrong with your game.

Session 1: Hands 67-70

10-6, **A-6**, 7-4 (UTG).

Session 1: Hands 71-72

I'm dealt **10♠-9♠** in the big blind. There is a raise with two callers. Pot odds of over 7-to-1 provide enough incentive to see the flop with that nice drawing hand. The flop is not much help: 3♣-6♠-Q♦. The original raiser bets the flop and I have no choice but to fold.

I pick up **J♠-10♠** in the small blind. Unfortunately it's three bets to me, so I fold.

On the button I look at **K♣-10♣**. An early middle-position player raised and there are no callers. I would make it three bets with this hand against a cutoff raise, but it's very unlikely I have the best hand against a raise from this position. Folding is the correct play here.

Session 1: Hands 73-92

7-2 (CO), **A-9**, 5-4, 7-6, 8-6, **A-8** (UTG), **J-4** (BB, RIF), 9-5 (SB, RIF), **K-J** (B, RIF), **K-5** (CO).

We are down to 8 players. **8-4**, **J-9s**, 10-6, **Q-J** (UTG), J-4s (BB, RIF, UTG shows Q-Q because nobody called), **9-6** (SB, RIF), **9-5** (B), **A-8** (CO, RIF), K-9, 6-3s.

Session 1: Hand 93

Since we are only 8 players at the moment, I'm already in second position. I peek at my hand and see **Q♥-J♥**. Ten-handed I would usually fold that hand (depending on the nature of the table), but here I call and hope some players will limp behind me. The player to my left raises and everyone else folds. I call. This is the worst-case situation. It's heads-up and I'm out of position with what is likely the worst hand, definitely not a +EV situation. Two players, pot $170.

To my delight the flop is K♥-Q♣-Q♠. I check with the intention to check-raise. My opponent disappoints me by checking behind (pot $170). The turn is the 8♦. Trying to check-raise again is too risky. I already lost a bet on the flop. I bet and my opponent calls. Two players, pot $290. The river is 3♠. At least I get a call from my opponent. He shows A-K. By playing very cautiously he lost the absolute minimum.

Session 1: Hands 94-104

A-9 (UTG), J-9 (BB, RIF), 9-7s (SB, RIF), 9-8 (B, RIF).

Barry Tanenbaum, a well-known poker theorist who writes articles for a poker magazine and has written several poker books, moves into the three seat. J-4 (CO), 8-7, Q-7, 7-3, K-3, 5-2 (UTG).

A middle-position player raises, the small blind calls and I call with 3-3 in the big blind. Three players, pot $180. The flop is 6-8-Q. It's checked around. The turn is an 8. The original raiser bets, and the small blind and I both fold.

Session 1: Hands 105-107

9-2 (SB, RIF).

It's folded to me on the button with 10-7. I would only steal with this hand if I knew that the blinds tend to fold. Since I don't know much about the blinds, I take the safe route and fold.

The next hand I'm in the cutoff seat. Three players limp and I call with 10♣-9♣. The button folds and both blinds call. We look at the flop six-handed (pot $180): 8♣-8♦-Q♥. One of the early limpers bets and we all fold. I had a gutshot and a backdoor flush draw. With a hand like that, pot odds of 7-to-1 looked about right, but the board was paired and there were several players to act behind me. Folding is reasonable.

Session 1: Hands 108-112

Q-9s (RIF), 9-5.

The table is full again. A-7s, 5-2s (UTG).

A middle-position player raises; the cutoff and button call. I call in the big blind with 10-9. Usually I would fold—it depends on the players in the hand. None of the players involved seems too experienced, hence the borderline decision to call. Four players, pot $260.

The flop makes me wish I had folded: A-3-5. The original raiser bets and only the button calls. I muck quickly. On the turn the betting escalates. When the smoke clears at the end it becomes apparent that we have a set-over-set situation. The original raiser holds A-A and the button 3-3. I don't have much sympathy for the button since he made a bad play pre-flop by calling a raise with a small pair and was punished for it.

Session 1: Hands 113-117

8-6 (SB, RIF), **K-J** (B, RIF), **8-2s** (CO), **K-7s.**

10-4s. Though I fold, this emerges as an interesting hand. The under-the-gun player limps, a middle-position player raises, Barry Tanenbaum in late-middle position reraises, and Suzanne, a lady who regularly plays $100-200, calls two bets cold on the button. The other two players call. Four players see the flop (pot $410): 2♣-3♦-4♥. It's checked to Barry, who bets. All three players call (pot $530). The turn is 5♥. Barry bets, Suzanne calls and the two other players fold. Two players, pot $650. The river card is 6♠, making a straight on the board. Both players check. Barry reveals Q-Q and Suzanne turns over A♦J♦.

> **Question 1/3:**
>
> How would you rate Barry's and Suzanne's play throughout the hand?

Let's analyze this hand. Q-Q is strong enough to reraise, so there is nothing wrong with Barry's pre-flop play. I don't like Suzanne's call. You can call a raise with A-Js in position, but I wouldn't call two bets cold with it. She can count on the original raiser calling, but the limper will probably not call two bets cold. Suzanne has a clear fold.

On the flop Barry has no reason to believe he doesn't have the best hand. His bet is mandatory. Suzanne has a gutshot, two overcards and a back-door flush. That looks like a lot of outs and a clear call, but it's not that simple. If Barry has an ace, then she is only drawing at half the pot with the gutshot. The value of the overcards is completely unclear. Suppose Barry has A-K, a very likely hand. In this case not only the gutshot is crippled; the ace is dead as well. The worst case is if Barry has aces. That would mean Suzanne has four outs to split the pot and a backdoor flush draw. One last point to consider: There are still two players behind Suzanne who could check-raise. Now the flop call no longer looks so sensible.

The turn brings a horror card for Barry, as any ace or six now makes a straight, leaving the queens drawing dead for the whole pot. The bet is courageous though it helps that two players before have already checked. Suzanne only calls. She probably reasons that if Barry has an ace, then the raise serves no purpose. If he has an overpair she might get another bet at the end.

There are problems with that reasoning. First, if Barry doesn't have an ace, he probably won't call on the river. If he has no intention to call the river, Suzanne is basically giving Barry a free shot to split the pot. Second, Barry probably has seven outs to tie her (any ace and any six). Third, the pot is too big to chance a mistake that could cost you half the pot. There is no question that a raise would immediately have won the pot for Suzanne.

Session 1: Hands 118-122

10-2, 8-5, A-3, K-10 (UTG).

The 7 seat raises in late position. I call in the big blind with **A-9**. You may recall that I folded A-9 in the big blind against a raise before (hand 1/54). This situation is different. It's a late-position raise from a passive player (the one who lost with A-K against my Q-Js, hand 1/93). Hence, he has a wider range of starting hands than an early-position player and he doesn't get full value from his hand. Two players, pot $140.

Flop: A-Q-7. I check, he bets and I call. Raising instead of calling is an option. But I will probably only get action when I'm behind. If I'm ahead, I don't want him to fold because with that flop he can't have many outs. Two players, pot $200.

On the turn a 4 falls. I check and he checks behind. His check is a clear indication that I have the best hand. With the exception of a queen, I will bet any river card. The dealer turns over a J (board: A-Q-7-4-J). I bet; he calls and shows K-J. The jack at the end was a lucky card for me. It didn't complete his gutshot and gave him enough of a hand to call my bet. Looking back, checking the turn and giving him a free card was a mistake, but it was the consequence of my just checking the flop. I didn't know if his flop bet was for value or to take down the pot. Therefore, betting the turn was too risky. I would have been in an awkward position had he raised.

Session 1: Hands 123-130

10-8 (SB, RIF), **Q-3** (B), 6-2 (CO), **A-3**, J-8s, 8-7 (UTG).

The 3 seat raises and gets four callers. I would call with many hands in this situation out of the big blind, but **Q-2** is not strong enough.

On the next hand only the 4 seat calls; I complete the small blind with **K-6**. The big blind gets a free play. At the end the board reads 9-9-Q-3-Q and I win with king high!

Session 1: Hands 131-142

Q-6 (B), **Q-6** (CO), **Q-8**, 4-3s, J-3, 10-3, K-8, **Q-7** (UTG), 7-3 (BB, RIF).

The button raises and I lay down **K-4s** in the small blind (button has 8-8, big blind wins with A-J). I fold **8-2s** on the button.

I pick up **A-A** in the cutoff seat. An early-position player has raised and I make it three bets. We see the flop heads-up: 4♦-6♦-8♦. My opponent checks. Having the ace of diamonds, this is a pretty good flop for my hand. I bet. Unfortunately, my opponent folds and shows K-Q (no diamond).

Session 1: Hands 143-148

Q-7s, J-7s, J-2, 4-2s, 9-2 (UTG).

In the big blind I get a free play with **Q♠-9♠**. Six players see the flop: K♦-J♥-6♦. I fold immediately to a bet and a call.

Session 1: Hands 149-155

6-5 (SB, RIF), **A-6** (B, RIF), **Q-8** (CO), **Q-J**, 7-6.

Under-the-gun I'm dealt **J♦-10♦**. Normally in middle-limit you are better off folding this hand in early position, but there are a lot of loose players at the table. Most pots have been multiway lately, so I call. My opponents don't disappoint me; I get four callers (pot $150). The flop creates a lot of possibilities: 9♣-9♦-A♦. Both blinds check and I bet my flush draw. All fold.

Next hand I chop with **A-9** in the big blind.

Session 1: Hands 156-159

K-7 (SB, RIF), **8-4s** (B), **J-5** (CO).

A middle-position player limps and I call behind with **Q♦-J♣**. Both blinds play. Four players, pot $120.

Flop: 5♦-A♦-K♦. The blinds check, the middle-position player bets, I call with the nut-flush draw and a gutshot, and both blinds fold. Two players, pot $180.

Turn: Q♥. My opponent checks. My bet is automatic (I don't want to give a king a free river card and make my opponent aware that he has the best hand). I win the hand[11].

Session 1: Hands 160-165

J-2, **10-8**, **Q-6**, **A-2** (UTG), **J-2** (BB, RIF).

Chico, an erratic player who suffers from FPS[12], limps from the 3 seat. Having **A-10** in the small blind, I throw in a $10 chip. Barry, sitting right behind me in the 8 seat (we have both changed seats), raises from the big blind. Chico and I call. The raise tells me I'm in trouble. Three players, pot $180.

The flop gives me some hope: 10-8-5. Though I have flopped top pair, top

---

[11] Most middle-limit players would have raised the flop to get a free card on the turn. I don't like that play in this situation. It's like telling your opponent, "I don't have a flush." My plan was to raise should my opponent bet the turn. That is a stronger play than the suspicious flop raise and gives you a much better chance to make a better hand fold.

[12] Fancy Player Syndrome, a term coined by Mike Caro (see *Caro's Fundamental Secrets of Poker*, 1991, p. 109).

kicker, my hand is vulnerable to overcards. Thus, I want to eliminate players as quickly as possible. So, what's the best course of action? If I check, Barry will bet and Chico will get 7-to-1 pot odds. With odds like that and a low flop, Chico will call with a lot of hands. I can check-raise, but it's quite unlikely that this will cause anyone to fold.

I can't get rid of Barry but I can make it tough for Chico to stay in the hand. I have played often enough with Barry that I'm sure he will raise when I come out betting in this situation. That will put a lot of pressure on Chico, especially because his call would not close the betting, opening him to my possible reraise. Therefore, betting instead of checking is the superior play. I bet and everything works as planned: Barry raises, Chico folds and I call. Two players, pot $300.

The turn brings a 6. Barry has either a pocket pair or a couple of high cards. In the latter case, I definitely don't want to give him a free card. I bet and Barry folds. Had I not bet, I would have given Barry a free card to beat me on the river.

Session 1: Hands 166-168

Q-7 (B), K-2 (CO).

Two spots to the right of the button I pick up **4-4**. There are already two limpers. Anticipating more limpers, I call. My assumption proves to be correct as six players see the flop: A-J-3. I fold to a bet.

Session 1: Hands 169-172

Q-6, 10-3s, Q-7s.

Under-the-gun I look at two **red kings** and raise the pot. Both blinds call. Three players, pot $180.

The dreaded ace comes on the flop: A♦-J♦-3♣. It's checked to me. Tough decision. I nearly always bet when I'm the pre-flop raiser, the pot is short-handed and it's checked to me. Here I figure, should I have the best hand, a free card can't hurt much. The exception is if someone has a diamond draw, but in this case I have a redraw with the king of diamonds if the turn completes the flush. The advantage of checking is that I probably lose less money if I'm beat, and one of the blinds might be induced to bluff the turn. I check. Still three players, pot $180.

The turn is another J. Again both blinds check. Looks like nobody has much, and taking down the pot would be nice, given the ugly board. I bet, the small blind folds and the big blind raises. I can't beat an ace and I can't beat a jack, hence the fold is easy. The big blind shows A-A. That ace on the flop saved me a lot of money.

Session 1: Hands 173-175

After folding **6-4** to a raise in the big blind, six players limp and I call with **7-6** in the small blind. The flop comes Q♦-K♦-10♣ and I'm done with the hand. I fold **K-9s** on the button since there is a raise in front of me.

Session 1: Hand 176

In the cutoff I pick up K♥-10♥. Since there are already three limpers and I have a drawing hand with some potential, I call. Barry calls behind me and the small blind surprisingly throws away his hand[13]. The pot is $200 and six players see the flop: Q♥-10♠-6♣. The first limper bets and everyone calls. Pot odds of 9-to-1 are enough to take another card off with middle pair plus backdoor flush and straight draws. Six players, pot $380.

Turn: 10♦. The flop bettor bets again. The next two players fold, I raise and Barry behind me makes it three bets. The remaining players fold and I call. Two players, pot $830.

The river is 4♠ (board: Q♥-10♠-6♣-10♦-4♠). What should I do? That Barry made it three bets on the turn means that he either has a ten or a full house. Of the possible hands he may hold, I can beat J-10, 10-9 and 10-8; I tie with K-10 and lose to A-10, Q-10 or 6-6[14]. Put another way, I beat 12 combinations, I tie three and I lose to 10 combinations. Being a favorite to have the best hand, should I bet? No! It's a common misconception that you should bet heads-up if you think you are a favorite. You can be an 80% favorite, but nevertheless you shouldn't bet if your opponent will

---

[13] He had pot odds of 20-to-1. A call is mandatory here regardless of the hand.

[14] Q-Q is unlikely as he would have raised pre-flop.

only call when he has you beat, in which case your bet loses money[15].

I can't bet here with the hope of forcing Barry to lay down the best hand; he's too good a player for that. He'll raise if he has me beat, and I cannot consider folding with this big pot. Taking that all into account, a bet on my part must have a negative expected value (-EV) because I most likely will only win one bet when I'm ahead and lose a double bet when behind. I check and Barry turns over J♣-10♣ immediately. A bet would have made me an extra 60 bucks, but the check was still correct.

Session 1: Hand 177

I'm two spots to the right of the button and everyone folds to me. I raise with **A-8**. That's a borderline play. On the button or in the cutoff seat I usually raise with that hand if no one has opened the pot. One position away from the button, it depends. The two players behind me are rather tight, so a raise will likely induce them to fold. The blinds are somewhat loose, but if they play I have position and probably the best hand. The cut-off and the button fold, the small blind calls and the big blind raises. I call and the small blind calls as well. Three players, pot $270.

Flop: 9-9-5. The big blind bets, I call and the small blind folds. The call is somewhat loose, but it's unlikely the flop has hit my opponent. Two players, pot $330. The turn is a 10. We both check.

A blank comes on the river (board: 9-9-5-10-3). The big blind bets and I call. My opponent takes the pot with 10-10. The river call probably wasn't one of my best. I called for two reasons. First, I had observed earlier that the big blind was capable of raising with any big suited cards such as Q-Js, hence there was some chance he was bluffing at the end. Second, when I check behind on the turn I call a fair amount of the time, so that an opponent can't automatically bet the river for an immediate profit.

Session 1: Hand 178

I bring it in for a raise with **A-K** from middle position. Only the big blind calls. The flop is all low: 8-5-4. I bet and the big blind folds.

---

[15] For a full treatment of this subject see David Sklansky, *The Theory of Poker*, 1992, p. 159ff.

Session 1: Hands 179-181

Q-7, K-3.

The cutoff raises and I call in the big blind with **10-9**. Though the cutoff seems to be rather loose and unimaginative, 10-9 is just enough to call. A fold is tenable. Two players, pot $140.

Flop: A♠-7♣-3♦. I bet, hoping to win the pot immediately. The cutoff calls (pot $200).

Turn: A♥. I fire another barrel. Again, the cutoff calls (pot $320).

River: 6♣. Now, I have no option. My ten-high is definitely not enough to win the hand. The only chance to win the pot is to bluff again. This is usually pointless on this sort of board, after the opponent has called both the flop and the turn. But there is a flush draw out that didn't come, so a bluff may succeed should my opponent hold a busted flush draw. I bet and the cutoff raises! There is nothing to think about. I fold and my opponent shows A-6. My loose call from the big blind became expensive.

Session 1: Hands 182-183

I fold **6-2** in the small blind.

Next hand I have the button and it's folded to me. With **4-4** I raise. Suzanne in the small blind makes it three bets and we play it out heads-up. At the end the board reads: 10-8-5-6-9. Suzanne bets all the way and I call her down. Her aces win the pot.

Session 1: Hands 184-188

Q-5, 6-3, K-8s (UTG).

I get a free play with **A♣-6♣** in the big blind, a pretty good hand in a seven-handed pot. Alas, the flop is no help: K-J-7 with no clubs. I make an exit at the first opportunity.

After running into aces two hands before, I pick up a big hand myself in the small blind: K♠-K♦. An early-position player raises, the button calls and I call as well. Of course, there is nothing wrong with raising here; I just like to mix it up once in a while. Three players, pot $230.

The flop couldn't be much better: K♣-6♥-7♦. I check, the original raiser checks, and the button bets. I'm not a proponent of slowplaying big hands. If you flop what is in all likelihood the best hand, you want to get as much money in the pot as possible, and that often means playing fast. But every situation is unique. If I raise, it gets tough for the early-position player to call, and the button might just have bet to pick up the pot, and will therefore fold to a raise. Raising and not getting more money is the last thing I want. I flopped the nuts, and unless my opponents have straight draws, they are close to drawing dead. That I didn't raise before the flop helps me now, since my hand is well disguised, and just calling doesn't look suspicious. I call and the original raiser calls as well. Three players, pot $320.

Turn: 10♣. That card opens a lot of drawing possibilities. I don't want someone to draw for free. Since I can't count on someone betting for me, I bet myself. Both players call. Still three players, pot $500.

The river card is ugly: J♣ (board: K♣-6♥-7♦-10♣-J♣). Any flush, A-Q or Q-9 beats me. Nonetheless, checking would be lame and would only invite a free showdown. The flush is not as dangerous because it's a backdoor flush, and with three high cards on the board, it's possible to get a call from a worse hand, such as K-Q or K-J. I bet and both players fold. Though I can't prove it, I think I got the most I could get.

Session 1: Hand 189

Four players call in front of me and I limp with **A-J** on the button. It's true that the value of unsuited high cards goes down in multi-way pots, but A-J is good enough to take a cheap look at the flop on the button. I would prefer a hand like 8-7s in this situation because it's easier to play after the flop.

Seven-handed, the flop comes 4♦-7♠-10♠. There is a bet with two callers before it gets to me. The key to playing unsuited high cards in volume pots is to release your hand if the flop doesn't help you. Thinking that your two overcards warrant a call usually leads to disaster. This is a mandatory fold.

Session 1: Hand 190

A very weak player in middle position raises the pot; I look at **A-Q** in the cutoff seat. How to play A-Q against a raise is a popular subject in the poker literature[16]. It all depends on the range of starting hands with which your opponent will raise. If a very good player raises in early position, a fold is in order because the only possible hands you can beat are A-Js and K-Qs. But in my experience, lacking knowledge of the raiser, you're better off reraising than folding because the typical player has looser raising standards than a very good player, at least from early and middle position.

I reraise and we see the flop heads-up (pot $170): 9-8-5. My opponent checks, I bet and he calls (pot $230). Turn: a 10. The weak player checks. The 10 is bad for me, but I still think I have the best hand. I bet and my opponent folds.

Session 1: Hands 191-207

K-4s, 3-2s, 9-4, Q-7 (BB, RIF), Q-5 (SB, RIF), 6-2 (B), 7-3 (CO), 9-3, Q-7s, A-4, J-7, K-8 (UTG), 8-2 (B, RIF), 6-4 (SB, RIF), 6-5 (B), A-J (CO, RIF). I bring it in for a raise with A♦-2♦ two to the right of the button and pick up the blinds.

Session 1: Hand 208

After I fold 8-4 on the next hand, two players leave the table; the button announces he will leave when the big blind comes around. It's my turn to take the big blind, a good time to take a break. I've played five hours straight. I usually break every two hours, but the game was very good and I was catching good cards.

When I come back the game is down. It's 2:00 a.m. and there are still two $30-60 games in progress. I go to the center podium and see that I'm second on the waiting list. Being up around $850 and not yet feeling tired, I decide to give it another try. I walk around the Bellagio poker room; after about ten minutes Lemlem calls me for table 17. As far as I can see, the table is alright. I sit down in the 7 seat and get a free play in middle position[17].

---

[16] For a good discussion of the A-Q problem, see John Feeney, *Inside the Poker Mind. Essays on Hold'em and General Poker Concepts*, 2000, pp. 33f.

[17] If you come from a broken game, you don't have to post.

Session 1: Hands 209-218

Q-4s, 10-6, J-9, 6-3, 6-5 (UTG), **A-2** (BB, RIF), **J-5** (SB, RIF), **9-5** (B), **K-5** (CO).

Two players have called in front of me; I limp with **Q-J**. The 8 seat, the player just behind me, raises. Not a good situation for my weak hand, but at least the pot is six-handed (pot $360).

Flop: 9-6-5. I fold quickly (turn and river are both fours; the original raiser wins with unimproved A-Q).

Session 1: Hands 219-221

J-4, 4-2.

I open with **9-9** for a raise, and the 10 seat, a young Asian guy, reraises. Just the two of us play, pot $170.

The flop is a good one: 6-4-6. I check, and the Asian player bets as expected. Against such aggressive players, I just call down if no ace comes. He will bet for me, should I have the best hand. I call (pot $230).

Turn is a Q. Not a good card, but much better than an ace or king. I check-call (pot $350).

River: 8 (board: 6-4-6-Q-8). I check and the Asian guy bets. Easy call for me. He shows A-K and I win the pot. Of course, my opponent misplayed that hand badly by betting A-K at the end. Many players, especially overly aggressive ones, fall into this trap.

Session 1: Hand 222

I raise under-the-gun with **10-10**. A middle-position player and the small blind call, so we are three players, and the pot is $210.

The flop is okay: J-8-7. I bet and both players call (pot $300).

Turn: Q. The small blind comes out betting. Pot odds of 6-to-1 are not enough to draw if I'm behind. I have probably 4-6 outs (a gutshot and two tens to make trips), however, if the small blind holds 10-9 I have only three outs to split the pot. Having two tens myself, this is rather unlikely.

I'm not completely convinced I'm beat. But if I call, I'll have to call the river as well, since the pot is so big. I've decided that I won't give up, so I raise. This costs the same as calling twice, with the added benefit that I can extract extra money if the river helps my hand. The drawback is that if I get reraised I'll have to fold, losing the opportunity to see the river card. Both players call; pot $660.

River: 2 (board: J-8-7-Q-2). It's checked down. The small blind wins the hand with J♣-7♣. He was rewarded for his bad pre-flop play. Well, that's poker.

Session 1: Hand 223

I get a free play in the big blind with **Q-J**. There are a total of five players (pot $150).

Flop: K♥-10♥-6♣. It's checked to the 10 seat, who bets. I'm the only caller (pot $210).

Turn card: 6♦. I check-call (pot $330).

River: K♠ (board: K♥-10♥-6♣-6♦-K♠). We both check. The 10 seat wins with 7-6. I'm glad I didn't play the hand more aggressively. By the way, since I'm in the 7 seat, the 10 seat called in early position with 7-6. The game is still good, but I'm still at the mercy of the cards.

Session 1: Hands 224-225

Q-3 (SB, RIF), **7-4** (B).

Session 1: Hand 226

I raise from the cutoff seat with **A-K** after two early players limp. The big blind, my friend in the 10 seat, of course calls as well. Four players, pot $260.

The flop misses me completely: J♠-Q♦-5♠. Everyone checks to me, I bet and only the 10 seats drops out. Three players, pot $350.

Turn: 2♥. Both early-position players check. A bet would only make sense if I had the best hand or if I could make both of my opponents fold. I don't think I have the best hand. If I bet and I'm raised, I lose the opportunity to complete my gutshot should a ten come on the river. I opt for the free card. Nothing has changed; still three players, and the pot is $350.

The river is a mixed bag for me: K♠ (board: J♠-Q♦-5♠-2♥-K♠). It gives me top pair, top kicker, but makes a flush and straight possible. The 1 seat bets; the 2 seat folds. I don't like my chances, but the pot is too big for a fold. I call and the bettor shows 10-9 for a straight. As I said, the game is excellent, but if you can't hit anything it quickly becomes expensive.

Session 1: Hands 227-232

A-7s, 6-4, 10-3s, A-9, K-3 (UTG), Q-4 (BB, RIF).

Session 1: Hand 233

Four players have already limped when I look at **K-10** in the small blind. I complete; the big blind raises. Five players, me included, call (pot $360).

Flop: A-10-4. The big blind bets and everyone calls. With pot odds of 17-to-1, I have an easy call with middle pair, especially since my call closes the action. Six players, pot $540.

Turn: 6. The big blind bets again, and only the 4 seat calls. On the river a queen falls (board: A-10-4-6-Q). The big blind bets and the 4 seat folds. The winner proudly turns over 7-7!

Session 1: Hands 234-236

10-7 (B), 7-4 (CO).

It's folded to me and I raise with **K-J**. The cutoff seat and the button call (pot $230).

Flop: Q-6-5. It's three-handed and I'm out of position, so I take the safe route and check. Both players check behind.

Turn: Q. Since both players checked, it's almost certain that no one has a queen. I see a good chance to pick up the pot. I bet, the cutoff folds and the button calls. Two players, pot $350.

River: 2 (board: Q-6-5-Q-2). The 10 seat is completely unpredictable, so I don't know where I stand. He could be hanging around with ace-high, in which case he might fold to a bet. I give it a try and bet. The 10 seat calls and shows 4♦2♦!

Sometimes you are just speechless. This guy made a ridiculous pre-flop call, and then called with two undercards and a gutshot on the turn with a paired board. Who said playing poker is fun?

Session 1: Hand 237

I raise with **A♦-9♦** in late-middle position and expect to get action, since the guy who called last hand with 4-2s is behind me. Surprisingly, everyone folds and I collect the blinds.

Session 1: Hands 238-244

A-4, **J-10**, **A-9** (UTG), **Q-4** (BB, RIF), **9-3** (SB, RIF), **4-3** (B).

The 4 seat limps in third position and I raise in the cutoff with **Q-Q**. Both blinds call, so the pot is four-handed (pot $240).

The flop looks excellent: J-3-2. It's checked to me and I bet. Both blinds fold and the 4 seat calls. Two players, pot $300.

I'm sure I hold the best hand. If no overcard shows up, I'm confident that finally one of my big hands will hold up. My hope is short-lived, as the turn brings an ace. The 4 seat checks. My opponent may have an ace, but since he didn't raise before the flop, it's probably not a big ace, in which case he will probably not raise. Therefore, my plan is to bet the turn and check down the river should he call my turn bet. I bet and he raises me.

I didn't expect the raise. It means that he either has a set; has A-J for top pair, top kicker; or is representing an ace and hoping that I will lay down a pocket pair. The latter is less likely, but the pot contains eight big bets, so I call. Two players, pot $540.

The river is a six (board: J-3-2-A-6). The 4 seat bets and I call. The call is the consequence of my turn play. It makes no sense to call the turn and then fold the river after a blank has come. The 4 seat shows 2-2 for a set. There is nothing you can do if the cards don't fall your way. I could have folded on the turn, but I still think going all the way was reasonable.

Session 1: Hands 245-246

I fold **4-3s**.

I pick up **A♥-A♠**. The first three players fold and I raise. In the cutoff seat is my friend who beat me with 4-2s. He calls, as does the big blind. Against two opponents I'm about a 2.8-to-1 favorite to win the hand (pot $200).

Flop: **K♥-J♠-6♠**. The flop is okay, but it presents a lot of drawing possibilities. The big blind bets, I raise and the cutoff folds. The big blind, a player from Kansas City, reraises. Few hands beat me at this point. K-J is the biggest threat; 6-6 and K-6s (maybe even J-6) are also possible. And he could have slowplayed K-K or J-J pre-flop. Nonetheless, I think I'm still ahead and the big blind is pushing a draw. Since I have position, I decide to just call, and will raise the turn if nothing threatening shows up. I call. Two players, pot $380.

The turn is **7♠**, making a flush possible. My opponent from Kansas bets. He could have a lot of hands I can beat, such as A-K, K-Q or Q-10, but I have a bad feeling. Given my recent results, I fully expect he has a flush. But folding is not an option, since I have a draw for the nut flush with the A♠. I call (pot $500).

A spade on the river would be nice. No such luck; the deuce of clubs comes on the river (board: K♥-J♠-6♠-7♠-2♣). The big blind bets and I call. Sure enough, the player from Kansas City turns over K♠-5♠ for a flush.

I can't fault my opponent for the way he played his hand. The pre-flop call is debatable, but given the fact that I raised from middle position and that the cutoff is extremely weak, I would have probably made the call as well. Then, with top pair and a draw to the second-nut flush, he flopped a monster. Even against my overpair, he is only a small underdog[18]. Playing as aggressively as he did was certainly correct.

Session 1: Hands 247-255

8-3, J-6 (UTG), 8-7 (B, chop).

I call with **A♠-7♠** in the small blind after a raise and two callers. The flop comes K-5-4 rainbow and I fold quickly.

---

[18] A♥-A♠: 55.76%, K♠-5♠: 44.24%

6-5 (B, RIF), **10-8** (CO), **Q-9**, 10-9, 4-2 (UTG).

It's my turn to take the blind. We were playing nine-handed for a while and on this round two players have left the table. It looks like the table will break down soon. It's 3:30 a.m. and I've played for 6½ hours with just one short break; time to call it a day.

Result Session 1		Total Results	
Hours	6:30	Hours	6:30
Win/Loss	-$275	Win/Loss	-$275

Session 1: Conclusion

This was a very disappointing and frustrating session. It has nothing to do with my $275 loss. First, even if you are a very good player in limit poker, you only win between 55 and 60 percent of the sessions you play[19]. Therefore, if you sit down at a limit hold'em table, you know you are only a little better than even money to have a winning session. Dealing with losses is part of playing poker. Second, if I lose $275 in a $30-60 game, I feel like I broke even. It's not that I have no regard for money. This is a lot of money for many people, but you must put it into perspective. A $275 loss is the equivalent of losing about $25 in a $3-6 game. Most $3-6 players, after losing 25 bucks, might think they broke about even. Just the day before, I lost $2,178 in the $30-60 game, so I'm not going to complain about a $275 loss.

No, I was disappointed because I was catching good cards and wasn't able to capitalize on them. Looking all all the hands I played, you saw a lot of trash, but I was actually dealt quite a few big hands.

It's 220-to-1 against being dealt a specific pair in hold'em. Put another way, after 221 hands, you should on average be dealt every pocket pair once. I was dealt 255 hands in the 6½ hours I played. That means I could

---

[19] Barry Greenstein states that he wins about 58% of his limit poker sessions; see Barry Greenstein, *Ace On the River. An Advanced Poker Guide*, 2005, p. 30. Though I don't play high-limit as Barry does, his findings tally with my experiences.

expect to catch any of the big pairs once. But I was dealt aces twice, kings three times, queens twice, tens once and nines twice. You don't often see that many good hands, which present excellent opportunities to score big wins.

At the first table I made about $850 in five hours of play. That was already disappointing, given the cards I was dealt. Much of the disappointment was due to my playing poorly by folding pocket kings on the turn (1/19). Had I not given up on that hand prematurely, I would have been up about $1,500, which would be reasonable if not great.

The real disaster occurred at the second table. The opposition was even weaker than at the first table. Though I didn't commit any serious blunders and still kept catching cards (I was dealt aces, queens, tens and nines once), I lost $1,100 in 1½ hours.

Looking through my notes, I realize that keeping track of my hands not only affected my play by limiting the amount of information I could process in order to make decisions; it also caused me to play differently than usual. I had been naïve in assuming that recording my hands at the table would not affect my play. Writing down the hands absorbed a lot of energy and took much time, time that I couldn't use to watch the action and observe my opponents. That's not a big problem against regular players, because I know how they play, but most people at the two tables I played were complete strangers to me.

Frequently I looked up from my notebook and saw a completely new face. I hadn't noticed when that player sat down and how he had played so far, and hence I had no read on him. It was like playing at a new online poker site where you only see the names. I saw faces that didn't have a playing history for me.

When I later looked calmly at the hand in which I folded the kings on the turn, I was puzzled by my play. The only explanation I could imagine was that since the hands were to be published, I didn't want to look like someone who stubbornly calls two big bets with a hopeless hand; instead I wanted to show how smart I was by making a big laydown. In a way, I'm happy that my play backfired, because it taught me a valuable lesson: I should just play my game and not try to be too smart.

Even a very good player has room for improvement. It's important to look at your play objectively and try to identify leaks in your game. The misplayed K-K hand is a perfect example. Though I can't remember that I ever folded a big overpair in a similar situation, one of my biggest weaknesses is that I tend to make big laydowns in multiway pots. Let's look at three examples, all from the same $30-60 game at the Bellagio.

Example 1

Four players have limped, I raise on the button with K-K and both blinds call. Seven-handed, the flop comes 10-5-3. It's checked to me, I bet my overpair and five players call. There are still six players contesting the pot. The turn pairs the five. Again everyone checks and I bet my hand. Now, the small blind raises and two players call. Though I know the small blind is a weak player, I put him on a five, probably A-5 or K-5. Since I am down to two outs at best, I fold. The river is a 9 (board: 10-5-3-5-9). It's checked around and the small blind wins the pot with 10-6!

It's easy to see what happened. The small blind had flopped top pair with a weak kicker. Unsure where he stood, he check-called the flop. The turn didn't bring an overcard, so he still had top pair. He checked, and again it was just me who showed interest by betting. He then figured (correctly) that I was the only threat at that time, and that he had the other players beat. He saw me raising pre-flop and betting both the turn and the river, and deduced that I must have had a big hand.

Even weak players know that it's more likely that a raiser has two high cards than a big pair. Hence, the small blind assumed he had a good chance to be ahead at the moment, and he raised to protect his hand. But I would not have bet the flop and the turn in a seven-handed pot with only overcards such as A-K or A-Q. I hadn't taken into account that he didn't understand that. Simply put, I gave him too much credit.

Example 2

I call on the button with Q♥-10♥ after four players have limped. Both blinds call. Seven active players. The flop is interesting: 10♦-7♠-2♦. Everyone checks to me, I bet, the small blind raises and four players call. Of course, I'm interested in eliminating players with my vulnerable hand, but raising would just make the pot bigger. Facing possible flush and straight draws, many turn cards can beat me, and I'm not even sure my top pair and medium kicker are best at the moment. I call. Still six active players.

Flop: 6♥. The small blind bets and three players call. I have little idea where I stand. The small blind could have anything, either a pair of tens, two pair or a set. The under-the-gun player is quite good, and from the way she has played the hand so far, it's clear she hasn't a ten, so the only logical hand is a flush draw such as K♦-Q♦. The other two players are weak and probably have some sort of draw.

I raise. The situation is somewhat unclear, but I can't fold with that big pot. I want to make it expensive for drawing hands, and a raise could make river play easy for me. If the river doesn't complete any draws, it will probably be checked to me, in which case I can check behind. As expected, everyone calls. Still five active players.

The river card is 8♠ (board: 10♦-7♠-2♦-6♥-8♠), making a one-card straight possible. The first three players check, then Johnny bets. Johnny, an Asian player, is quite a character. He is the only player I never saw winning. In poker even the weakest player can win once in a while, and Johnny is no exception. But if Johnny is winning, he won't stop until he's lost every-thing. He must be a masochist. He isn't happy when he is winning because he knows it's only temporary, nor is he happy when he loses. Over the years he must have lost hundreds of thousands of dollars.

Now here comes Johnny, betting at the end into four players. Having played with him for years, I know him very well. He is not only extremely loose, but likes to bluff as well. Heads-up I would have called him without looking at the river card. Here, the situation is different with three other players to take into account. I fold.

I have four reasons for this. First, it's very easy to beat my hand—any nine will do, and with four opponents, it's likely to be the case. Second, since the pot is protected[20], bluffing makes absolutely no sense. Hence, I think Johnny must have a nine. Third, even if I exclude Johnny from the equa-tion, it's doubtful I can beat the small blind. Fourth, since I'm first to act after Johnny, I'm in the worst possible position. One of the players behind me might raise, in which case I've wasted a big bet by calling.

---

[20] Bluffing at the end in large multiway pots is usually not a paying proposition, as you can expect at least one opponent to call due to the size of the pot. Therefore, it's said that the pot is 'protected'. See David Sklansky, *Sklansky on Poker*, 1994, p. 55f.

Only the small blind calls. Johnny turns over Q-J and the small blind takes the pot with Q-10. After seeing the hand, Johnny's thoughts become clear to me. Three players checked on the river, so Johnny figured none of them had a nine and that he had just to bluff one player, the player behind him who hadn't acted yet. Johnny didn't understand that bluffing was pointless, and I couldn't imagine that he wasn't aware of that. So I folded and threw away half the pot.

Example 3

A weak player limps in middle position, I raise from the cutoff with Q-Q and a loose-aggressive Asian guy calls on the button.

Three-handed, the flop comes 9♦-8♠-3♦, a pretty good flop for my hand. I bet and both players call.

Turn: 4♥. Again, I bet my overpair and my opponents call. One of them probably has a flush draw. Therefore, I don't want to see a diamond on the river, and no ace either, as many weak players hang around with an ace.

With the exception of A♦, the river brings the worst possible card: K♦ (board: 9♦-8♠-3♦-4♥-K♦). That makes a flush possible and puts an overcard to my queens on the board. The middle-position player checks, I check as well and the young Asian guy bets. I'm probably beat, but I've already made up my mind to call, since I know that player well enough to realize he couldn't resist bluffing after his opponents had checked at the end.

Then something unforeseen occurs: the middle-position player calls. Now I start to question my decision to call. One player can bluff, but at least the caller must have a hand. I can't beat a flush and I can't beat the king, and it appears that at least one of them has such a hand, so I fold the queens. The Asian guy shows J-10 and the middle position player 8♥-6♥. I hadn't considered that weak players often call with substandard hands, not taking into account that there are likely better hands behind them.

All my folds would have been correct against competent opponents. It was (and sometimes still is) a weakness in my game to assume that players act rationally in situations that seem obvious to me.

Since most players call too much, making tough laydowns may not be your problem. But that's not my point. Nearly all players have leaks in their game. Don't assume that you are an exception. Take a realistic look at your game, identify your leaks and then work on them. I try to work on my game constantly, and you should, too.

Session 2: Bellagio, Tuesday, September 6, 8:40 p.m.

I arrive at a half-empty Bellagio poker room at about the same time as yesterday. Usually this is not a bad time, since between 7:00 and 9:00 p.m. many tourists go to dinner, returning between 9:00 and 10:00. Three $30-60 tables are in progress; I get a seat immediately at table 28. Two seats are open and I choose the 10 seat.

Session 2: Hand 1

I let the button pass to post behind. I'm dealt **A-9** in the cutoff. A player in first position raises and it's folded to me. I usually wouldn't call an early-position raise with this hand, but since I'm already halfway in, I call, as do the blinds. Four players, pot $240.

Flop: 4-6-8. The blinds check, the original raiser bets and I fold. Only the small blind calls. The turn is a ten and the river an ace. The original raiser wins with K-K. Sometimes bad play is rewarded. Had I stubbornly, foolishly called down with my ace, I would have won the pot.

Session 2: Hands 2-5

I fold **K-6**.

Since we are playing six-handed at the moment, I'm already under-the-gun. I pick up **K-J** and raise the pot. Usually I don't even play K-J in first position, but high cards gain value in a shorthanded game, and you must be more aggressive. My raise wins the blinds.

In the big blind I chop the blinds with **9-5**. Chopping means that if everyone folds to the blinds, they may take their money back, and the next round is dealt. To chop or not often stirs up a fierce controversy. I will say more about this interesting subject at the end of the chapter (see p. 69).

I fold **Q-6** in the small blind to a middle-position raise.

Session 2: Hand 6

It's folded to me and I raise on the button with **A-6**. It's some sort of a semi-steal raise. You don't mind if the blinds fold and you can collect the pot. This is different than raising with a big pair like A-A or K-K, in which case you hope for a call because your EV is higher than just the value of the blinds. Only the big blind calls. Two players, pot $140.

Flop: 4♠-7♠-9♦. My opponent checks, I bet and he folds. That's the beauty of being the aggressor and having position: If you and your opponent both miss the flop, you can usually pick up the pot. Aggression always puts your opponent to the test.

Session 2: Hands 7-22

K-2 (CO), **7-6s**, **7-2**. Two players are back, so we play eight-handed now. **3-2s**, **Q-10** (UTG), **9-2** (BB, three bets to me), **7-5** (SB, RIF), **10-3** (B), **5-4** (CO), **6-4**, **9-8**, **A-4**, **10-9** (UTG), **10-6** (BB, RIF), **7-6s** (SB, three bets to me), **8-3s** (B).

Session 2: Hand 23

An early-position player limps; a loose player in the 8 seat raises. I'm two seats behind in the 10 seat, one before the button, and look at 8♣-8♥.

The situation is often ambiguous when there is action in front of you and you hold a middle pair. You are usually better off folding against a player with solid raising standards. He has either two overcards or a higher pair. Even in position, it's not a good situation. You're either a very small favorite (against overcards) or a big underdog (against an overpair).

In this case the raiser is pretty loose, in which case the best course of action is normally to attempt to isolate the loose raiser with a reraise. This hand is complicated by the presence of an early-position limper. The correct play for him (if he is not slowplaying a big hand) is to fold if I make it three bets. In my experience, average players nearly always call the double-bet. They already have money in the pot and see that a big pot is developing.

Therefore, if I reraise, I will probably play my pocket eights three-handed, and they don't play well in that situation. If I just call, the players behind me may be attracted by the good pot odds, giving me the right price to draw for a set. I call, as does the button. Both blinds fold and the early position limper calls. Four players, pot $290.

Flop: 4♦-4♠-7♥. The early-position player checks and the raiser bets. The flop is pretty good for me. I want to eliminate the other players as quickly as possible. I raise, the button calls two bets cold and the early-position limper folds. The original raiser raises again, I call and the button calls. Three players, pot $560.

Turn: J♥. The 8 seat bets again. Things get tough for me. On the one hand, the pot is large (pot odds 10.3-to-1), but the pot is too small for me to profitably draw with just two outs. I should only call if I think there is a good chance my hand is best, and if I call the turn, I must call on the river as well (the exception may be if an ace falls on the river and my opponent still bets). My opponent showed a lot of strength by reraising on the turn. However, I am not completely convinced he wouldn't do that with a hand such as A-K or 6-6. I call and the button folds. We are heads-up now, pot $680.

River: 5♦ (board: 4♦-4♠-7♥-J♥-5♦). My opponent bets and I call. He turns over K-K. Unfortunately, even though my opponent is a loose player, he can still pick up a big hand once in a while. Even a drunken squirrel finds an acorn now and then.

Session 2: Hands 24-26

Q-3, Q-8s.

I'm in third position. The two players in front of me limp, and I call with A♠-9♠.

Six players (pot $180) see the flop: J♦-9♥-10♠. It's checked to the button, who bets. Only the UTG and I call. I have probably five outs and a backdoor flush draw. That's just enough, given the 8-to-1 pot odds. I would have folded to a bet in front of me, but since only the button bet, I'm more likely to really have outs and not be running into a made straight. Three players, pot $270.

The turn is 4♠. The UTG player checks. I now have a four-flush, but I believe betting is pointless. I might have bet if K♠ or Q♠ had come on the turn, which could give someone with a pair of jacks or tens an incentive to fold. With the innocent looking 4♠ it's out of the question that both of my opponents will fold. I check, the button bets again and the two remaining players, including me, call. Three players, pot $450.

Alas, the river is the 5♣ and I don't make my flush (board: J♦-9♥-10♠-4♠-5♣). Everyone checks. The UTG player shows A-10 and the button takes the pot with J♥-7♥.

Question 2/1:

What are my chances of winning on the flop, and should I have called, given my opponents' hands?

Session 2: Hands 27-50

I fold **8-2**.

The UTG player takes a break, so I'm already in the big blind. Everyone folds and the small blind raises. Obviously, he doesn't chop. I call with **J-8**. Heads-up you can't be too selective or your opponent shows an immediate profit by always raising. The flop is no help: 2-A-6. The small blind bets. I can raise, trying to represent an ace, or fold. I take the safe route and fold.

J-2 (SB, RIF), **10-6s** (B), **K-9** (CO), **Q-J**, **10-3s**, **9-6s** (UTG).

I get a free play in the big blind with **6-5**. Three players are in the pot ($90). Flop: A-Q-9 and I'm done with the hand.

10-7s (SB, RIF).

It's folded to me on the button and I raise with **5-5**. Only the big blind calls. Flop: 4-9-7. The big blind checks and I win the hand by betting.

8-7 (CO), **Q-6s**, **Q-3**, **Q-3** (BB, RIF), **A-8** (SB, RIF), **5-3s** (B).

A new dealer sits down and we are again down to six players. I raise with **A-7** in the cutoff seat after everyone has folded to me. The small blind three-bets and I call. Two players, pot $210. Flop: K-J-6. The small blind bets. With that flop I'm forced to fold. It's too likely that my opponent started with the better hand or got help from the flop.

A-5, **7-4**, **8-6** (UTG), **10-5** (BB, RIF), **8-4** (SB, RIF). Now we are down to five players. **7-3s** (B).

Session 2: Hand 51

The UTG player limps and I raise with **A-Ks** one off the button. Only the UTG player calls. Two players, pot $170.

The flop comes 8-A-4. My bet wins the pot. Another player leaves the table, so we are just four players. Two of them refuse to play four-handed, so the game comes to a halt.

I have played for one hour and 10 minutes and I'm down about $600. Since there is currently no game anyway, I decide to take a break.

Session 2: Hands 52-57

Upon my return the table is broken. The floorman has a seat for me on table 38. Since I am from a broken game, I don't have to post.

10-4s (CO), **J-3**, **8-7**, **A-9**, **10-5**, **K-4**.

Session 2: Hand 58

I'm dealt **J♦-10♦** under the gun. Usually that's a clear fold, but all the hands I've seen have been multiway, so I decide to call. This is probably not a good decision, since the player behind me raises and a middle-position player makes it three bets. The button calls cold and the blinds fold.

You may recall my saying that if you limp, you should generally fold to a raise and a reraise. This is different. There is another caller (the button), giving you better pot odds. Furthermore, J-10s not only plays well in multiway pots, it's usually easy to play; you hit something or you're gone. I call the double bet, accepting the risk that the original raiser will raise again and the middle-position player will cap it. J-10s is not a hand I like to play four-handed for 150 bucks pre-flop. Fortunately the MP player only calls. Four players, pot $380.

Flop: Q♦-J♥-8♠. The middle-position player bets and the remaining players all call. Admittedly, my call is rather loose. Don't be fooled by the pot odds of 14.7-to-1 with five outs and a backdoor flush draw. It's impossible to know how many outs I really have. For example, a ten on the turn gives me two pair, but it makes a straight for A-K, and that's a very likely hand in a double-raised pot. In addition, I don't know if a jack or even a flush would be good. But I'm willing to take some risks for a large pot. Four players, pot $500.

Turn: 8♣. I check and to my surprise, everyone checks behind. Good news: I get a free card (I couldn't have called if someone had bet), and none of my opponents seems to have much of a hand. I might even be best. Still four players, pot $500.

The river shatters my hopes: A♣ (board: Q♦-J♥-8♠-8♣-A♣). The player behind me (the original raiser) bets and we all muck.

The floorman says he has an open seat at the other $30-60 table. I'd put my name on the transfer list because that table looked better. I grab two racks and put my chips in them.

The dealer at the new table tells me there is no open seat. I point to the 3 seat and say, "Looks like an empty seat to me".

The dealer replies, "The player in that seat will be back. He went to get more money."

I tell the floorman what has happened and reclaim my seat. Meanwhile, the blinds have passed me by. The dealer lets me post behind the button[21] and no one objects.

Session 2: Hands 59-61

When the action comes to me in the cutoff seat there is already a double raise and my **J-8** goes into the muck. **9-7, 7-2.**

Session 2: Hand 62

The UTG player raises and I see **A-Q** in middle position. This is just my second premium hand. The raiser is not one of the really good players, so I reraise; only the UTG player calls. Two players, pot $170.

Flop: K-7-4. My opponent checks, I bet and he folds.

---

[21] In my opinion, this isn't the correct decision. Technically, I'm not a new player. Therefore, I should be required to post the small and big blind or wait until the big blind comes around.

The floorman tells me that my transfer is ready now. I move to table 39 and take the open 5 seat. As usual, I wait until I can post behind.

Session 2: Hands 63-66

K-6 in the cutoff seat is not much of a hand. At least nobody raised, so I get a free play six-handed (pot $180). Flop: 10-6-J. An early-position player bets, the player in front of me raises and I quickly release my hand.

10-2, 10-3.

Now an interesting hand develops. Pizza Mike, a tough pro who got his name because he likes to order pizza from a delivery service right into the Bellagio poker room, raises the pot under-the-gun. Behind him is a rather loose player who makes it three bets. I'm in third position with A♦-K♣ and decide to call. Just behind me sits a young Asian action guy. The large pot clearly captures his interest. He calls the three bets cold and everyone else folds. Four players, pot $410. The flop comes 10♦-J♠-7♥.

Pizza Mike checks in first position and the loose guy behind bets. The pot is currently $440; it costs me $30 to call (pot odds 14.7-to-1). I probably don't have ten outs, but I have at least four outs (any queen) to the nuts, and the overcards might be worth something. Easy call. The Asian guy behind me folds and Pizza Mike calls. Still three players, pot $500.

On the turn I hit the jackpot: Q♣. Pizza Mike checks and the loose player bets. I currently hold the nuts, but I still have to survive the river. Any A or K can cost me half the pot and if the board pairs it may make one of my opponents a full house. There is $560 in the pot. If I just call to keep Pizza Mike in, he gets about the right odds to draw with two pair. No time to fool around. I raise, Pizza Mike folds and the 4 seats calls. Two players, pot $740.

The river is 6♦, and it doesn't change anything (board: 10♦-J♠-7♥-Q♣-6♦). My opponent checks, I bet and he calls. He shows K♠-K♦. I got lucky this time. K-K is about a 7-to-3 favorite against A-K before the flop. Took me 66 hands to win the first showdown.

Session 2: Hands 67-69

3-2, 10-7 (UTG).

The Asian action player limps under-the-gun, the 9 seat calls and then Pizza Mike raises on the button. The small blind folds and I call with Q♥-10♦ in the big blind. The limpers call. Four players, pot $260.

The flop comes 8♠-10♥-4♣. Top pair with a decent kicker may currently be the best hand. But a pair of tens is vulnerable to overcards. First priority is to protect my hand by reducing the number of opponents. What's the best course of action to achieve that goal? The two limpers are pretty loose. They probably won't fold to my bet on a ten-high flop. If I check, there is a good chance that Pizza Mike, the pre-flop raiser, will bet and I can raise, confronting the two loose limpers with a double bet. I check with the intention to check-raise.

The first part of my plan works as expected. It's checked to the button who bets, and I make it two bets. But then the plan goes astray. Both limpers call and Pizza Mike reraises—bad news for me. I had assumed I had the best hand. Pizza Mike raised pre-flop on the button after two loose players had limped. He would do that with a wide range of starting hands. But he would only make it three bets on the flop against three active players if he could beat top pair, decent kicker. With pot odds of 17.7-to-1, my call is automatic. The two limpers call as well. Four players, $620 in the pot.

Turn: 9♦. It's checked to Pizza Mike at the button. He bets and we all call. The nine on the turn gives me just enough to call. The gutshot alone is not very strong; if a jack comes on the end, any queen makes a non-nut straight. Queens are most likely not outs, but if Pizza Mike doesn't have a set, another ten would probably give me the winning hand. I estimate that I have about four outs (counting the gutshot as two outs)[22]. Pot odds of 11.3-to-1 are just enough to keep me in. Four players, pot $860.

River: 5♠ (board: 8♠-10♥-4♣-9♦-5♠). Pizza Mike bets after it has been checked to him, and only the second limper calls. I still hold top pair, but there is no point in calling. I have played with Pizza Mike often enough to know that my hand can't be good under these circumstances. Pizza Mike's pocket aces win the pot.

---

[22] See Ed Miller/David Sklansky/Mason Malmuth, *Small Stakes Hold'em. Winning Big With Expert Play*, 2004, pp. 99f. It contains a good discussion about estimating the number of outs you have.

Session 2: Hands 70-83

J-7 (SB, chop), **5-3** (B), **8-4** (CO), **3-2**, **10-5**, **A-6s**, **7-2** (UTG), **A-9** (BB, RIF), 6-5 (SB, RIF), **6-3** (B), **10-8s** (CO), **6-3**, **3-2**.

There are three limpers and a late-position raiser when the action comes to me. I call in the big blind with **A♥-10♥**. The limpers call. We have five players, pot $320.

Flop: 3♥-6♦-9♣. It's checked to the late-position raiser, who bets. I don't like to call with overcards in multiway pots, especially with players behind me. However, I don't believe the limpers have strong hands. A check-raise is unlikely. Pot odds of 10.6-to-1, two overcards and a backdoor flush draw give me enough reason to call. Only the under-the-gun limper calls behind. Three players, pot $410.

Turn: 5♠. I fold quickly when the original raiser bets. The UTG player calls (pot $530).

River: 8♠ (board: 3♥-6♦-9♣-5♠-8♠). The UTG player check-calls. The late-position raiser turns over J-J and his opponent wins the pot with 4♦-2♦! It would be hard to play the hand worse than the lucky winner did. With the exception of the flop, he misplayed every street.

Session 2: Hands 84-95

There are three limpers and I pay 10 bucks with **7-4** in the small blind. Five-handed (pot $150) the flop comes 2-Q-Q and I'm done.

I fold **8-4** on the button.

It's folded to me and I raise with **K-J** in the cutoff. The button and both blinds call. Four players, pot $240. With three opponents, I need help from the flop. I don't get it, as the flop comes A-6-8. The small blind bets and we all fold.

10-8, **Q-6**, **K-4**, **6-2**, **8-5** (UTG), **J-7** (BB, RIF), **10-9** (SB, RIF), **A-6** (B, RIF), **8-3** (CO).

Session 2: Hand 96

Two off the button, I'm dealt **A-Q** for the second time. Everyone has folded so far. I raise. The player behind me and the two blinds call. Four players, pot $240.

Flop: 2-3-4. Both blinds check. Having two overcards, a gutshot and possibly the best hand, I bet. The player behind me folds and the blinds call. Three players, pot $330.

Turn: 4. The small blind bets and the big blind folds. Does the small blind hold a 4? I don't think so. The player in the small blind is Donna, a very good player. She wouldn't call a raise out of the small blind with a hand like 5-4s or 6-4s. Maybe with A-4s, but in that case she would have played the hand differently.

I put her on an overpair, which would mean I have probably ten outs, more than enough to call. But given my read, there's a chance I can make her lay down the best hand. I raise, representing a big pair. She simply calls. Two players, pot $570.

River: J (board: 2-3-4-4-J). She checks and I check behind. There is no point to a bluff. She called the turn, and she will call the river as well. At least my assumption was correct: Donna shows 9-9.

Session 2: Hands 97-100

8-7s, 8-3, K-8.

I pick up **A-K** UTG and raise the pot. Only the big blind calls. Two players, pot $140.

Flop: 10-10-6. My opponent checks, I bet and he calls. Two players, pot $200.

Turn: 6. The big blind checks and I check behind. Heads-up with A-K, I normally bet the turn, but there is little to gain by betting here. With what hands would my opponent call the flop? He either has a pocket pair or is waiting to check-raise with a ten or six. In neither case should I bet. He could also hold two overcards. Giving a free card is not too dangerous as long as he doesn't hold Q-J. Two players, pot $200.

River: 3 (board: 10-10-6-6-3). The big blind bets and I call. My opponent wins the pot with a pair of jacks.

Session 2: Hands 101-102

I get a free play with **10-5** in the big blind. There are five players (pot $150). With a flop of A-J-4 there is nothing I can do.

The session so far is much like yesterday's. I can't hit anything or make a hand hold up. But yesterday I was catching good hands pre-flop and today I haven't seen a big pair. That's about to change.

Two early-position players limp and the button raises. I reraise in the small blind with K♣-K♦. As expected, the two limpers call the double bet and the original raiser calls. Four players, pot $390.

The flop looks promising: 9♥-4♦-3♥. Being first to act, I bet. The first limper calls and the second raises. The original raiser folds. I just call. One of the limpers probably has a flush draw; I want to see what comes on the turn. The first limper calls. Still three players, pot $570.

Turn: 3♦. The flush card didn't come. Convinced that I hold the best hand, I bet. Both limpers call. Three players, pot $750.

River: 8♥ (board: 9♥-4♦-3♥-3♦-8♥). My hopes to win the pot sink. With two opponents and a low board like that, someone usually has a flush draw. I check. Surprisingly, both of my opponents check. Perhaps I still hold the best hand. I show my kings. The first limper reveals 10♥-7♥ for a flush and the second turns over K-9 for a pair of nines.

Session 2: Hands 103-127

Three players limp and I call with **A-6s** on the button. Both blinds call, so the pot is six-handed ($180). Flop: K-7-9. The small blind bets, there is one caller and I fold.

The table is extremely loose for a $30-60 game. There are regularly 4-6 players contesting the pot. Therefore, a hand like **6♠-5♠,** which I'm dealt now in the cutoff seat, is often playable. Three players limp in front of me. I call and both blinds call. Again, we have six players (pot $180), an excellent starting point for my small suited connectors. However, the flop of 2-2-9 with no spades makes me wish I hadn't called.

J-3, 10-7, 6-3s, 10-2 (UTG), **Q-3** (BB, RIF), **J-4** (SB, RIF), **9-8** (B), **K-6** (CO), **J-2s, K-J** (RIF).

I raise from middle position with **A-K**. Only the big blind calls (pot $140). Flop: 10♣-8♣-6♠. The big blind checks, I bet and he folds. It's taken a long time to win another hand. The pot was small, but it's better than nothing.

K-3, **10-5**, **8-6** (UTG).

I get a free play in the big blind with **A-J**. Six players (pot $180) see the flop: Q♥-9♥-5♦. Another flop that missed me completely. I fold to a bet and a call.

K-10 (SB, RIF), **Q-4** (B), **10-7** (CO), **8-2**, **A-9**, **K-7**, **5-4s**, **Q-J**.

Session 2: Hand 128

Though I had folded Q-J the hand before, I call with **K-Q** (UTG). In tough games I routinely fold that hand in early position, but it becomes playable in weak games. Again, six players (pot $180) look at the flop: 6-5-6. Everyone checks. Turn: 6. The small blind bets and all the remaining players fold.

Session 2: Hand 129-130

Q-7s (BB, RIF).

A loose woman player raises from the cutoff. I call in the small blind with **K♣-10♣**. If you play from the small blind against a late-position raiser, you should usually reraise to get it heads-up. However, the big blind already has chips in his hands, so I doubt he will fold to my raise. So, should I play K-10s for three bets or for two? I opt for the latter and just call. The big blind calls. Three players, pot $180.

Flop: J♥-Q♣-6♥. I bet my open-ended straight draw. The big blind calls and the lady in late position folds. Two players, pot $240.

Turn: 9♦. Thanks to the Poker Gods, finally I hit something. I bet the nut straight and to my delight my opponent calls. Two players, pot $360.

River: 2♠ (board: J♥-Q♣-6♥--9♦-2♠). Still with the nuts, there is nothing to think about. I bet and the big blind calls. He mucks his hand when he sees the winner, so I don't know what he had.

Session 2: Hand 131

On the next hand I'm on the button. An early-position player and two late-position players limp, I call with **5-5,** the small blind folds and the big blind raises. To my surprise, the early-position player raises again and the two limpers call behind. It costs me 60 bucks to stay in the hand. I'm getting 6.3-to-1 pot odds (6.8-to-1 if the big blind calls) and I'm about a 7.5-to-1 underdog to flop a set. I call. The big blind makes it four bets, the early-position player caps it and we all call. I got trapped for five bets with my pocket fives. Since we are five players and I have implied odds should I hit a set, I get about the right price for my hand, although I don't like to invest $150 with just a small pocket pair. Five players, pot $770.

The flop is Q-10-6 and I miss my set. The big blind checks, the early-position player bets and the two players behind call. Now we have an interesting situation. Normally, when holding a small pocket pair in a multiway pot, you either flop a set (or an open-ended straight draw) or you're gone. Here I have pot odds of 28.7-to-1 and I am a 22.5-to-1 underdog to turn a set. Clearly, the pot is so big that it's justified to take a card off with just two outs. I call and the big blind calls as well. Five players, pot $920.

It would have been great had my $30 investment won me a monster pot. Unfortunately, the turn is a J. The early-position player bets and only the big blind calls (I fold; my pot odds have dropped to 16.3-to-1). Pot $1,040.

River: A (board: Q-10-6-J-A). Both players check. The early-position player has Q-Js and the big blind wins with A-J! No question, Q-Js and A-J are not the kind of hands with which you want to make it four or five bets pre-flop, but these guys did, and it paid off for once.

Session 2: Hands 132-134

A-7, J-4.

In early position I raise with A♦-K♦ and get six callers. Yes, the game is really good. When someone calls, they all follow like lemmings. With A-Ks I don't mind if I get a lot of callers, since it's a hand that plays well in multiway pots. Seven players, pot $420.

The flop opens some possibilities for me: 10♦-7♦-4♥. I bet, the cutoff raises and I call. Astonishingly, the other players all fold. Two players, pot $540.

The turn is Q♣, not what I was hoping for, but at least it's not a complete blank. It gives me three additional outs to win (or split) the pot. I don't think my opponent has a straight draw; it appears that he raised on the flop to protect his hand. If this is the case, then a bet on my part doesn't make much sense because he will not release his hand, and he may even raise. I check, and am surprised when my opponent checks behind. This reinforces my suspicion that he just has a pair of tens and that the overcard keeps him from betting. Two players, pot $540.

River: 6♥ (board: 10♦-7♦-4♥-Q♣-6♥). All I have is ace-high. There is no doubt in my mind that my opponent will call should I bet. Trying to bluff here is just wasting money. I check and he checks behind. My opponent turns over 10-7! He was so timid that he checked his two pair twice. That's the only good news for me on this hand: I saved money.

Session 2: Hands 135-137

9-8 (UTG), 5-4 (BB, RIF).

A middle-position player player limps and I complete the bet from the small blind with Q-6. The big blind gets a free play.

Three-handed (pot $90), we look at the flop: A-A-10. I check, the big blind checks and the middle-position player bets. His play looks like a move to pick up the pot. It's nearly impossible that he has an ace. A typical player does not bet trips in a shorthanded pot. He is afraid that everybody will fold and he won't get paid off. Therefore, I think he either has a ten, a pocket pair or absolutely nothing. I suspect the latter, so I raise. The big blind folds quickly and the middle-position player calls. Two players, pot $210.

Turn: 5. My steal-raise didn't work. I doubt that another bluff will make him lay down. I check and he checks behind. Two players, pot $210.

River: 4 (board: A-A-10-5-4). My queen-high will not be good enough to take down the pot. His check on the turn gives me some hope that a bluff will work. I bet and he calls. Not wanting to show my hand, I say, "You win.", who proudly turns over 10-9.

Session 2: Hands 138-139

I fold 7-5 (B).

Next hand, the UTG player limps. Since some players are walking, I'm already in middle position. I raise with **Q-Q**. Only the button, the small blind and the limper call. Four players, pot $270.

Flop: K-9-2. The small blind and the UTG player check to me. The board contains an overcard, but I must assume that I have the best hand, in which case I must bet to protect it. The button and the small blind fold; the UTG player calls. We are heads-up, pot $330.

Turn: 4. My opponent checks. Nothing has changed. If I had the best hand on the flop, I still have the best hand. This is confirmed by my opponent's passive play. I bet and he calls. Two players, pot $450.

River: 2 (board: K-9-2-4-2). The UTG player checks and I check behind. My opponent turns over A-J and my queens take the pot. Admittedly, my check at the end was lame. However, I doubt that my opponent would have called, so at least my weak play didn't cost me a bet.

Session 2: Hands 140-150

J-6, **8-3**, **5-2s**, **10-2** (BB), **A-3** (SB, RIF), **A-2** (B), **A-4** (CO), **J-9s** (RIF), **10-7s**, **A-8**.

I'm dealt K-Q UTG. I mentioned earlier (2/128) that K-Q is playable from early position if there is not a lot of raising and reraising. I call, the 9 seat in middle position raises and only the small blind calls. I call. Just three players this time, pot $210.

The flop is good: K-10-7. The small blind checks. With top pair, second-best kicker, I take the initiative by betting. The 9 seat calls and the small blind folds. Two players, pot $270.

Turn: 2. A perfect card for me. I bet and my opponent calls. Two players, pot $390.

River: 2 (board: K-10-7-2-2). Another perfect card for me. Since the 9 seat only called on the flop and the turn, I'm sure I hold the best hand. I bet and my opponent folds.

Session 2: Hands 151-152

In the big blind I get a free play with **10-2s**. Four players (pot $120) see the

A-7-2 flop. The small blind bets and I give up.

On the next hand a late-position player limps and I complete the bet from the small blind with **7-5**. The big blind asks if we want to do a three-way chop. The limper shrugs his shoulders and says, "Okay, why not?" I don't object, of course, since I'm in the worst possible position with what is probably the worst hand. Getting back one-third of the pot is definitely a +EV situation for me. Three-way chops are usually not allowed in raked games because the house loses money. But this is not the case in our time-fee game. The dealer doesn't say a word when we take our money back.

Session 2: Hand 153

The 2 seat in middle-position limps. Right behind him is Ray, a player who tries to make a living as a pro. He certainly is an above-average player, but not good enough to make it as a pro in the long run. He raises the pot. I hold A♥-Q♥ two spots behind him at the button. Reraising is an option. But A-Qs plays well in multiway pots, so I just call to let the blinds in. But both blinds fold and the limper in the 2 seat calls. Three players, pot $230.

Flop: A♠-J♣-9♣. The limper checks and Ray bets. Though I have top pair with a good kicker, the board opens up several flush and straight possibilities. There is no way I can eliminate the draws by raising. I just call to see the turn. The limper in the 2 seat calls also. Three players, pot $320.

Turn: A♣. The 2 seat checks and Ray bets. Though my hand has improved to trips, the flush card is awkward. Ray could have any of the following: a) a flush; b) a full house (perhaps J-J or A-J); c) trips with a better kicker (A-K); d) a hand that got help from the board but is worse than mine (A-10 or Q-Js); d) a flush or straight draw; or f) a busted hand like 7-7.

Obviously in cases a) through c) I'm better off calling than raising. The same is true for case f). If he has a busted hand he will fold to a raise, but if I just call I can probably induce a bluff at the end and collect another big bet. However, in cases d) and e) I should raise to make him pay for his draw. Tough decision. What tips me towards calling is that there is still another player in the hand who called the flop and checked the turn. It wouldn't be unusual if this player made a flush on the turn and checked with the intention to check-raise. In that case it would cost me $180 instead of $60 trying to make a full house. I call and the 2 seat folds. Two players, pot $450.

River: 7♥ (board: A♠-J♣-9♣-A♣-7♥). Ray bets and I call. He shows K♠-Q♣. No pair. My trips are good.

How did I play that hand? Probably too passively. The good news is that it cost me no money. Had I raised on the turn, Ray would have called with the nut-flush draw and a gutshot, but he wouldn't have put more money in the pot on the river when he missed. By not raising on the turn I let him draw cheaply; it was a weak play and I was lucky he missed his flush. Of course, when you look back at the hand you are always smarter. Nonetheless, I didn't pay enough attention to the fact that with two opponents it's likely that at least one has a club for a flush draw. That asked for a more aggressive approach on the turn.

Session 2: Hands 154-156

A-10 (CO, RIF), **6-5**, **J-8**.

Four players are walking and it looks like the game will break down or come to a halt soon. Since it is my turn to take the big blind, I don't want to put money in the pot and then have the table break up. I have been playing for over four hours; good time to take a break.

When I come back, my table is indeed down, but there are still two $30-60 tables in progress. They look okay, but neither is really very good. I go to the center podium and see that there are four names on the list. I don't think it's worth the wait, and decide to end the session. Tomorrow is another, hopefully better, day for me.

Result Session 2		Total Results	
Hours	4:15	Hours	10:45
Win/Loss	-$832	Win/Loss	-$1107

Conclusion

Another disappointing session, my fourth consecutive losing session if you include those before I started recording hands for this book. From a philosophical point of view, this is perfectly acceptable, since anything can happen in the short-run. That the game is good and you are the best or one of the best players at the table doesn't imply that you will win any given session.

Winning takes patience, an adequate bankroll and the ability to shrug off temporary setbacks. The last two games were really, really good, with lots of loose players giving me plenty of action. With all due modesty, I think I was a big favorite at the table. Maybe I played a little worse—specifically less aggressively—than usual because I was distracted by taking notes, but I committed no serious blunders (with the exception of the K-K laydown in the first session). However, playing poker requires a capacity for suffering. If you don't catch cards, or if your opponents draw out on you, there is nothing you can do. Always keep that in mind. That's one lesson you can learn from these two disappointing sessions.

To Chop or Not to Chop?

I chop for two reasons: It speeds things up, and it makes my opponents happy, since most of them want to chop. However, chopping is often the subject of heated debates among poker players. Should you chop or not? The answer is quite simple.

Is chopping profitable? Even the best hold'em players in the world lose money in the blinds. No one can overcome the disadvantage of putting money in the pot in the worst position with two random cards. The key to being a successful player is to make more money when you voluntarily put money into the pot than you lose in the blinds. Even the worst player in the world could break even if he could chop every time. He would do this by folding any hand he was dealt. This way his expected value would always be zero. Therefore, there is no question that chopping indeed is profitable.

If chopping is profitable, could not chopping be even more profitable, especially if you are a good heads-up player? To answer this question, we have to look at raked and time-fee games separately.

The maximum rake at the Bellagio is $4 per hand. Most casinos will not take a rake if there is no flop or if one player folds to a flop bet. But the specific procedure is irrelevant. No reasonable player would play heads-up with a $4 rake. But that's exactly what you are doing if you don't chop in a raked game. The rake is simply too high to make playing worthwhile.

Let's do some simple arithmetic. The game is $4-8 heads-up. We will assume that the rake is $4, you play 50 hands per hour and that on average, 20 hands are fully raked, in which case the house collects $80 per hour. That means the better heads-up player has to beat his opponent for more than ten big bets per hour to show a profit. Even in the $10-20 game, the highest raked game in Las Vegas, the superior player must beat his opponent for over four big bets per hour to show a profit.

Things are different in a time-fee game. Since there is no rake, every player keeps what he wins. In this case, a good heads-up player has an advantage over a not-so-skilled opponent, and playing instead of chopping makes sense. Of course, it makes a difference whether you have the small or the big blind, but the argument generally holds true: In raked games chopping is always better than playing; in time-fee games a good heads-up player makes more money by playing.

One last word of caution: Chopping is not done on a case-by-case basis. If you do it once, you have to do it every time during a session[23]. It is unethical (and against the rules in some card rooms) to suddenly not want to chop because you have pocket aces.

A Typical Problem in Middle-Limit Hold'Em

Are you ready for the $30-60 limit hold'em game? Here is a hand problem to test your skill. This is neither overly complicated nor trivial; it's just the type of hand you are confronted with all the time in limit hold'em.

In a full-ring game you are dealt A♥-Q♠ under the gun. What do you do?

A-Q is too strong to fold and too weak for a call. The latter may sound surprising, but it's true. If you just call, you give the players behind you better pot odds and invite them to call. Therefore, you usually do this with hands that play well in multiway pots. But A-Q doesn't play well out-of-position in this situation. Two unsuited high cards lose a lot of value in multiway pots. Thus, the correct answer is that you should raise. You hope that you get just one or two callers. This goal can be achieved best by rais-

---

[23] The exception is when the game gets short-handed; many players refuse to chop when there are five or less players at the table. That is a sensible arrangement.

ing. A hand like A-Q gains a lot of its value from its ability to win unimproved. But this only happens if you have few opponents.

You raise. A loose player right behind you reraises, a solid player calls the three bets cold and a loose/aggressive action guy calls as well. All other players, including the blinds, fold. There are three opponents, the pot is $380 and it costs you $60 to call. What do you do?

Two of your opponents are loose players. Though weak players can wake up with big hands, it's just possible that one of them has, for instance, 8-8 and the other A-Js, in which case you would be in good shape. The real problem is the solid player. A solid player doesn't call three bets cold with a worse hand than A-Q. Therefore, raising is out of the question[24]. But you get pot odds of about 6.5-to-1, which is too good to fold.

You call. There are four players and the pot is $410. The flop comes 10♦-J♠-7♥. You are first to act. What do you do?

Betting is pointless. In a double-raised pot with a flop like that, there is no way that all three opponents will fold. With your weak hand you don't want to put in a lot of money, and the less the better.

You correctly check. The pre-flop reraiser bets, the solid player calls and the action guy folds. There are three players, the pot is $470 and it costs you $30 to call. What do you do?

You have flopped a gutshot and you have two overcards. It's hard to determine the value of the overcards, but you have four nut outs (any K). With pot odds of 15.7-to-1 the call is automatic.

You call. There are three players and the pot is $500. On the turn the Q♣ comes. What do you do?

On the turn you got what you are always hoping for when you have a hand like A-Q: top pair, top kicker. However, the board is dangerous and it's questionable that you have the best hand. You should check and see what happens.

You check, the player behind you bets and the solid player raises. There is

---

[24] If you assume that the solid player hadn't called, you still shouldn't raise. Even loose players need some sort of hand to make it three bets and to call three bets cold. A-Q is not strong enough to four-bet in this situation.

$680 in the pot and it costs you $120 to call. What do you do?

In this situation, it's crucial to ask the right questions. The first question is: Can I be in the lead? At least one of your opponents likely has a straight, a set, two pair (very unlikely) or an overpair. If you don't have the best hand, the second question is: Do I have the right odds to draw? The pot is $680 and it costs you $120 to call (pot odds 5.7-to-1). With pot odds like this you need about seven outs, or slightly less if you can expect to win one or more bets at the end.

You have nine outs to improve your hand (three aces, four kings and two queens). How many of these outs are good? It's to be assumed that none of the aces will give you the winning hand. Any king would make a straight, and even in the unlikely case that no king is out, then the probability increases that one of your opponents has a set. Any king would give you the nuts, but if an ace is out, you are only drawing at half the pot, and if one or more kings are out, you have fewer nut-outs. If you hit a queen on the end, you still lose against a straight or a set that would fill up. You lack the pot odds to draw, and thus you must fold.

By the way, this is not a constructed hand problem. In fact, I've already discussed it, but from a different point of view. It's hand 2/66. I won that hand with A-K, the pre-flop reraiser had K-K and the player with A-Q was Pizza Mike, a tough pro. Now that you know Pizza Mike's hand, look back at that hand and notice how expertly he played. In my experience, nearly all average players, and even some good ones, wouldn't be able to resist the temptation to call with top pair, top kicker in a fairly large pot.

If you got all the answers right for the right reasons, you're well on the way to becoming a successful middle-limit hold'em player.

Session 3: Bellagio, Wednesday, September 7, 8:35 p.m.

When I enter the Bellagio poker room there are three $30-60 tables in progress but no open seats. I take a quick look at the lineup. At least two games look good. I go to the center podium and Boba, the floorman, already has my name on the waiting list. We have known each other for over ten years. Every time he sees me coming he immediately puts my name on the list. He knows how to take care of me. Boba calls my name after a 20-minute wait. I get a seat at table 28.

Session 3: Hands 1-3

I post behind the button in the 8 seat. The player right in front of me raises. I look at my hand, **6-5**, and fold. Though I had position and could have played for half-price, 6-5 is not a hand I like to play heads-up. With one or more additional players, I would have looked at the flop.

On the next two hands I fold **7-5s** and **J-8**.

Session 3: Hand 4

The tourist in the 7 seat raises again. I fold **10-4** in middle position. Right behind me is Ray, a would-be pro we already met (2/153). He makes it three bets and all the players behind him fold. The 7 seat raises again and Ray calls. Two players, pot $290.

The flop is 3-2-3. The 7 seat bets, Ray raises and the tourist calls (pot $410).

Turn: 3. The tourist checks and then calls Ray's bet (pot $530).

River: 10 (board: 3-2-3-3-10). The 7 seats check-calls again. It looks to me like the tourist must have a couple of high cards and Ray a pocket pair. My assessment proves to be right. The 7 seat shows A♣-K♣ and Ray 6 6 for a baby full house.

Ray played the hand well post-flop, but I don't like his reraise with just a pair of sixes before the flop. This play, three-betting a raiser with a small pair in an attempt to isolate him, has spread like a disease in middle-limit games. The logic behind this play seems convincing, especially to aggressive players, but it's actually flawed[25].

Session 3: Hand 5

I'm in third position. The tourist in the 7 seat plays again. But this time he just limps. I raise with A♥-Q♦.

Only the big blind, a solid regular, and the limper call the raise. Three players, pot $200.

Flop: K♦-J♠-K♠. The big blind checks and the 7 seat bets. It's very unlikely

---

[25] See p. 229 for explanation.

that the bettor holds a king. Since I have position and showed strength by raising pre-flop, an average player would attempt a check-raise with a king on the flop or turn. Therefore, I put him on a jack, a pocket pair or a flush- or straight-draw. Even if I'm currently behind, I have ten outs[26] if my opponent has a pair. The solid player in the big blind is another concern, but so far he's shown no strength. I call and the big blind folds. Two players, pot $260.

Turn: Q♣. The 7 seat bets and I call. I'm pretty sure I have the best hand. So, should I raise or call?

In case my opponent has a flush draw, I should definitely raise, which gains me a bet on the turn I wouldn't get at the end. However, my instinct tells me that he wouldn't bet a flush draw on that board. That means he has just two outs[27]. If I raise, it's very unlikely that he'll call with a jack or a pocket pair. Calling is not too dangerous, and has two advantages: I may get another bet from him on the end, and I lose less money if my analysis is wrong and he really has a king. Still two players, pot $380.

River: 4♠ (board: K♦-J♠-K♠-Q♣-4♠). My opponent bets and I call. Raising is out of the question, since he will only call (or raise) with a better hand. Though I didn't put my opponent on a flush draw, I certainly didn't want to see a spade. But my worries dissipate when he shows J♣-9♣ for a pair of jacks.

Session 3: Hands 6-9

9-5, **K-3** (UTG), **K-Js** (BB, three bets to me), **K-10** (SB, RIF).

Session 3: Hand 10

It's folded to me on the button and I raise with **Q-10**. Only Ray in the small blind calls. Two players, pot $150.

Flop: K-9-6. Ray checks and I bet. The bet is automatic. I bet almost every

---

[26] If an A, Q or 10 comes on the turn, I can beat a pair of jacks. Notice that even if my opponent has A-J or Q-J and duplicates one of my hole cards, it doesn't help him.

[27] Notice again that because of the pair of kings on the board, hitting the kicker doesn't help my opponent if he has a pair of jacks.

time in this situation. You don't want to miss an opportunity to pick up the pot with air. Ray calls (pot $210).

Turn: 9. Ray checks. The 9 is a bad card for me. What can Ray hold? Since there is not much of a draw out (only 8-7, and that's very unlikely) I have to put Ray on a K, 9, 6 or pocket pair. If I bet and he raises, I lose the opportunity to hit my gutshot. So I check behind (pot $210).

River: A (board: K-9-6-9-A). Ray checks. Clearly, my queen-high can't be the best hand. The ace on the river is an excellent bluffing card. Ray will call with an A or K, raise with a 9, and possibly fold with a 6 or a pocket pair. I think it's worth a try, and I bet. Ray calls. I say, "No pair," and Ray turns over K♥-7♥. I don't like Ray's pre-flop call but it won him the pot.

Session 3: Hands 11-12

I fold **9-5** in the cutoff seat. On the next hand an early-position player limps. I hold **K-6s**, two seats before the button. A weak hand like that with just one limper typically goes into the muck. But, not only the limper but the two players in the blinds are extremely weak, increasing the value of my hand considerably. I have position against the weak players and may get a lot of action if I hit something. I call. Ray calls behind and the two blinds play. Five players, pot $150.

Flop: 7-6-3. The blinds check and the early limper bets. My second pair with a good kicker could be the best hand. I raise to protect it. Ray and the small blind fold; the big blind and the bettor call. Three players, pot $330.

Turn: 9. Both players in front of me check. The last thing I want to do with my weak hand is give my opponents a free card. I bet and they both call. Three players, pot $510.

River: Q (board: 7-6-3-9-Q). Both players check and I check behind. Betting my small pair with three overcards on board against two opponents seems a bit too optimistic. The big blind turns over 10-9 and the early-position limper shows 5-5. The pair of nines wins the pot.

The big blind is weak, but you can't fault his play. He got a free play with 10-9. On the flop he called two bets with a gutshot and two overcards. I'm not sure I would have done it, but the call is justifiable. Then with top pair and a gutshot, he had an easy call on the turn.

Session 3: Hands 13-25

6-5, Q-5, 9-4.

The UTG player limps; I call behind with **Q-10s**. The game is loose and my hand has excellent drawing potential, hence the call. Seven players, pot $210. Flop: 5♠-3♠-K♥. Since I have no spades, I fold quickly to the big blind's bet.

K-10 (UTG), **Q-8** (BB, RIF).

There are three limpers; I call in the small blind with **K-9**. The big blind gets a free play. Five players, pot $150. Flop: A-6-A and I'm done with the hand.

J-9 (B), **6-5** (CO), **10-3**, **3-2s**, **6-2**, **7-4** (UTG).

Session 3: Hand 26

I get a free play in the big blind with **6-6**. There are two limpers, and the small blind has called. Four players, pot $120.

Flop: A♥-9♥-9♣. The small blind checks. I think it's time to make a move at the pot. There are just two limpers behind me. I can take down the pot if none of them has an A, a 9 or a flush draw. I bet. Only the two seat, the guy who beat me with 10-9 a couple of hands before, calls (pot $180).

Turn: 3♥. I have no idea what my opponent holds. I decide to shoot as long as the third spade doesn't show up. I bet and my opponent folds. Strange. With what hands would you call on the flop, then fold on a blank turn? Be that as it may, I'm happy to take the pot.

Session 3: Hands 27-34

9-6 (SB, RIF), **8-2** (B), **Q-2** (CO). The tourist in the 7 seat leaves the table. He was all-in, now he goes with two racks. **K-9**, **9-2**, **Q-6s**, **2-2**, **3-2** (UTG).

Just when it's my turn to take the big blind, the floorman calls me for a table change. Perfect timing, since two weak players at the table have left, to be replaced by tough locals. I grab my chips and head over to table 25, where seat 6 is open.

Session 3: Hand 35

I post behind and I'm dealt 7♣-3♦. There are limpers in front of me; I check and both blinds play. Six players, pot $180. The flop is A♣-K♥-Q♠.

It's checked to me in last position. I check behind (pot still $180).

Turn: A♦. The first four players check and then Pizza Mike bets. I reraise and everybody, including Mike, folds. Without a doubt, this is the best play you've seen from me so far.

How could I know Mike was bluffing and no one else had a hand? Actually, the play is quite straightforward, and I was virtually certain of its success. Let's look at the hand in detail.

The key is that Mike just checked the flop in second-to-last position, a clear indication of weakness. Let's assume Mike would have flopped the nuts with J-10. Would he check on the flop? Of course not! The board is way too dangerous. Any J or 10 on the turn would probably cost him half the pot, and any A, K or Q could give someone a full house. If he had a hand he would have bet the flop to protect it.

Why did I wait until the turn to make a move? Simply because there is not just Mike, but four other players that are of concern. It's quite possible that one of them checked the flop with the intention to check-raise. In that case I would have just wasted a bet. A-K-Q is not the kind of flop you want to bluff at in multiway pots.

That all changed when the second ace came on the turn and none of the early players bet. None of them would check an ace twice with that board (one of them might have a king or queen, but that's not strong enough to call a double bet). Of course, Mike could add up two and two as well as I could, so he correctly sensed weakness, and that it presented an excellent opportunity to bluff. I knew that no one held an ace, Mike was making a move at the pot and no one had the strength to call two bets cold, so I raised. The reasoning behind the play is easy to understand; the art is to recognize the situation and take advantage of it.

Session 3: Hands 36-40

9-5, 8-5s, 8-6 (UTG).

We are down to six players. I get a free play in the big blind with **K-7**. Four players, pot $120. Flop: J♦-6♥-4♥. The small blind bets and I fold.

On the next hand there are again two limpers. I call from the small blind with **A-Q**. Raising is certainly an option here. With unsuited high cards I often just call from the small blind if there is more than one caller. That allows me to take a cheap look at the flop, and my hand is well disguised. The big blind checks. Four players, pot $120.

Flop: K♦-Q♠-7♠. I check, the big blind checks, the first limper bets and the second calls. I have no idea if my second pair is best. The board presents many drawing possibilities, giving me some hope that my A-Q may be good. I call. The big blind folds. Three players, pot $210.

Turn: 4♥. I check, the first limper bets and the second one calls. Nothing has changed from the flop to the turn. If I had the best hand on the flop, then it's still best. I call (pot $390).

River: 3♠ (board: K♦-Q♠-7♠-4♥-3♠). A bad card. It's pretty much impossible that I'm best, so I check. The first limper bets and the second raises. At least that makes things easy for me. I fold and the first limper calls. The first limper shows 7-7 for a set of sevens and the second wins with K♠-8♠.

I was not only beat on the flop, I was drawing close to dead[28]. The passive play of the second limper cost me 90 bucks. He just called on the flop with top pair and a flush draw. Had he raised, I would have folded.

Session 3: Hand 41

I open-raise with **4-4** on the button. Only the big blind calls, pot $140.

Flop: 8-8-5. The big blind checks, I bet and he calls (pot $200).

Turn: 9. My opponent checks. I probably have the best hand, and I don't want to give my opponent a free card. I bet and he calls (pot $320).

River: Q (board: 8-8-5-9-Q). The big blind checks. I don't think betting has a positive expected value. If my opponent has a pocket pair himself, it's probably higher than mine. He'll call if he has a pair (fives, nines or queens). He probably won't call with nothing. And I could run into a check-raise. I call. The big blind turns over A-J and my fours win the pot.

---

[28] Winning percentages on the flop: A♣-Q♦ 2.10%, 7♦-7♥ 66.33%, K♠-8♠ 31.56%.

Session 3: Hands 42-67

9-7 (CO), **9-3s.** The game is nine-handed now. **J-2, 9-5, K-10** (UTG), **A-7** (BB, RIF), **Q-3s** (SB, RIF), **Q-4** (B), **K-6** (CO), **J-9.**

One player has limped in front of me; I call from middle position with **K-Q.** Both blinds play, pot $120. Flop: 3♥-2♣-4♥. The small blind bets, the big blind raises, the first limper folds, and I have to release my hand.

10-3, 8-5s (UTG).

I get a free play in the big blind with **8-4.** Five players, pot $150. Flop: 2♦-2♣-9♦. The small blind bets and I fold.

A-2s (SB, three bets to me), **8-5** (B), **6-2** (CO), **Q-7, K-4, 9-2s, 9-7, 9-3** (UTG).

I move into the 9 seat. Two players come from a broken game, one of them the guy who made me lay down K-K in the first session. Hopefully, this is not a bad omen. The table is full.

6-4, K-2, Q-6s (BB, three bets to me).

I **chop** in the small blind. I muck without looking at my hand.

Session 3: Hand 68

A player wearing a faded "Howard Dean for America" T-shirt limps from middle position and I raise on the button with **Q-Q.** The big blind calls. Three players, pot $200.

Flop: 10♣-2♣-3♦. The big blind and the limper both check. I bet and the big blind folds. The limper raises and I call. Two players, pot $320.

Turn: 8♥. The guy with the Howard Dean T-shirt bets. I start to wonder if I should raise or just call. I decide to call for a couple of reasons. It's quite possible that this obviously aggressive player is trying to move me off the pot. He will fold to a raise if he has nothing, but will bluff again on the river if I just call. If he has a flush draw, I lose less by not raising if he completes his hand on the river, and I make probably the same amount if he misses, because he will bluff the river. And he might have flopped a set. In that case, to not raise is much better. All that speaks for calling. The exception is if he has a pair with A-10 or 7-7, for instance, in which case raising is clearly the superior play. Two players, pot $460.

River: 5♠ (board: 10♣-2♣-3♦-8♥-5♠). My opponent bets and I call. He shows A♣-8♣ and my pocket queens are good. All in all, my opponent didn't play the hand too badly. Pushing a draw heads-up is often the right thing to do. However, at the end he should have checked. With his pair of eights, he had something to show down. It remains unclear why he bet. Did he do so because he was value-betting or because he intended to bluff? At least the bet at the end didn't cost him anything. Had he checked, I would have bet.

Session 3: Hands 69-75

6-6 (CO), **5-4**, **10-6**, **8-4** (BB, RIF), **6-3** (SB, RIF), **Q-8s** (B).

The 6 seat, the player who made me lay down K-K, brings it in for a raise from middle position. I make it three bets with K♣-K♠ in the cutoff seat; only the 6 seat calls. Two players, pot $230.

Flop: 6♦-K♦-6♥. My opponent checks. I've flopped a monster and don't want to lose my opponent. Should I check? I sometimes slowplay big hands, but the situation has to be right. Checking after I made it three bets pre-flop in this spot would just look odd and alert my opponent that something fishy is going on. I bet, and to my delight he calls (pot $290).

Turn: 5♦. Again the 6 seat checks. The 5♦ is an excellent card, since it might make my opponent a flush, in which case I could get three bets, or it may give him a flush draw. Anything but a bet would be wrong. I bet and he calls (pot $410).

River: 9♠ (board: 6♦-K♦-6♥-5♦-9♠). My opponent checks, I bet and he raises. The raise comes completely unexpected. I wasn't even sure I would get a call. I was hoping for a fourth diamond, and that he had the ace of diamonds. I don't worry about what he may have—only quad sixes beat me—and reraise. He calls and shows A-K. That's quite a coincidence. Two times I've played against him and both times I had K-K against his A-K; this time I got the better end of it.

Session 3: Hands 76-91

Q-2, **A-10** (RIF), **10-3**, **J-8s**, **10-9** (UTG), **J-6** (BB, RIF), **7-2** (SB, RIF), **Q-9** (B).

Two players limp and I call with **K-J** in the cutoff. The button raises and the small blind makes it three bets. One limper folds; the other calls; I fold. K-J is not a hand you want to play for three bets. No need to throw good money after bad. I got trapped; that happens sometimes.

Next hand I'm two spots off the button and raise with **Q-J** after all the players in front of me fold. Only the button calls (pot $170). Flop: 9♦-3♣-10♦. That's pretty good for me. I have an open-ended straight draw and my opponent has probably missed the ten-high board. I bet and he folds.

Q-3s, 5-5, 9-5, 6-3, 5-2 (UTG).

Two middle-position players limp and the small blind completes. I check **A-10** in the big blind. Flop: Q♥-J♥-8♠. The small blind checks, I check my gutshot, the first limper bets, the second raises and the small blind makes it three bets. Easy fold.

Session 3: Hand 92

The Howard Dean fan in the 5 seat raises, the 7 seat calls and I call in the small blind with **K♥-Q♥**. The big blind also plays. Four players, pot $240.

Flop: 4♠-K♦-8♠. I check, the big blind bets, and the 5 and 7 seats both call. My intention was to raise should one of the late-position players bet. But since the bet came from the player to my left and the others have already called, my raise would eliminate no one, so I call. Still four players, pot $360.

Turn: 8♥. People often see the turn with second pair in multiway pots, hence it's usually bad when the second-highest card pairs. But if I'm in the lead, I don't want to give anyone a free shot to beat me, and I can't count on someone to bet the hand for me. I bet, and all three players call. At least that tells me no one has an 8, and that I probably have the best hand. Four players, pot $600.

River: 8♣ (board: 4♠-K♦-8♠-8♥-8♣). Another not-so-good card. At least it's not a spade, but it's possible I'll only get a half or a third of the pot (depending on how many kings are out). I bet, and am delighted that all my opponents fold.

Session 3: Hands 93-94

I fold **A-2** on the button after two players have limped.

Two middle-position players limp and I call with **K-J** from the cutoff seat. Both blinds play. Five players, pot $150.

Flop: Q♥-J♥-8♠. It's checked to the 7 seat (the second limper), who bets. I have a pair, a gutshot and an overcard. It's hard to tell how many outs I really have (or if I hold the best hand), but 6-to-1 pot odds are good enough to call and take off another card. The other players fold. Two players, pot $210.

Turn: 5♣. The 7 seat bets again. My pot odds have dropped to 4.5-to-1, and the turn was no help, so I fold.

I might well have folded the best hand. It would have probably been better to raise on the flop, trying to quickly find out where I stood.

Session 3: Hand 95

It's folded to me in late-middle position and I raise with **A-10**. Only the big blind calls (pot $140).

Flop: 8♣-4♠-2♣. The big blind checks. This is a pretty good flop to steal the pot. I bet and my opponent calls (pot $200).

Turn: J♠. The big blind bets. I don't think he has a flush (most players would try to check-raise in this situation) but I have nothing, so I fold.

Session 3: Hands 96-115

3-2, **K-6s**, **10-8s** (UTG).

A middle-position player raises; the cutoff and the button both call. I call with **Q-10** in the big blind. Four players, pot $260. Flop: 5-7-3. I check, the original raiser bets and the two players behind him call. My two overcards are certainly not good enough to call. I fold (the original raiser wins the hand with 10-10).

7-6 (SB, RIF), **K-Q** (B, raise from UTG), **7-2** (CO), **5-2**, **10-6**, **A-10** (RIF), **J-7s**, **4-2**, **8-4** (UTG), **J-8** (BB, RIF).

Five players limp and I complete the bet from the small blind with **10-6**. Seven players, pot $210. Flop: 8-Q-8. I check-fold.

4-4 (B, RIF), **Q-3** (CO), **J-6**, **10-8**, **8-3s**.

Session 3: Hand 116

I limp in first position with K♦-Q♥. I did this because the game is pretty loose, but interestingly, everybody behind me folds. Only the blinds play. Not a bad result, having position against two random hands. Three players, pot $90.

The flop is Q♠-4♠-3♥. The small blind bets and the big blind folds. My top pair, second-best kicker is a strong hand. The small blind is the young guy who made me lay down K-K in the first session. He is a very aggressive player. If I just call, he will bet the turn no matter what comes. He may be bluffing, and would fold to a raise, so I just call, intending to raise on the turn. Two players, pot $150.

Turn: 7♠. My opponent bets out as expected. The turn card makes a flush possible. If my opponent was semi-bluffing on the flop with a flush draw, he's made his hand. But tricky players tend to check when they hit their hand, hoping to induce a check-raise. That speaks against a flush. Also, if I call on the turn I will have to call on the river. If he has picked up a flush draw, I should make him pay to draw out. I raise and he calls (pot $390).

River: 8♦ (board: Q♠-4♠-3♥-7♠-8♦). The small blind checks and I check behind. He turns over A♠-5♦ and the dealer pushes me the pot.

My opponent played the hand aggressively but well. His pre-flop call out of the small blind was correct. He flopped a gutshot and went ahead and bet that hand. With just two opponents and only one picture card on the flop, he had an excellent chance to pick up the pot. The third spade on the turn gave him a powerful draw. Against top pair, my most likely hand, he had as many as 15 outs (9 spades, 3 aces and 3 sixes). Betting his draw was better than just checking, since it gave him an additional way to win.

Session 3: Hands 117-120

K-8 (BB, chop), **5-3** (SB, RIF), **K-6** (B).

The UTG player raises the pot and the next three players call. I call in the cutoff with A♣-K♦. I would have reraised if I were right behind the raiser, but A-K isn't strong enough in multiway pots to make it three bets. The small blind folds, the big blind calls. Six players, pot $380.

The flop is 4♣-4♠-3♦. The original raiser bets and three players call behind. Had I been right behind the bettor, I would have raised to thin the field. But after three players have already called, raising only makes the pot bigger. I call and the big blind folds. Five players, pot $530.

Flop: 4♦. The four players in front of me all check. Looks like nobody has a hand. I can't give all these guys a free card to beat me, so I bet. Two players (including the original raiser) fold and two call. Three players, pot $760.

River: 2♥ (board: 4♣-4♠-3♦-4♦-2♥). Both opponents check. You usually shouldn't bet an unimproved A-K at the end because you normally only get a call when you are beat. But it's unlikely that one of my opponents has a pocket pair, since it would be an overpair to the board and he would probably have played it faster. There is a small chance that someone holds a deuce or trey, but it's more likely I'll get a crying call from someone with ace-high just because of the size of the pot. I decide to bet my A-K for value, and my opponents reluctantly fold. What a strange hand! It's not often that you win a six-handed pot with unimproved A-K.

Session 3: Hands 121-131

I fold **8-4**. Then three players limp and I call from middle position with **Q-10**. The button calls and the small blind raises. The big blind folds and the limpers (including me) call. Six players, pot $390. Flop: 9-7-9. The small blind bets and two of the limpers in front of me call. I muck my hand.

10-5, **6-2s** (BB, RIF), **Q-7** (SB, RIF), **J-4s** (B), **9-6** (CO), **10-3s**, **10-9s**, **10-5**, **A-8s** (UTG).

Session 3: Hand 132

The cutoff limps, the button raises and I look at **A-A** in the big blind. While I occasionally call with a big pair from the blinds to mix up my play, I never do this against late-position players. They don't necessarily have strong hands, so I want to charge them as quickly as possible. I reraise and both players call. Three players, pot $200.

Flop: 6-4-7. It makes no sense to worry if my opponents have hit anything. I have a big overpair, I made it three bets before the flop and I have just two opponents. In this situation you just have to assume you have the best hand. I bet and both players call (pot $290).

Turn: A. Not a good card because it usually kills the action. There is just one ace left and not much of a draw (with just two players in a raised pot, it's unlikely that someone has a five). I would have preferred any picture card, since it may have made someone top pair. The ace on the turn makes it a near certainty that I will win the pot. I bet, the cutoff calls and the button raises. I hadn't foreseen such a development. I don't know what the cutoff holds, but the button has either slowplayed a set or has the case ace. Either way, the ace on the turn was excellent for me. I make it three bets and both opponents call. Three players, pot $830.

River: 6 (board: 6-4-7-A-6). I bet, the cutoff calls all-in and the button calls. My aces full are good. The button has A-K and the cutoff leaves the table without showing his hand.

Session 3: Hands 133-135

J-8 (SB, chop), A-7 (B, RIF).

It's folded to me in the cutoff. With **8-8** my raise is automatic. The big blind makes it three bets and I call. Two players, pot $200.

Flop: 10-10-9. The big blind bets and I call (pot $260).

Turn: 6. The big blind fires again. He made it three bets before the flop. That usually means he has a couple of high cards or a pocket pair (probably higher than eights). There is a decent chance that I have the best hand, in which case I don't want to give a free card[29]. I raise and he calls (pot $500).

River: J (board: 10-10-9-6-J). We both check. My opponent mucks his hand.

---

[29] Because my opponent's bet is already in the pot, calling is basically the same as giving him a free card.

Session 3: Hand 136

It's folded to me and I raise with **A-Q**. Only the big blind calls (pot $140).

Flop: K-K-J. The big blind checks, I bet and he calls (pot $200).

Turn: 10. My opponent checks and I check behind. I know that check looks pretty odd. I believe my opponent has either a very big hand or nothing. My check saves money if he holds a full house, and might induce a river bluff if he's sitting on air. Should he have three jacks or a king, then I've made a bad play (pot still $200).

River: 4. The big blind bets and I call. He shows 5-4! My seemingly strange turn play has paid dividends.

Session 3: Hands 137-144

A-7, **8-2s** (UTG), **8-3** (BB, RIF), **7-2** (SB, RIF), **9-3** (B), **A-7** (CO), **K-7**, **K-3**.

A new dealer comes in and starts to collect the six bucks for the time fee. It's 1:00 am, I've been playing for four hours and I'm getting hungry. Good time for a break. I cash in my chips and go to the Noodle Kitchen, the Chinese restaurant at the Bellagio that's still open after midnight. I order my favorite meal there, roasted duck. I'm back in the poker room at about 2:00 a.m. There is only one $30-60 game going, and there are three names on the list. I ask Joe, one of the pros who is still playing, how the game is. He shrugs his shoulders. "It's okay. Not really good." That coincides with my evaluation, so I return to my room.

Result Session 3		Total Results	
Hours	4:15	Hours	15:00
Win/Loss	$1844	Win/Loss	$737

Session 3: Conclusion

This was an interesting session, not because I finally made some money, but because of the way I won the hands. I won 13 out of 144 hands and chopped once. Three times I won with a bluff[30]. Of the remaining ten wins, with one exception[31], I always had the best hand on the flop. That means I never drew out on my opponents. I didn't hit a straight- or flush-draw, nor did I need to improve to win the pot.

You might believe such a session proceeded normally and that's the reason you won. Since you never drew out on your opponents and your opponents didn't draw out on you, that seems to suggest itself. That's a big self-delusion.

I played 4.25 hours and won $1,844, or 7.23 big bets per hour. It's not normal to win at this rate. The only explanation is luck. But how could I get lucky if I didn't draw out on my opponents? I was really lucky in three areas:

1) Flop

2) No draw-outs

3) Opponents' hands

Let's look at these areas more closely.

Flops

I certainly saw good flops. I flopped a full boat with K-K, and I twice made top pair with K-Q. Moreover, I saw safe flops. The first flop was 4♠-K♦-8♠ (3/92) and the second Q♠-4♠-3♥ (3/116). With these flops, I very likely had the best hand, and my opponents had few outs to beat me.

If you have the best hand and no flush draw is out, your opponent has between two and five outs. He has two outs if he holds an underpair like 7-7, three outs if he has top pair with a worse kicker (e.g., K-10 vs K-Q), and five outs if he has second or third pair and his side card doesn't match your kicker (e.g., A-4 vs K-Q on a Q-4-3 board).

---

[30] 3/26, 3/35 and 3/85. I may not have made a better hand fold, but I count them as bluffs since I held weak hands and my opponents didn't show their cards.

[31] 3/15. My opponent flopped a pair and I made a better pair on the turn.

Compare this to a Q♠-J♥-9♠ flop. K-Q still has top pair, but the flop is anything but safe. First, it's totally unclear if you've flopped the best hand. Many players will play any two high cards, in which case you may face a straight, a set or two pair. And even if you have the best hand, you have a long way to go against a lot of powerful draws. Anybody with a ten has an open-ended straight draw, and someone with A♠-10♠ has no less than 17 outs against you, making him the favorite to win the hand.

A flop is sometimes good because, rather than helping your hand, it doesn't help your opponents. When I had 4-4 heads-up against A-J, the flop came 8-8-5 (3/41). My opponent stayed until the end. A small pocket pair is only a marginal favorite against A-J. My expected value was just a couple of dollars, yet I won the whole pot. In another heads-up pot with Q-Q against A-8s, the flop was T-2-3 and I was able to avoid an ace on the board.

When you hold two aces against two opponents you are a big favorite. But we have seen (1/246) that much can go wrong. This can be expensive because it's tough to get away from aces in shorthanded pots, especially on a safe-looking board. When I had pocket aces I saw a good flop: 6-4-7 rainbow (3/132).

Conclusion: In the hands I won, I not only hit good flops, but mostly safe ones.

No Draw-Outs

A good flop puts you just halfway there. You still must survive two additional board cards. In this session, I was a solid favorite to win most of the hands in which I lead after the flop. It appears that it was not unusual that I won these hands. That's correct if you look at the hands individually, but if you look at them as a whole, it's pretty amazing I won them all.

Let's just discuss two hands. On the first hand I had Q-Q and my opponent hold A♣-8♣ (3/68). The flop came 10♣-2♣-3♦. My opponent had a flush draw and an overcard. My queens were a 53.74% favorite to win the hand. In the second hand I had K♦-Q♥ against A♠-5♦ with a Q♠-4♠-3♥ flop (3/116). My opponent had a gutshot, an overcard and a backdoor flush draw. This time I was an even bigger favorite: 67.07%. I was a favorite to win each hand. However, I'm an underdog to win both hands. The probability that this will occur is 36%. And these are just two hands!

One last example from this session is really stunning. In a six-handed pot I had A-K and the flop came 4-4-3 (3/120). It's extremely rare that an unimproved A-K is best against five opponents on the flop. And to survive the turn and the river without improving was amazingly lucky.

Conclusion: with one exception (3/12) I was very fortunate that every time I flopped the best hand, it held up.

Opponents' Hands

More important than winning is how much you win, and that has a lot to do with your opponents' holdings. If you flop a monster and no one can call a bet, you've lost an opportunity to score really big. You only win a fraction of what you could have made if another player had a strong, but second-best hand.

Let's look again at some examples from the last session. On hand 3/75 I had pocket kings and the flop came 6♦-K♦-6♥. My hand was almost certain to win, so the main concern became how to get the most out of it.

It's hard to get action with the top full house because there are usually very few draws out. A flush draw could have helped, but I had just one opponent, and he didn't have a flush draw. However, he had A-K and raised me at the end, winning me three bets on the river. Had he had A-Q instead of A-K, I would have probably won a $230 pot instead of a $770 pot. I made an extra 270 bucks because of my opponent's holdings.

When I had pocket aces I could even trap two players (3/132). The flop was 6-4-7 rainbow. Since the pot was raised before the flop this is a pretty safe flop for my aces. However, it's tough to get action with a board like this. Because my two opponents probably had overcards, I could expect to get a call with this low board. If no picture shows up on the turn it's usually all over.

The turn brought another ace, giving me a set of aces. This is usually the worst card for action because there is only one ace left. Again I got lucky. One of my opponents had A-K and played back at me on the turn, and the second player was trapped for three big bets (I have no idea what he had, as he didn't show his hand at the end). Had the ace not shown up on the turn, and had an opponent not held the case ace, I would have probably won a $400 pot instead of a $1,000 pot.

Conclusion: I got a lot of action with my big hands because my opponents had strong hands themselves.

Poker players tend to immediately recognize when they're unlucky in a session, but not when they're lucky, instead attributing the positive result to their superior playing skill, or simply thinking that the cards finally broke even. That's one of the reasons why so many poker players erroneously believe they are good, winning players.

Session 4: Bellagio, Thursday, September 8, 7:55 p.m.

I arrive a little earlier at the Bellagio poker room than the days before. Three $30-60 games are going on, none of them full. I get a seat immediately at table 28 and, out of three spots, I choose the 8 seat. After yesterday's results, I feel fresh and confident. Perhaps my good run of cards will continue.

Session 4: Hand 1

I post behind the button in an eight-handed game. The 4 seat in early position opens the pot with a raise and it's folded to me. I glimpse at my hand: J♦-10♠ – definitely good enough to call for 30 bucks. The button calls, the small blind calls and the big blind folds. Four players, pot $270.

Flop: J♥-10♦-7♣. The small blind checks and the original raiser bets. I've flopped the top two pair, in all likelihood the best hand. The possibility that someone has 9-8 or a set is remote. However, the board offers a lot of drawing possibilities. Not the time to slowplay my hand. I raise. The button and the small blind call the two bets cold, and the raiser stays in the hand. Four players, pot $510.

Turn: 3♣. The small blind checks and the original raiser bets. The situation is obvious. Had the original raiser had a better hand than me, he would have three-bet the flop. He didn't, so he must have either an overpair or a jack with a big kicker. He bets because there is a decent chance he has the best hand, in which case he doesn't want to give a free card. He interprets my raise on the flop either as an attempt to get a free card on the turn with a hand like Q-9, or as a ploy to drive out the other players with a semi-strong hand like Q-J or A-10. It's safe to assume I hold the best hand, so I raise. The button and the small blind both fold and the bettor calls. Two players, pot $750.

River: 7♠ (board: J♥-10♦-7♣-3♣-7♠). My opponent checks and I check behind, fearing that I may have been counterfeited. My opponent has me beat if he holds an overpair. I can only win if he has a jack with a big kicker. My opponent turns over A-J; my jacks and tens beat his jacks and sevens.

Session 4: Hands 2-18

8-3s, 4-2s, K-8 (UTG).

I get a free play in the big blind with **7-5**. Since one player is walking, we have a family pot with all seven players ($210). Flop: K-Q-3. Three players play and I fold.

In the small blind I fold **7-4** to a raise.

I'm dealt **5-4s** on the button and everyone folds to me. Both blinds are complete strangers to me. So far I haven't seen a hand from them. I take the safe route and fold my small suited connectors.

10-8 (CO), 7-6s, 6-3s, 10-3 (UTG).

I get another free play in the big blind. This time we have six players and my hand is not much better than last time: **J-2** (pot $180). Flop: 10♠-7♦-8♣. There is a bet, then two callers and a raise before I fold.

The hands don't get any better. I complete the bet from the small blind with **3-2**. Four players, pot $120. Flop: K-5-9. I check and nobody behind bets. Turn: J. If a 5, 9 or a small card had come, I would have tried a move, but with the jack showing, I have to check-fold.

There are two limpers in front of me and I call with **A-9** from the button. Both blinds play. Five players, pot $150. Flop: Q♦-8♥-5♦. It's checked to me. With a two-flush and a Q-8 on board, I doubt that everyone will fold to a bet. I check. Turn: J. The small blind bets, one of the limpers calls and I fold.

J-2 (CO), 7-3, Q-7 (UTG), 4-2 (BB, RIF).

Session 4: Hand 19

We are down to five players. The 4 seat raises in early position and I three-bet from the small blind with **10-10**. The big blind and the original raiser call. Three players, pot $270.

Flop: J-6-6. A good flop for my tens. I bet and both players call (pot $360).

Turn: J. An excellent turn card. The best card I could get, besides a ten, since it reduces the likelihood that one of my opponents has a jack. I bet, the big blind folds and then the original raiser makes it two bets. I don't like the raise but there is no way I can fold. I have no idea what my opponent holds. He could be making a move or betting a worse pocket pair than mine. Hence, I call.

River: A (board: J-6-6-J-A). I didn't want to see an ace, since it is quite possible that my opponent raised with a hand like A-K or A-Q (though it's questionable he would have raised with a such a hand on the turn). I check and he checks behind. I turn over my tens; he nods and shows 9-9.

Session 4: Hands 20-39

On the button I fold **10-5**.

In the cutoff seat I pick up **A-3s**. No callers, so I raise and collect the blinds. **9-5**, **J-5**.

Three walkers are back, so that the game is eight-handed again. **Q-7** (UTG), **Q-3** (BB, chop), **10-5** (SB, RIF), **K-8** (B), **10-8** (CO).

Two seats before the button I call with **Q-J**. Six players, pot $180. Flop: 10♦-A♠-5♥. The big blind bets and one limper calls. I have 8-to-1 pot odds for my gutshot. I have implied odds, and there is no flush draw, so I call. The small blind raises, the big blind makes it three bets and the caller folds. I've been trapped, and I release my hand.

Two new players arrive, so the table is full. **A-4**, **8-5s**, **7-3**, **J-3** (UTG).

There is a raise with five callers. I see **2-2** in the big blind. I'm about a 7.5-to-1 underdog to flop a set, and I get 13-to-1 pot odds. Easy call. Seven players, pot $420. Flop: 7♦-10♦-4♣. I give up.

There is just one limper and I call from the small blind with **A-3**. The big blind gets a free play. Three players, pot $90. Flop: Q♦-J♦-7♣. That's not a good flop for stealing the pot. I check, the big blind bets and the limper calls. I take the exit door.

7-4 (B), **8-3** (CO), **J-8**, **K-3**.

Session 4: Hand 40

I pick up **7-7** under the gun. The game has been pretty loose, so I call. The button and the blinds call. Four players, pot $120.

Flop: J♣-4♦-7♣. Both blinds check, I bet and only the small blind calls.

Turn: 3♣. The small blind checks. The flush card means that I could run into a check-raise; nonetheless I must bet to keep from giving a free card. The small blind folds.

Session 4: Hands 41-48

9-5 (BB, RIF), **J-8** (SB, RIF), **10-2s** (B), **9-6** (CO), **A-9**.

In middle position it's folded to me and I raise with **A-10s**. Everyone folds and I win the blinds.

9-4, **10-7** (UTG).

Session 4: Hand 49

The button raises and gets a call from a new player who is posting between. The small blind folds and I just call with **J-J** from the big blind. Three players, pot $210.

Flop: Q-7-3. The new player checks, I bet, the button calls and the new player folds. Two players, pot $260.

Turn: 4. I bet and the button folds, showing K♦-10♦. In hindsight, raising pre-flop would have been better.

Session 4: Hands 50-67

Q-10s (SB, raise from first position with no callers), **10-2s** (B), **Q-3** (CO), **9-5**, **7-7** (RIF), **Q-6**, **K-4s**, **K-8** (UTG).

I get a free play in the big blind with **A-6**. Six players, pot $180. Flop: 8-9-Q. That's it for me.

A-7 (SB, RIF).

Korean Joe, a decent-playing regular, limps from under the gun. It's folded to me on the button. I raise with **A-J**. Both blinds and Joe call. Four players, pot $240. Flop: 8-K-5. It's checked to me. The flop missed me completely. But with just one picture card on the board, I have an opportunity to pick up the pot. I bet, the blinds fold and Korean Joe check-raises. I have no choice but to fold.

A-5 (CO), **2-2**, **5-3s**, **10-3**, **K-6**, **K-2s** (UTG).

A middle-position player raises, the button calls and I call from the big blind with **K-Q**. Three players, pot $200. Flop: 3-4-7. I check, the original raiser checks and the button bets. The button's bet looks like a move to pick up the pot, but with my hand and one player behind, I fold.

Session 4: Hand 68

Four players have limped, and I see **8-8** in the small blind. I complete the bet and the big blind knuckles. Six players, pot $180.

Flop: 6♠-5♣-6♣. With no overcards, this is a pretty good flop for my hand. However, there are plenty of flush and straight draws possible. I can't eliminate these draws by betting, but can probably induce the overcards to fold. I bet. A young, fast, Asian player in the 5 seat raises, and all fold to me. I call, pot $300.

Turn: 8♠. I check, and my aggressive opponent bets, as expected. I raise. The Asian guy goes into the tank. Finally, he folds reluctantly. He probably held something like A-5 and assumed I had a six or eight. Looking back, I probably played the hand too aggressively. Just calling the turn and betting the river may have been better.

Session 4: Hands 69-72

A-9 (B, RIF), **10-2s** (CO), **8-4**.

The young Asian guy in the 5 seat limps under-the-gun and an old, cautious guy behind him raises. In the 8 seat I reraise with A♠-A♦.

The big blind, the Asian limper and the old guy all call. Four players, pot $380.

Flop: 6♥-6♦-3♥. All check to me, the aggressor. I bet and everyone calls. Four players, pot $500.

Turn: Q♥. The big blind and the Asian guy check, then the old player in the 6 seat bets. The turn card makes a flush possible. But he may be betting with A-Q or K-Q. I decide not to give up my overpair, though I don't have the ace of hearts. Raising doesn't seem wise, since I may be badly beat, and two players behind me could check-raise. I call, the big blind folds and the Asian guy calls. Three players, pot $680.

River: K♥ (board: 6♥-6♦-3♥-Q♥-K♥). A horror card for me. The young Asian player bets and the old guy behind him folds. The bettor called the flop and the turn, so he must have something, most likely a big heart[32]. However, this player is not only very aggressive, but likes to bluff as well. I don't have high hopes to win the hand, but the pot is large (my pot odds are over 12-to-1) and my aces are at least good enough to catch a bluff. I call. The Asian player mucks his hand.

Session 4: Hands 73-85

7-3s, A-J (UTG), 5-4 (BB, RIF), J-6 (SB, RIF), A-3 (B), A-5 (CO), K-2, Q-6, A-4, 4-4, 9-5, Q-5 (BB, RIF).

Jimmy, a very strong player who plays mostly mixed games and higher limits, limps from under the gun. The button calls, I complete with 3-3 from the small blind and the big blind gets a free play. Four players, pot $120.

Flop: 3-Q-10. I check with the intention to check-raise. The big blind checks, Jimmy checks and the button bets. That isn't what I was looking for. I had hoped the big blind or Jimmy would bet and the button would call, enabling me to trap all the still-active players for an additional bet. Since the player to my right bet, if I raise, the big blind and Jimmy will probably fold, and the button may not call, since he could have been bluffing at the pot.

---

[32] The way the hand was played, you can rule out a full house.

You don't flop a set that often, so I don't want just the five small bets that are currently in the pot; I want more action. With a queen and a ten on the board, calling is not risk-free, but I'm willing to take the risk, given the prospect that I may win more when the bets double. I call, the big blind folds and Jimmy calls. Three players, pot $210.

Turn: 7. This is a safe card for me. I check, hoping one of my opponents will bet. Jimmy bets, the button folds, I raise and Jimmy calls. Two players, pot $450.

River: J (board: 3-Q-10-7-J). That's a pretty good card. I don't think Jimmy has a set, so the only hands that beat me are A-K, K-9 and 9-8. Jimmy usually would have raised A-K before the flop, and even if he just called, he would not have bet the turn. He wouldn't play K-9 from first position. Because the game is loose, he may play 9-8s. However, on the flop he lacked the pot odds to continue with a gutshot, and a player of Jimmy's caliber knows this. I bet my small set. Jimmy calls. I show my hand and take the pot. (Jimmy doesn't reveal his hand.)

Session 4: Hands 86-98

K-6 (B), 9-5s (CO), 5-3, Q-J, 5-2, A-2, 10-3 (BB, RIF), J-2 (SB, RIF), J-4 (B), Q-6 (CO), 8-3, 9-2, 7-4 (UTG).

I've been playing for two-and-a-half hours and I'm up about $1,600. Time to take a break and relax.

Session 4: Hands 99-113

I return 15 minutes later to an eight-handed game. I wait for the big blind.

When the action comes to me there is a bet, a raise and a reraise. I quickly fold 8-3s.

An early-position player raises and gets two callers behind. I call from the small blind with 3-3; the big blind folds. Four players, pot $270. Flop: Q♥-K♥-8♦. I check-fold.

K-2 (B), J-6 (CO), K-5, 9-5, 10-9s, Q-J (UTG), 6-3 (BB, RIF), 6-4s (SB, three bets to me), 10-5 (B), Q-2, 7-4, 10-3 (UTG), 7-5 (BB, RIF).

Session 4: Hand 114

It's folded to the button, who just calls. I complete the bet from the small blind with **K-4**. The big blind taps the felt. Three players, pot $90.

Flop: K♥-J♦-8♥. I check, the big blind checks and the button bets. You often face tough decisions with trash hands like K-4 offsuit. With top pair, no kicker, it's easy to make the wrong play. The button's pre-flop call means either he was trying to trap the blinds with a very strong hand (usually A-A or K-K) or he is inexperienced and just plays his cards, which would indicate a mediocre hand.

I shouldn't raise if the button holds A-A or K-K. But I welcome action if he's bluffing or has hit a pair smaller than kings, since he has few outs. Should he have a flush- or straight-draw, I should raise and charge him to see a card. The situation is far from clear, and there is still the big blind behind me. I call and the big blind calls as well. Three players, pot $180.

Turn: 5♠. I check, the big blind checks and the button bets again. The five on the turn hasn't changed anything. I call and the big blind folds. Two players, pot $300.

River: 2♠ (board: K♥-J♦-8♥-5♠-2♠). We both check. I show my king and my opponent mucks his hand. I don't feel good about my play of this hand. It looks like my opponent had some sort of draw, in which case I let him draw too cheaply.

Session 4: Hands 115-124

10-3s (B), **5-2, 7-6, 6-3**. We get two new players and the table is full again. **K-3s, 10-5** (BB, RIF), **A-10** (SB, RIF), **J-4s** (B), **A-7** (CO).

The 5 and the 6 seat both limp. I'm in the 8 seat, two spots from the button, and see 7♠-6♠.

If both blinds play, we have five players. That's enough for me. I call. The button calls and the blinds play. Six players, pot $180.

Flop: 9♠-6♦-7♥. The small blind bets, the big blind calls, the 5 seat raises and the 6 seat calls two bets cold. Seems like everybody likes the flop. There is a decent chance that my bottom two pair are the best hand. I decide to see the turn before making a move. With that many players it's very likely one of them has an eight. I will play it fast if no 10 or 5 comes on the turn. We all call. Still six players, pot $540.

Turn: 6♣. It's checked to me, a good sign because with that many players it's not unusual that someone has a set. I bet. The button calls, the small blind calls all-in, the big blind and the 5 seat call, and the 6 seat folds. Five players (one all-in), pot $840.

River: A♦ (board: 9♠-6♦-7♥-6♣-A♦). I was hoping for a 10 or 5, but the ace is not a bad card, since the 5 seat bets out after the big blind has checked. I raise, the button folds, the big blind folds and the 5 seat calls. My full house is good (nobody shows his hand).

Session 4: Hands 125-126

I fold **J-5**. Then the 5 seat limps and I raise with **K-K**. The 9 seat right behind me makes it three bets. The blinds fold and the 5 seat calls. I just call to disguise my hand. If I reraise it's pretty obvious that I have aces or kings. Three players, pot $320.

Flop: 6-J-6. The 5 seat bets, I raise, the 9 seat calls and the 5 seat calls (pot $500).

Turn: 2. The 5 seat checks, I bet and both opponents call (pot $680).

River: K (board: 6-J-6-2-K). I don't know if I needed that king, but I definitively didn't want to see an ace or jack. The 5 seat checks, I bet and both opponents call. As expected, my kings full are good. The 5 seat had K-J (bad for me that there was a pair on board; otherwise he would probably have bet or check-raised the river with top two pair). The 9 seat folded without showing his hand[33].

Session 4: Hands 127-153

7-6 (UTG), **J-8** (BB, RIF).

---

[33] It's hard to put him on a hand. Originally I thought he had Q-Q, 10-10 or 9-9 (remember, he made it three bets before the flop) though the call on the end looks strange. With A-J it seems odd that he would play so aggressively pre-flop but just call on the flop and turn with top pair, top kicker. A-K or A-Q are also possible. That would explain the reraise before the flop, but the turn call is hard to justify.

I call from the small blind with **6-4**. Four players, pot $120. Flop: 2♠-K♦-J♣. Everyone checks to the button, who bets. I fold.

10-6 (B), **K-4** (CO), **8-6**, **Q-2**, **10-2**, **Q-3** (BB, RIF), **J-9** (SB, RIF), **A-6** (B), **10-6** (CO), **8-6**.

We are eight-handed at the moment. **10-8** (UTG), **6-4** (BB, RIF), **K-2s** (SB, chop), **J-7** (B), **8-3**, **10-5**, **K-10**, **10-6** (UTG).

I get a free play in the big blind with **A-10s**. Four players, pot $120. Flop: Q-J-5. The button bets and I fold.

J-5 (SB, RIF), **6-5** (B), **10-6** (CO), **10-9**, **K-9**.

Session 4: Hand 154

I raise with **K-K** in middle position. The two players behind me call, as do the blinds. Five players, pot $300.

Flop: Q♦-2♦-8♥. The small blind bets and the big blind calls. All my opponents are pretty loose and aggressive. The player in the 10 seat, a middle-aged Chinese wearing black sunglasses, is especially loose. Like many Asians, he likes to play a lot of hands and loves action, the more the better. I raise and all call. Still five players, pot $600.

Turn: 3♠. Both blinds check. The turn card is a good one for me—no reason to slow down. I bet, the player behind me folds, Chinese sunglasses and the two blinds call. Four players, pot $740.

River: 10♠ (board: Q♦-2♦-8♥-3♠-10♠). The blinds check. There is some danger that the river card made someone a straight or two pair. However, I have absolutely no idea what these guys could have, and checking is lame. I bet. Only the big blind calls. My kings are good and I grab an $860 pot.

Session 4: Hands 155-167

10-4 (UTG), **J-2** (BB, chop), **A-10** (SB, two bets to me), **J-5** (B), **10-4** (CO), **3-2s**, **8-6**, **9-8** (UTG), **7-4** (BB, chop).

I call from the small blind with **K-J**. Five players, pot $150. Flop: A-4-8. There is a bet followed by a call. I fold.

Q-3 (B), **10-8**, **10-9s**.

Session 4: Hand 168

I raise from middle position with **A♣-K♣**. The 9 seat behind me reraises and the button calls. Three players, pot $320.

Flop: 8♦-Q♥-Q♠. We all check.

Turn: A♥. I bet, the 9 seat folds and the button raises. I fold. That both players behind me checked the flop caused me to suspect that one of them was slowplaying a queen. However, when the ace came on the turn, I had to bet to find out where I stood. If I checked, then I would have to call the turn and river as well. I couldn't comfortably fold on the turn after I had just checked. By the way, the button showed Q♦-J♦. I wouldn't call three bets with that hand, but you see it all the time.

Session 4: Hands 169-195

8-4s (UTG), **8-5** (BB, chop).

I call with **6-5** from the small blind. Five players, pot $150. Flop: 9♣-5♥-K♣. It's checked to the button, who bets. I fold bottom pair.

A-5 (B, RIF), **K-5** (CO), **Q-8**, **J-10**, **K-8**, **9-6** (UTG), **10-3** (BB, RIF).

I give it a try from the small blind with the worst hand, **7-2**. Five players, pot $150. Flop: 6♦-4♣-3♦. I fold my weak gutshot to a bet and two calls.

8-6s (B, RIF), **9-3**.

I raise with **A-K** from middle position and win the blinds. **J-5**, **Q-8** (UTG). We are down to seven players, and one of them is walking. **5-3** (BB, RIF).

I call from the small blind holding **7-5**. Four players, pot $120. Flop: K-A-9 and that's that. **Q-2** (B).

It's folded to me in the cutoff seat, where I hold **K♦-2♦**. We are playing six-handed. Shorthanded, you can't wait for premium hands. You have to get something going once in a while or the blinds will eat you up. I raise. Chinese sunglasses at the button and the small blind call. Three players, pot $210. Flop: A-7-5. The small blind checks, I bet and both opponents fold. An ace on the flop is always a good card if you were the aggressor before the flop, there are few possible draws, and none of your opponents holds an ace, of course.

Q-7, **A-4** (UTG), **Q-4** (BB, RIF), **10-8** (SB, RIF), **A-3** (B), **J-6** (CO), **A-7**.

Session 4: Hands 196-198

Andrew, a local pro, limps from UTG. I raise with **A-Q**; the big blind and Andrew call. Three players, pot $200.

Flop: 7-8-J. It's checked to me, I bet, the big blind folds and Andrew raises. I call. Two players, pot $320.

Turn: 6. Andrew bets. I have two overcards, making me a 6.7-to-1 dog to draw an ace or queen. If I call I'll be getting 6.3-to-1 pot odds, but I don't know if I really have six outs. Because Andrew limped from UTG, it's just too likely that he has a hand like A-J or Q-Js, duplicating one of my hole cards. I fold.

8-2s (UTG), **J-8** (BB, RIF).

Session 4: Hand 199

Two loose players limp and Andrew raises on the button. I'm sitting right behind him in the small blind with A♣-J♥.

I usually don't call a raise with A-J from the small blind. But Andrew raised two loose, weak players from the button, so he doesn't necessarily have a premium hand. Under these circumstances my hand warrants a call. Chinese sunglasses in the big blind and the limpers call. Five players, pot $300.

Flop: A♦-Q♥-7♦. Everyone checks to the button. Andrew bets. Time to thin the field and determine if Andrew really has an ace. I raise and everyone calls except Andrew, who folds. Four players, pot $570.

Turn: 6♣. There is not much to think about. No one played back at me on the flop, so I have to assume that my ace is good, and it's unlikely that the turn card changed that. I bet, Chinese sunglasses calls, the first limper folds and the second calls. Three players, pot $750.

River: 9♦ (board: A♦-Q♥-7♦-6♣-9♦). With the flush card at the end and two opponents who are obviously on draws, betting doesn't look like a good idea. I check, Chinese sunglasses checks and, as feared, the second limper bets. He is a young business guy who is in for four grand and down three. I think he is desperate enough to run a bluff. I call and Chinese sunglasses folds. The businessman turns over 5♦-4♦ for a flush. At least the money went to a contributor and not to Andrew (nothing personal; it's just better for the game).

Session 4: Hands 200-204

I pick up **A-Q** on the button. Only the 5 seat has called. I raise, Chinese sunglasses, who nearly always defends his blinds, calls from the small blind, the big blind folds and the 5 seat puts another 30 bucks in the pot. Three players, pot $210. Flop: 8-K-5. It's checked to me and I bet. Both opponents call (pot $300). Turn: 4. Chinese sunglasses and the 5 seat check. It doesn't look like my opponents are holding much. I bet and they both fold.

4-4 (CO), **6-2s**, **5-3** (UTG).

A middle-position player raises, the button calls and I call from the big blind with **4-4**. Three players, pot $200. Flop: 8♥-6♣-Q♠. I've flopped sets twice in this session, so I can't complain. This time I fold after the button bets.

Session 4: Hand 205

A middle-position player limps and I call from the small blind with **A-6**. Andrew, who has moved to my left, raises from the big blind. The limper and I call. Three players, pot $180.

Flop: 4-3-7. I check, Andrew bets and the limper calls. I have 8-to-1 pot odds, slightly short for my gutshot. But aces and even sixes may be additional outs. I know Andrew—his raise does not necessarily mean he holds a big pair. He would raise in this situation with 9-9, K-Q or A-10s. So, I call. Three players, pot $270.

Turn: 2. We all check (pot still $270).

River: 9 (board: 4-3-7-2-9). We all check again. Andrew's A-J wins the pot.

Session 4: Hands 206-215

J-9 (B), **8-3** (CO), **J-5**, **6-3** (UTG), **Q-7** (BB, RIF), **9-3** (SB, chop), **J-5s** (B).

There is an early-position limper. I call with **K-10** in the cutoff. Both blinds play. Four players, pot $120. Flop: 10-8-5. The blinds and the limper check.

I have top pair, second-best kicker, a good but vulnerable hand. I bet and all three opponents fold.

A-9, 8-6 (UTG). We are playing five-handed. The game is still excellent, but I'm very hungry. I've had nothing but a candy bar, so I end my session and get something to eat.

Result Session 4		Total Results	
Hours	5:45	Hours	20:45
Win/Loss	$2,791	Win/Loss	$3,528

Session 4: Conclusion

No doubt, this was an excellent session. I have had bigger wins over the years, but I don't often make three grand in a single session in the $30-60 game. My records indicate that I book a win that big about once a month. Wins such as my last session, where I netted about two grand, are more frequent.

The effect of good play on the size of the win is grossly overestimated by most players. The deciding factor is not your playing skill so much as luck, how many hands you play, how aggressive you are, and your appetite for risk. As a tight player, my big wins are usually smaller than those of my opponents. My losses are usually smaller as well[34].

On Sunday, the day before I recorded my first session for this book, I lost about $2,000, a pretty big loss for me. While walking from the Bellagio through the warm Las Vegas night back to my room, I thought to myself, "Had I stayed in my room I would be two grand richer. Heck, instead of playing poker, I could have gone to the best restaurant in town, ordered the most expensive meal, a great bottle of wine and a delicious dessert, and I would have still been ahead."

Thoughts like that are human. However, it's easy to see that such reflections are silly and miss the point. Would I have those thoughts today after winning $2,791? Of course not! In poker, you never know in advance if

---

[34] See chapter 9, section "Who scores the big wins at the table?" (p.272).

you are going to win or to lose. Therefore, you shouldn't lay too much emphasis on day-to-day results.

At the end of the year you sum up your results and determine your hourly rate. Let's say you net 0.75 big bets per hour. Then instead of saying, "I lost $2,000 in four hours," you should say, "I played for four hours; that means I won 3 big bets per hour, or $180." That's the attitude you should be striving for; otherwise, the ups and downs will drive you nuts.

Session 5: Bellagio, Friday, September 9, 6:05 a.m.

I go to Denny's for a late-night dinner. It's amazing, after a good session like the last one, how the food tastes better, the grass looks greener, the sun shines brighter and your wife looks prettier. Of course, its just the opposite after a losing session. After dinner I return to my room, check my email and work a bit on the computer.

Three $30-60 games were still going when I left the Bellagio poker room. All of them were good. Not feeling tired, I think there still might be a game in progress in the early morning, and I can catch some overtired, losing players who are desperately trying to get even. I decide to return to the Bellagio; perhaps my good run will continue.

I arrive in the Bellagio poker room shortly after 6:00 a.m. Indeed, there is still a $30-60 game going on. There are eight players at the table. Andrew in the 4 seat is stacking his chips, ready to leave. The young business guy I played with before is still in the 6 seat. He obviously likes that seat because he switched tables and is in the same seat. When I left, he had about $1,200 in chips; now he has about three grand in front of him. He either made a nice comeback or bought in again. In the 7 seat is the Chinese guy with the sunglasses. In the 8 and 9 seats are two elderly players, tourists probably. In the 10 seat is a young one who plays okay. Left of the dealer, in the 1 seat, is a tough, young, Asian guy. In the 2 seat is a younger player I haven't seen before. He is short-stacked and doesn't look too happy.

The lineup is not great but looks okay, especially Chinese sunglasses, because he gives a lot of action. I buy a rack of chips from Andrew, take the 3 seat and wait for the button to pass by. Chinese sunglasses misses his big blind.

Session 5: Hand 1

I post behind the button. Everyone folds to me. I raise with **J-7**. You might ask what I'm doing here. I fold all sorts of good hands, and now I raise with J-7? This is pretty standard when you post behind the button and it's folded to you. Your two cards don't matter; the raise is automatic. Raising gives you a good chance to knock out the button and make the two blinds fold.

Look at the odds. There is already $80 in the pot and it costs you only $30 to raise. This play shows an immediate profit if the three players behind you fold more than 27.3 percent of the time. It's not even necessary that they fold that often because you have three ways to win: 1) everyone folds; 2) the flop misses everyone and you steal the pot with a position bet; and 3) you out-flop the competition. This play has another possible benefit: in case you have to show your hand, which can change the image of a tight player like me.

I once made this play with 5-2 offsuit. The button three-bet and the blinds folded. That's the worst case scenario for this play, but you have to call because the pot is offering you 20-to-3 (6.7-to-1) odds. No hand is that much of an underdog, not even 5-2[35]. The flop was something like 4-2-8. I checked, he bet, I called. The turn was a ten. He bet again and I called. The river card was a trey. He bet and I called him down. He showed A-K and was disgusted when I took the pot with a measly pair of deuces.

You can be sure that it makes a lasting impression when you're seen playing 5-2 for three bets. This helps you tremendously to get action if you are a tight player. It's surprising that even strong players don't know this play. They just check when it's folded to them and they don't have a good hand. But why give the blinds a cheap or free play? Bet and give them a chance to fold!

The post-behind-the-button play is powerful, but don't do it carelessly. The situation has to be right. The following conditions must be met:

1) It has to be folded to you. If there are limpers in front of you, you should only raise with a strong hand. You can lower your raising standards slightly because you are already in for one bet, but don't raise with trash.

---

[35] For instance, 5-2 is a 6.3-to-1 underdog against pocket aces.

2) Don't raise if the button is a loose player who calls with all sorts of hands. When the button calls, your play is essentially ruined. You no longer have position, and the blinds get better odds for a call. Be cautious if the button is an expert player. He may see through your play and three-bet you. That's the worst-case scenario because you have to put more money into the pot out-of-position with the worst hand.

3) Don't raise if either of the blinds always defends, in which case your raise achieves nothing. You only make the pot bigger, making it harder to bluff if you and your opponent(s) don't flop anything.

Returning to the hand, I raise with J-7, the business guy at the button folds and the blinds call. That's not what I was hoping for. Three players, pot $180. The flop comes 8-9-K. The small blind bets and the big blind folds. There is no way I can call. All I have is a gutshot with poor odds[36]. I fold.

Session 5: Hands 2-5

6-2 is an easy fold.

I'm dealt **Q-10** in second position. This is usually a clear fold, but our game is seven-handed, and high cards go up in value in shorthanded games. You have to loosen up because you are not dealt enough premium hands to make up for the blinds, which come around much faster. Most players realize that they have to play more hands. So they start playing hands like 9-8 and 6♥-4♥ that look good because of straight and/or flush possibilities. But that's exactly the wrong adjustment. Small (suited) connectors go down in value because you usually don't get the right odds to play them. Shorthanded, I would prefer K♠-2♠ over 8♦-7♦ anytime. The high card is of more importance than the possible straight.

With only three players behind me, I usually raise with Q-10. But I have no read on my opponents. The elderly player in the 8 seat called my raise before. Maybe he did that with a good hand, or maybe he's a habitual caller. You're better off just calling if it's the latter. By calling, you keep the pot smaller, making it easier to get away with a bet if nobody flops anything. Not being sure if I should raise or just call, I take the safe route and fold.

---

[36] The pot is offering me 6-to-1 while I'm about 11-to-1 to hit the gutshot.

I'm dealt **A-6** under the gun. Yes, you should loosen up seven-handed, but not that much. Fold.

Next hand I have the big blind when the 10 seat raises in the cutoff and the small blind makes it three bets in a desperate bid to go all-in. I doubt the small blind has a premium hand, but I still can't call with **J-8s**. My read on the small blind was correct. The flop comes 9-K-3. The small blind bets, the 10 seat raises and the small blind reraises all-in. The turn is a ten, and the river a seven (board: 9-K-3-10-7). The small blind shows 9♦-7♦ and wins with two pair. The 10 seat has K-Q. At least we didn't lose the 2 seat.

Session 5: Hand 6

Two players limp; I toss in a chip with **6-3** in the small blind; the big blind knuckles. Four players, pot $120.

The flop is Q-8-6. I doubt that my bottom pair is best with this flop. I check. To my surprise, everyone checks behind. I'm prepared to bet if a card lower than a six falls on the turn. Alas it's a jack. Everyone checks again. The river is a five (board: Q-8-6-J-5). I check. If someone bets, I'll face a tough decision. But no one is interested in betting.

Being first, I turn over my hand thinking I have a decent chance to take down the pot. The second elderly gentleman in the 9 seats turns over 9-8 and the button shows K-8 for a pair of eights with a better kicker.

Without a doubt, the button played the hand horribly. It was a big mistake to not bet second pair with an excellent kicker after everyone checked. At least the player with 9-8 in his hands would have given him action. The button missed at least one bet and gave two free cards that could have easily beaten him.

Session 5: Hands 7-12

A-2 (B), **A-8s** (CO, RIF), **8-6**, **7-2** (UTG).

We are down to six players—the 2 seat who was all-in a couple of hands ago went broke. **K-8** (BB, three bets to me).

There are three limpers; I call from the small blind with **5-3**. The big blind gets a free play. Five players, pot $150.

Flop: J-10-5. I flop bottom pair, just as I did last time in the small blind. With four opponents and J-10 on board, it is unlikely I have the best hand and even more unlikely that a bet will win the pot. It's checked around to the button, who bets. The button is the tough young Asian guy. He is definitively able to bet to pick up the pot. I call and the 9 seat calls as well. Three players, pot $240.

Turn: 10. We all check. That confirms my suspicion that the button was betting with nothing (pot still $240).

River: 7 (board: J-10-5-10-7). I check, the 9 seat bets and the button quickly folds. Tough decision. All I have is bottom pair. The elderly gentleman in the 9 seat looks like a solid player. On the other hand, it's obvious that the button has nothing, and he could try to take advantage of that knowledge by running a bluff. He could have a drawing hand that missed, such as K-Q or Q-9, or maybe he was hanging around with ace-high. I call. My opponent turns over A-10! He is either an extremely passive player or he went for a check-raise on the turn.

Session 5: Hand 13

I open-raise on the button with A♥-5♥. Both blinds call. Three players, pot $180.

Flop: Q♦-3♣-6♦. Both blinds check. I bet, hoping to pick up the pot. The blinds call. Three players, pot $270.

Turn: 4♦. The small blind bets and the big blind calls. I have an open-ended straight draw but I fold quickly. It's too likely that I'm drawing dead.

After the hand is over, two players leave the table and the game breaks down.

Result Session 5		Total Results	
Hours	0:15	Hours	21:00
Win/Loss	-$360	Win/Loss	$3,168

Session 5: Conclusion

I made two mistakes in this session, both involving table selection. The first mistake was not checking out the other games before I took a seat in the $30-60 game. When our game broke down the floorman came over and told us that he had a $15-30 game with one seat open. The remaining four players, me included, drew for the seat. I got the lowest card, so I was third on the waiting list.

I checked out the $15-30 table to see if it was worth the wait. The game was fabulous, with seven extremely loose-passive players, most playing nearly every hand. I waited for about an hour but nobody left. I would have been better off playing the $15-30 game from the start.

Because of the previous session's good result, I was too fixated on Chinese sunglasses, one of the big contributors during that session. There was no rush to get a seat in the $30-60 game, as three seats were open. I should instead have taken the time to look at the $15-30 table. That game was easily worth 40 bucks an hour, much more than the mediocre $30-60 game, especially when Chinese sunglasses was not playing.

The second mistake was playing in the $30-60 game in the first place; the table wasn't that good, and due to the better players, my edge wasn't that great. However, when I came to the table, I was excited to see Chinese sunglasses. I had played with him the session before and knew him to be extremely loose, and willing to give a lot of action. When I sat down, the Chinese sunglasses guy had money on the table but had stepped away, and I didn't know if he would continue playing upon his return. I was fixated on the opportunity to win money from a single player instead of assessing the table as a whole—a variation on the first mistake. Though none of the remaining players was very good or excellent, the fact that you are the best player at the table doesn't mean that you should play—at least if you don't play high-limit.

Most players grossly overestimate what they can make if there are no really bad players like Chinese sunglasses at the table. If all your opponents have some basic idea of what they are doing, which means they know what hands to play pre-flop, understand the importance of position, don't chase with hopeless hands and are able to make the occasional move, then your win rate goes way down, even if you are the best player at the table. Thus, table selection is a crucial issue.

Without any scientific proof, I estimate that in such a situation even a very good player makes no more than 0.25 big bets per hour. If you play $4,000-8,000, that's no small deal. $2,000 per hour is a nice income, more than most people will ever dream of. In low- and middle-limit, however, the picture is different. I can't realistically expect to make much more than about $15 per hour in a $30-60 game like the previous one. It's not that I don't appreciate 15 bucks, but the point is that instead of playing eight hours in a mediocre game, I could play two hours in a good game and, on average, expect to make about the same amount of money. So, why should I play in a bad game? Moreover, instead of playing $30-60 I could play $8-16 with an hourly rate a bit higher than $15, and the risk (my standard deviation) is much lower.

This brings up an interesting subject. How does the presence of a tough pro influence your win rate? When I started playing $20-40 at the Mirage in Las Vegas, I had a friend from Colorado who played $6-12 for a living. During a break I went to his table and chatted with him. He asked me how I was doing in the $20-40 game. "Not too good," I replied, and then I added that we had David Sklansky at the table. He said, "Maybe that's the reason you're losing." That was said in jest, but it made me think about how much I lose to an excellent player like Sklansky.

To solve that problem I did a thought experiment. How would I fare against nine excellent players? I would lose, of course, but how much? At that time I was a decent $20-40 player. Now, let's assume that I'm correct that even an excellent player against a bunch of reasonable players can expect to make about 0.25 BB/h. That translates to a loss of 0.023 BB/h for the reasonable player. In other words, each reasonable player loses on average 0.023 BB/h to the excellent player[37].

We can now answer the original question: how much would a reasonable player lose against nine experts? If we replace eight reasonable players with excellent players, the remaining player loses nine times as much as before, i.e., 9×0.023 = 0.25. On average a reasonable player loses as much to nine experts as an expert wins against nine reasonable players. So, the presence of an excellent player like David Sklansky cost me about 0.023 BB/h, which isn't much, as we will see.

---

[37] Notice that I said 'on average'. Position does play a role. The player to the right of the excellent player will lose more than the player to the left.

Now, let's assume that I, as a reasonable player, could play against nine truly horrible players. A conservative guess is that I could make about 1.5 BB/h against such a lineup, i.e., every bad player is worth on average 0.17 BB/h to me. If you compare the 0.17 BB/h I can win from a bad player to the 0.023 BB/h I lose against an expert, it becomes clear that the decisive factor in table evaluation is not the expert players but the bad players. Even if you disagree with my assumptions, you will surely reach the same conclusion.

Let's look at it from a different point of view. If you have some idea what you are doing, your starting hand selection is not much different from that of an expert. In a full-ring game you play about 15% of the hands, sometimes a little more, sometimes a little less depending on the playing conditions. That means you will only cross swords with the expert about every six or seven hands you play. A truly horrible player plays about 50% of the hands dealt to him (I have seen some that played every hand), so you happily play against him about every second hand you play[38]. Since you will play the bad player far more often than the expert, we again conclude that the presence of bad players at a table is much more important than the presence of those who can outplay you. Therefore, the presence of excellent players should not deter you from playing, but the absence of bad players should[39].

Session 6: Bellagio, Friday, September 9, 9:10 p.m.

Friday and Saturday are the busiest days of the week in the Bellagio poker room; tourists stream in from all over, and the local players are there to get some of the action. When I come in at about 9:00 p.m., there are three full $30-60 tables. I go to the center podium to put my name on the waiting list just as the floorman is opening a new $30-60 game, and there is still an open seat. Since the game hasn't started yet, the players are still buying chips and I have time to size up the lineup.

---

[38] The probabilities of the events are not completely independent . For instance, that a bad player is in a hand may be an incentive for you to play, and the fact that an expert has called or raised may be a reason for you not to play. So, you are even more likely to play the bad player and less likely to play the expert.

[39] Remember that I don't talk about high-limit games, in which all the players at the table are often at least decent or pretty good. The stiffer competition is the reason why the win rate goes down even for an expert in high-limit games.

I'm in the 2 seat. In the 7 seat is Adam, a young pro. Right behind him in the 8 seat is Boris, a Russian player with maniacal tendencies. Obviously, the limit is too small for him. I have seen him play fairly rationally and conservatively in a $100-200 game. In lower-limit games like this, he tends to play a lot of trash, right on the edge of nutsy. In the 10 seat is Mason Malmuth, who operates poker/gambling publisher 2+2. I used to play with Mason a lot in the $20-40 game at the Mirage, but now because of his successful business activities, he no longer plays that often. I don't know the other players. Usually a good sign, probably mostly tourists on a weekend trip to Sin City.

Finally, everyone has his chips and we can draw for the button. The 4 seat has the highest card and gets the button.

Session 6: Hands 1-6

I nearly get a full round for free, but I can't catch anything playable: **K-9s, 10-7s, 8-5, 6-4, 7-6** (UTG).

Boris raises on the next hand. That doesn't mean much, since he always brings it in with a raise. The 9 seat and the small blind call. I have **10-7** in the big blind and fold quickly. Just because Boris plays a lot of substandard hands doesn't mean that I have to play trash against him. I can loosen my starting hand requirements against him, but not so much that I play 10-7 out of position against an extremely aggressive player. Also, Boris raises with good and bad hands alike, and this could be a good one. Lastly, there are two others players in the pot that I have to worry about.

I have pot odds of 20-to-3 (6.3-to-1) which looks seductive. I said before that I had an automatic call with 5-2 and exactly the same pot odds (5/1). I was heads-up then; here I'd be playing four-handed.

Against three random hands, 10-7 has 23.24% equity, which translates to odds of 3.3-to-1. This tells you two things: First, 10-7 is a below-average hand. Second, 3.3-to-1 odds compare nicely to 6.3-to-1 pot odds, but your opponents' hands are not random—not even Boris plays every hand—and it's easy to lose money after the flop with 10-7. If you flop a ten or a seven it can cost you a lot of money to find out that your hand is no good, so into the dumper it goes.

By the way, Boris had Q-J and made three queens.

Session 6: Hands 7-14

I fold **Q-3** in the small blind to another Boris raise. **9-5** (B), **Q-3** (CO), **K-5s** (RIF by Boris. He flops quad sixes and wins a monster pot), **Q-10**, **Q-5**, **9-8**.

I raise with **J♠-J♥** in second position. The 4 seat calls and Adam makes it three bets on the button. I call, as does the 4 seat. Three players, pot $320.

Flop: A♣-Q♣-7♠. It doesn't get much worse for a pair of jacks. I check, the 4 seat bets and Adam folds. Originally I thought this was the perfect flop for Adam. But his fold makes it clear that he had the same type of hand as I hold, a big pair below aces (probably K-K, J-J, 10-10 or 9-9).

I muck my hand. There is a small chance that the 4 seat is betting a flush draw. If he has me beat, which is very likely, my chances to improve to the best hand are remote (two jacks and a backdoor straight draw), and if he really has a flush draw, he has 2-to-1 odds to complete it. Hence, the fold is mandatory.

Session 6: Hands 15-24

I fold **K-5** under the gun.

The first-position player limps, the 4 seat raises and it is folded to me in the big blind. I call with **3-3**. Three players, pot $200.

Flop: Q-7-5. Having flopped nothing, I check. The UTG limper checks and the 4 seat bets. With just one big card and the bettor in steal position, there is a good chance I have the best hand. I call and the UTG player behind me calls as well. Still three players, pot $290.

Turn: A. It doesn't take a rocket scientist to realize that this was the worst card for my hand. I check, the limper checks and the 4 seat bets. I release my hand immediately. The 4 seat wins the hand with A-J. The limper doesn't reveal his hand.

It's folded to the button, who raises. I make it three bets with **10-10** in the small blind. The big blind folds and the button calls. Two players, pot $210. Flop: Q-8-7. I bet and my opponent folds.

I fold **A-5** on the button.

On the next hand there are two limpers in front of me and I call with **7-7**. Both blinds play. Five players, pot $150.

Flop: **9♠-K♦-10♣**. Everyone checks to me. With so many straight possibilities, I see no chance to pick up the pot with a bet. I check behind for the free card.

Turn: **2♦**. The small blind bets and we all fold.

9-4. Boris leaves the table; he always does that after a quick win. **J-7s**, **J-2**, **K-8**, **A-5s**.

Session 6: Hand 25

I hold **J♠-10♠** in first position. Though Boris is gone, the table still seems loose enough to profitably play J-10s from under the gun. The player behind me in the 3 seat limps and the two blinds play. Four players, pot $120.

Flop: **A♥-10♥-6♣**. Both blinds check. The ace on the flop is awkward. But I have middle pair, the blinds have shown no interest in the pot and there is just one player behind me, so I bet. The 3 seat calls, Mason in the small blind folds and the big blind calls. Three players, pot $210.

Turn: **A♠**. Surprisingly, the big blind, who just check-called the flop, now bets out. Though I normally act quickly, I take my time to think the situation through. The big blind's bet looks suspicious. Most people realize that if the top card pairs on the turn, it's less likely that one of the other players holds a card of this rank. For this reason, players often represent trips by betting into the field. On the other hand, the bet could mean the big blind really has three aces. He may have check-called the flop because he had a pair of aces with a bad kicker and didn't know where he stood. When the third ace showed up on the turn, he figured he probably had the best hand. By betting, he wants to ensure that a potential flush draw doesn't get a free card.

I would have probably called in this situation on the river. But on the turn it's significantly worse for me. First, if I call the turn I will have to call the river as well; otherwise my turn call makes no sense. Second, if my opponent has three aces, then I'm drawing dead. Additionally, the river can only help my opponents. Even if I'm ahead with my pair of tens, many river cards will beat me. Third, my call doesn't close the action. There is still a player behind me whose most likely hand is a flush draw, which means he won't fold. Should he hold an ace, he may raise, and then I've wasted a big bet. I fold and the player behind me calls. Two players, pot $330.

River: 5♣ (board: A♥-10♥-6♣-A♠-5♣). The big blind bets and the 3 seat folds. Looks like the big blind had three aces and the 3 seat a flush draw.

Session 6: Hands 26-34

8-2 (BB, RIF), **J-4s** (SB, RIF), **J-7** (B).

Boris's replacement in the 8 seat raises from early position. The table has tightened up considerably since Boris left. I make it three bets with **J-J** in the cutoff. The big blind and original raiser call. Three players, pot $290.

Flop: 4♣-6♥-J♣. The big blind and the 8 seat check, I bet and both fold.

The fold, at least from the 8 seat, was unexpected. A raise from an early-position player usually means a pocket pair or a couple of high cards. With a non-threatening flop like this, such a player is normally tempted to call. No question, he made a good laydown and I was understandably a little bit disappointed that my top set didn't win a bigger pot.

4-3, **A-4s**, **J-5**, **4-3**, **4-2s**.

Session 6: Hand 35

Under the gun I pick up K♦-Q♦. The table is still a bit less than tight. I would normally fold K-Q under-the-gun, but under these circumstances K-Qs is good enough to play. I call. Two middle-position players, the cut-off, the button and the two blinds call. Seven players, pot $210.

Flop: 6♣-K♣-2♦. Both blinds check. With a flop like this, I expect I have the best hand. There is a remote possibility that someone has hit a set of sixes or deuces. With six opponents and a flush draw on board, I want to reduce the field and charge the remaining players to play. I bet, and only the two middle-position players call. Three players, pot $300.

Turn: 4♥. A good turn card for me. I bet, the first middle-position player calls and the second folds. Two players, pot $420.

River: 4♠ (board: 6♣-K♣-2♦-4♥-4♠). I almost certainly have the best hand. My opponent has either a flush draw or a king with a worse kicker. In both cases, the river card is no help to him. I bet and the 5 seat calls. I show my hand and it's good. The 5 seat doesn't show his hand, but it's pretty sure he had a king with a lesser kicker.

Session 6: Hands 36-45

Q-9 (BB, RIF), **A-6** (SB, RIF).

Mason in the 10 seat raises and the 1 seat calls. Right behind him, I hold **K-Q** on the button. Though I have position, K-Q doesn't play well against a raise and a call. I would make it three bets with that hand against a lone late-position raiser to get it heads-up, but K-Q is not a calling hand, and reraising against a raiser and a caller is overplaying the hand. I fold.

It's folded to me in the cutoff seat. I raise with **9-9**. The button and the big blind call. Three players, pot $200.

Flop: K♥-Q♥-7♦. The big blind checks, I bet and both opponents call (pot $290).

Turn: 8♣. The big blind checks, I check, the button bets and the big blind folds. When I bet the flop it was clear to me that this was a one-shot attempt. They both fold or I'm done with the hand. Unfortunately, they both called. If I would get a free card on the turn, good, but I would not invest another dime given the ugly board for my pocket nines. Consequently, I fold to the button's turn bet.

J-2. I raise with **A-K** from middle position and win the blinds. **10-6, Q-5s, J-2, 10-3s** (UTG).

Session 6: Hands 46-48

Everyone folds, including the button. The small blind throws in a $10 chip, indicating that he refuses to chop. I raise in the big blind with **A♦-2♦**. I have position and probably the best hand, and raising gives me the initiative, which is often important in heads-up play. Two players, pot $120.

Flop: A♠-5♦-6♦. The small blind checks, I bet and he folds. Another monster flop for my hand and I only won the minimum (see 6/29). At least raising before the flop made me an extra 30 bucks.

A middle position player limps, I complete the bet from the small blind with **A-7** and the big blind gets a free play. Three players, pot $90. Flop: K-J-8. I check, the big blind bets, the limper calls and I muck my hand.

10-6 (B).

Session 6: Hand 49

I raise from the cutoff with **A♣-K♣**; the button and big blind call: the same line-up as one round before when I raised from the same position with 9-9 (6/39). Three players, pot $200.

Flop: Q♥-9♥-3♠. The big blind checks, I bet and both players call. Still the same. Three players, pot $290.

Turn: A♥. The ace is excellent except that it makes a flush possible. None-theless, I have to bet. I can't risk an opponent's making a flush on the river with a baby heart in his hand because I gave him a free card. The disad-vantage of betting is that I face a tough decision if I'm raised. I bet and both opponents fold.

Session 6: Hands 50-54

8-2s, 2-2, 10-5, 7-4.

I raise with **A-Q** from under-the-gun and only the button calls. Two play-ers, pot $170.

Flop: K-8-9. I bet and the button calls. Turn: K. I check and the button checks behind.

River: 4 (board: K-8-9-K-4). I check and the button bets. I often call in heads-up situations with just ace-high. But what draws might my oppo-nent have missed? The only possible drawing hand is J-10. (I don't think he would have called a raise with 10-7 or 7-6.) My instinct tells me he has a pocket pair. I fold. I might have called had the pot been bigger.

Session 6: Hand 55

The player in the 6 seat limps and everyone folds, including the small bind. Holding **K♥-K♦** and facing just one limper, I raise from the big blind. You want to get the money in as fast as possible—you may not get more later. The limper calls. Two players, pot $140.

Flop: A♦-K♣-Q♦. I bet the third-nuts and am delighted that my opponent calls (pot $200).

Turn: 2♠. I bet again and the limper calls (pot $320).

River: 5♦ (board: A♦-K♣-Q♦-2♠-5♦). Should I bet my set for value and risk a check-raise, or should I lamely check and possibly lose a big bet? It's usually not a clear decision, but it is this time, because my opponent has only 10 bucks left. I throw in a chip and he gladly calls. My opponent shows 9♦-6♦ and takes the pot.

Session 6: Hand 56

It's folded to me on the button. I raise with **6-6**; both blinds call. Three players, pot $180.

Flop: J♠-7♠-2♦. The small blind bets and the big blind folds. The small blind could be betting on one of many hands I can beat—flush draw, gutshot, overcards—or is he just trying to move me off the pot? I call. Two players, pot $240.

Turn: 8♦. The small blind bets again. The eight is an overcard to my pair, but the situation hasn't changed much. If I call now I have to call the river as well. I raise. This costs the same as calling the turn and river, and may cause my opponent to lay down a better hand, such as A-7. The small blind simply calls (pot $480).

River: J♦ (board: J♠-7♠-2♦-8♦-J♦). The small blind bets out. Clearly, he has three jacks, so I fold. As you can see, raising on the turn didn't cost me any extra money. Had I just called on the turn, I would have had to call the river because there was no way I could know that my opponent had a jack. Had I known that he held a jack, I wouldn't have called the flop.

Session 6: Hands 57-61

8-3 (CO), 8-3s, 5-3.

I limp from middle position with **Q-J**. Only the blinds play (pot $90). Flop: 5♦-A♠-6♠. The blinds check, I bet and both players fold.

8-7.

Session 6: Hand 62

In early position I raise with A♥-K♠. Only the 5 and the 6 seat in middle position call. Three players, pot $230.

Flop: K♦-K♣-6♥. A monster flop for my hand. But it would look suspicious if I were to check to keep the two players behind me in the pot. I bet, the 5 seat folds and the 6 seat calls. Two players, pot $290.

Turn: 2♦. I bet and my opponent calls (pot $410).

River: 7♣ (board: K♦-K♣-6♥-2♦-7♣). Given the action so far, I'm sure I have the best hand. I bet and the 6 seat calls. I show my trip kings, ready to grab the pot, when my opponent turns over 6-6!

Sometimes you are just speechless at your opponent's play. This elderly gentleman in the 6 seat is one of the most passive players I have ever seen. He flopped a full boat but only called me down on an extremely non-threatening board. He held the third nuts on the flop (only quad kings and K-6 beat him). His call was acceptable if he intended to raise the turn. He still had the fourth nuts on the turn (only losing to K-K, K-6 and K-2) but just called again. What was he thinking? His passive play saved me a lot of money. I would have definitively capped the flop with my hand. I would have lost about three additional big bets on this hand to a competent opponent.

Session 6: Hands 63-70

4-3 (UTG), **8-5** (BB, RIF), **7-7** (SB, chop), **A-6** (B), **K-4** (CO), **Q-5**, **J-7s**.

The game is quite passive at the moment, so I limp with A♦-10♣ from middle position. Two seats back, the 4 seat raises. The 5 seat, the big blind and I call. Four players, pot $260.

Flop. A♣-9♦-6♥. The big blind checks, I bet my pair of aces, the 4 seat raises, the 5 seat calls and the big blind folds. It's doubtful I'm ahead, but 13.6-to-1 pot odds are good enough to see another card. I call. Three players, pot $440.

Turn: 8♠. I check, the 4 seat bets and the 5 seat calls. I have 9.6-to-1 pot odds, a bit short for my gutshot, but the three outs for my ten kicker may be worth something. I decide to call.

River: 7♠ (board: A♣-9♦-6♥-8♠-7♠). Bingo, I hit the gutshot. I bet. The 4 seat, looking depressed, calls and the 5 seat raises. There is no point in reraising. I either split the pot with the 5 seat or I lose to the nuts (J-10). Just calling and hoping that the 4 seat will overcall is the right play. The 4 seat flashes 9-9 and mucks. The 5 seat has A-10 also, and we split the pot.

I was extremely lucky. I wouldn't have called the turn — or even the flop — had I known my opponents' hands. My ten kicker was no good, and I didn't have the pot odds to call with just a gutshot. And the 5 seat had the same hand, so I was drawing at half the pot, meaning my pot odds were effectively halved.

Session 6: Hands 71-93

J-8s (UTG).

I get a free play in the big blind with **Q-4**. Six players, pot $180. Flop: K-J-7 and I fold at the first opportunity.

Q-5s (SB, RIF), **3-2s** (B).

The 8 seat has left the table and Mason moves into that seat. Sam, a strong regular player, takes the 10 seat. **Q-2s**, **9-6**, **Q-4**, **10-2**, **9-5**, **8-3** (UTG).

Mason leaves the table. **J-6** (BB, RIF), **A-8** (SB, RIF), **7-2** (B), **J-4s**, **10-2s**, **10-3**, **A-5**, **3-2**, **10-3s** (UTG), **8-3** (UTG).

A middle-position player raises; the button and small blind call. I decide to see the flop with **A♠-7♠** in the big blind. Four players, pot $240. Flop: Q♦-6♠-5♦. I release my hand after a bet and a call.

9-4 (SB, RIF), **J-7** (B).

Session 6: Hands 94-95

The game has deteriorated slowly but steadily since Boris left. I had put my name on the transfer list, and now the floorman tells me my transfer is ready. I put my chips in a rack and head to table 17. I'm down $300 so far. The new table looks much better. The only good players I recognize are Barry Tanenbaum (see 1/97) in the 3 seat and Joe, a very good pro, in the 9 seat. I take the 7 seat and post behind the button when it's my turn.

The 4 seat raises and I fold my **7-2** though I'm already in for 30 bucks. It makes no sense to throw good money after bad just because you get a discount. The next hand, however, is worth the money.

A young Asian guy raises the pot from under the gun and the 5 seat calls. Two seats off the button I call with Q♥-Q♦.

A rather unusual play for me. Q-Q is definitely strong enough to make it three bets. By just calling, I leave the initiative with the raiser. He is very aggressive, so as the pre-flop raiser he will bet the flop no matter what comes. This gives me the option to raise and confront the other players with a double-bet should I get a favorable flop. The 8 seat right behind me calls, Joe folds at the button, the small blind folds and the big blind calls. Five players, pot $320.

Flop: 2♣-6♥-7♦. The big blind checks, the original raiser bets and the 5 seat folds. Raising to protect my hand and to put pressure on the two remaining players is the natural choice. But I decide to wait for the turn, giving me a much better chance to eliminate my opponents after the bet size doubles. I'll take the risk of an A or K on the turn, which could put me in second place. I call. The 8 seat and the big blind call as well. Four players, pot $440.

Turn: 5♣. Again, the young Asian guy bets after the big blind has checked. I raise as planned. The five on the turn makes a straight possible, but it's not a big concern. It's not likely that someone is playing 9-8, 8-4 or 4-3 in a raised pot. The real threats are that one of my opponents has flopped a set or that the original raiser has A-A or K-K. The 8 seat and the big blind fold; the bettor calls. Two players, pot $680.

River: 5♥ (board: 2♣-6♥-7♦-5♣-5♥). The Asian guy checks. That he only called my turn raise makes it very likely that I hold the best hand. He is the type of player that would have reraised with a big pair like A-A or K-K. I bet and he calls. I turn over my queens and they're good. My opponent doesn't show his hand, but I assume he had a pocket pair, probably 8-8 through J-J.

Session 6: Hands 96-104

6-3s, K-10s (RIF), J-7s, J-8.

I get a free play in the big blind with 9-7. Seven players, pot $210. Flop: A-A-10. Two players (holding A-J and A-10) start a raising war and I fold.

J-4 (SB, RIF), J-5 (B), A-8 (CO), 9-3s.

Session 6: Hands 105-109

A middle-position player limps and I raise with **A-Q**. The 8 seat, both blinds and the limper call. Five players, pot $300.

Flop: K♦-4♦-2♥. It's checked to me. A bet would likely achieve nothing against a gaggle of loose players, so I check. The 8 seat bets. Tommy, an extremely loose player who has finished second in a WSOP no-limit event, calls from the small blind. The big blind and the middle-position limper fold. I have 12-to-1 pot odds, but with two players putting money in on the flop, there's little chance I have the best hand. If one of them has a king, my pot odds aren't good enough to draw for three outs, and there is a flush draw on board. I fold. Tommy wins the pot with 6-2; the 8 seat has A♦-Q♦.

I fold the next few hands: **9-5, 10-2, Q-7** (UTG).

A middle-position player raises; the button and small blind call; I call with **K♣-Q♣** in the big blind. Four players, pot $210. Flop: J♦-6♦-2♦. The small blind bets and my hand goes in the muck.

Session 6: Hand 110

Tommy raises in third position and the 4 seat calls. I call from the small blind with **A-Q** and the big blind plays. Four players, pot $240.

Flop: A♦-10♣-9♥. A pretty good flop for me. But there's no need to bet— Tommy will do that for me. I check, the big blind checks, Tommy bets and the 4 seat calls. The 10-9 on board opens a lot of straight possibilities. I want to see the turn before I get deeply involved with my hand. I call and the big blind stays. Four players, pot $360.

Turn: 5♥. Clearly a good card for me. I can no longer count on Tommy to bet for me. He may be a loose, action guy but he's no fool. With three opponents, an ace and a straight draw on board, he will not bet with air. I bet. The big blind folds; Tommy and the 4 seat call. Three players, pot $540.

River: J♥ (board: A♦-10♣-9♥-5♥-J♥). The J♥ makes a backdoor flush and a gutshot straight possible. Someone could possibly hold K-Q or Q-9 for a straight; I doubt anyone has 8-7. If I'm beat, it'll probably be because an opponent holding a jack made two pair. I bet and both players fold.

Session 6: Hands 111-133

J-8s (B, RIF), 9-8 (CO), A-9.

Tommy moves from the 1 seat to the 2 seat. **10-2s**.

I raise with **Q-Q** and win the blinds. **Q-2s, Q-7s** (BB, RIF), **Q-3** (SB, RIF), **8-6** (B), **7-4** (CO), **3-2, 5-2s, Q-2s, Q-10** (UTG), **K-9s** (BB, three bets to me).

I call from the small blind with **5-2**. Seven players, pot $210. Flop: 4-K-10 and I have to let it go. **7-6** (B).

On the next hand we nearly have a family pot. I call with **5-5** in the cutoff. One player folds and one is walking, so we have eight players (pot $240). Flop: 9-9-2. Tommy bets from first position and everyone folds. I'm not convinced Tommy has a nine, but with three players to act behind me, it's best to fold.

A-3, Q-J (RIF), K-7, 6-4s, 10-9s.

Session 6: Hand 134

A middle position player and the button limp. The small blind completes the bet and I get a free play in the big blind with **Q♣-J♦**. Four players, pot $120.

Flop: Q♥-10♥-K♥. The small blind checks. I bet my pair of queens and weak open-ended straight draw. The first limper folds; the button and small blind call. Three players, pot $210.

Turn: 5♣. The small blind bets. My hand (second pair with an open-ended straight draw) only looks good on paper. I can't beat the flush, I can't beat the straight, I can't beat a king and I could very well be drawing dead. The only hand I can imagine that the small blind may bet and that I can beat is A♥-x, where x is any non-heart ten or below. Clear fold (the button folds also).

Session 6: Hand 135

A loose player in the 1 seat opens with a raise. I call in the small blind with **A-Q**. The big blind folds, so we are heads-up (pot $150).

Flop: 8♦-2♦-8♣. I check, the 1 seat bets and I call (pot $210).

Turn: A♠. I bet and my opponent folds. Damn, I should have gone for a check-raise. I bet because I didn't want to give a free card; that wasn't a well-thought play. If he had nothing, then checking might have induced a bluff, which would have earned me an extra bet. A check behind wouldn't have been a disaster, since the board wasn't too dangerous, and I might have collected an additional bet at the end. I played the hand too fast, which probably cost me sixty bucks.

Session 6: Hands 136-146

8-7 (B), **K-7** (CO).

Two players limp and I call with **6-6**. Everyone calls behind, then Barry raises in the big blind. All call. Eight players, pot $420. Flop: J-10-3. Barry wins the hand with 10-10.

A-8, **6-3** (UTG), **J-9** (UTG).

I get another free play in the big blind, this time with **6-3**. Five players, pot $150. The flop (J-K-J) is no help and I fold immediately.

A-2 (SB, RIF), **J-2** (B), **9-7** (CO), **K-7**.

Session 6: Hand 147

I raise a limper with **Q-Q**. Tommy in the small blind and Barry in the big blind both call. Four players, pot $240.

Flop: A♠-4♠-4♦. Tommy checks and Barry bets. Since there are two spades on board and I know that Barry would bet a flush draw, I call in spite of the ugly ace. The limper and Tommy fold. Two players, pot $300.

Turn: 6♠. Barry checks. The turn card is bad news for me. I'm almost certainly beat. If Barry doesn't have the flush, he either has an ace (very likely) or a four (less likely). I don't think he'll believe me if I represent a flush, so I check behind (pot $300).

River: J♥ (board: A♠-4♠-4♦-6♠-J♥). We both check and Barry's A-10 wins the pot[40].

---

[40] I will say more about this hand at the end of the chapter.

Session 6: Hands 148-152

8-6 (UTG), J-4 (BB, RIF).

We are down to eight players. It's folded to the button who limps. I raise from the small blind with **A-K**. The big blind folds and the button calls. Two players, pot $150.

Flop: J♦-10♦-J♥. Not a good flop for my hand. It could have helped my opponent in many ways. At least it gives me a gutshot. I bet and the button calls (pot $210).

Turn: K♠. Though the king makes two straights possible, with top pair, top kicker my hand has improved considerably. I bet and the button calls.

River: J♣ (board: J♦-10♦-J♥-K♠-J♣). Only the case jack and pocket kings beat me. We could split the pot if my opponent holds a king. I bet and he folds, telling me that he had a flush draw, which sounds plausible[41].

K-8 (B), **A-7** (CO).

Session 6: Hand 153

It's folded to me in middle position and I raise with Q♣-Q♦.

Tommy in the small blind makes it three bets and Barry in the big blind calls two bets cold. I call. Three players, pot $270.

Flop: J♠-6♥-3♣. Tommy checks, Barry bets and I raise with my overpair. Tommy and Barry both call. Three players, pot $450.

Turn: Q♥. Tommy and Barry check. I was confident that I had the best hand on the flop, but hitting a set on the turn makes me feel much better. I bet, Tommy calls and Barry raises. Holding the nuts at the moment, there is nothing to think about. I raise, Tommy folds and Barry calls. Two players, pot $970.

River: 4♣ (board: J♠-6♥-3♣-Q♥-4♣). Barry checks, I bet and he calls. My pocket queens win the pot. Tommy announces that he had A-A. I don't know if that's true. He talks a lot, and his flop play looked strange for A-A. Barry didn't show his hand.

---

[41] Another, albeit less likely possibility is 9-8. With a ten my opponent would have called at the end.

Question 6/1:

What is Barry's hand?

Session 6: Hands 154-167

K-7, **10-7s** (UTG), **10-3** (BB, RIF), **J-10s** (SB, Bill, a strong player, raised from early position and there were no callers), **Q-3s** (B), **Q-9**, **9-4s**, **Q-3**, **J-6** (BB, RIF).

Barry Tanenbaum leaves the table. **7-2s** (SB, RIF), **A-2** (B).

Two players limp and I call in the cutoff with **A-J**. The button and the two blinds call. Six players, pot $180.

Flop: A♦-K♣-6♦. It's folded to me. I bet and only the 5 seat in front of me calls. Two players, pot $240.

Turn: 10♠. The 5 seat checks, I bet and he calls (pot $360).

River: 3♦ (board: A♦-K♣-6♦-10♠-3♦). The 5 seat bets and I fold. He obviously hit a flush at the end. Keep in mind that the pot was six-handed at the flop. Heads-up or in a three-way pot, it would have been a different story.

6-3s, **6-2** (UTG). The game is still good, though not as good as when I sat down. I've played enough for today. I grab my chips and head to the cashier's cage.

Result Session 6		Total Results	
Hours	4:45	Hours	25:45
Win/Loss	$697	Win/Loss	$3,865

Session 6: Conclusion

The characteristics of a table change constantly. Players leave the table; new players arrive. It's amazing how one player can change the character of the entire table. When I started playing we had Boris at the table. He plays 60-70 percent of all hands and likes to raise and reraise a lot. When people see a player like Boris, they tend to loosen up considerably, since they want a piece of the action. Suddenly you have an extremely loose and profitable table. Unfortunately, Boris won a couple of big hands and happily left with a nice profit, after which the table gradually lost its extremely loose characteristics, with most players reverting to their regular playing style.

The best decision I made in this session was to switch tables when the original table no longer looked that good. If you play to make money you should carefully observe table conditions, and if they take a turn for the worse, watch for a more profitable table. Don't be shy; put your name on the transfer list if you spot a better table!

At the first table I lost $300; at the second I won $1,000. That alone doesn't tell you much. I have won big at bad tables and I have lost big at unbelievably good tables. But there is no question that the second table was far better than the first, and that if you play more often in good than in bad games it makes a difference at the year's end.

In the $30-60 limit game at the Bellagio, you often face extremely good players, some of whom have written poker books or columns for poker magazines. Most people who are watching these experts are disappointed because they expect to see one great play after the other. First, the opportunity to make 'great' plays is limited, and second, the plays that make them so good are so often subtle and concealed that the average player doesn't recognize them. Here are two examples from the last session.

The first example is hand 6/147. I had raised a limper with Q-Q, the small blind called and Barry Tanenbaum called from the big blind with A-10. The flop came A♠-4♠-4♦. Barry bet and only I called. Turn: 6♠. We both checked. River: J♥ (board: A♠-4♠-4♦-6♠-J♥), and we both checked again.

How do you judge Barry's check at the end? Most players in Barry's shoes would think something like this:

"I bet the flop but my opponent who raised pre-flop just called. That means either he can't beat the ace or is waiting for the turn to raise. On the turn I checked because the third flush card came and if I got raised I would have been in an unpleasant situation. But my opponent just checked behind. Clearly, he can't have a flush, or he would have bet that hand. And he would have bet a better hand than mine because he couldn't give a free card with three spades on board. So, my pair of aces must be good. The jack at the end doesn't change anything in most cases, so I should bet the river."

The conclusion is right—A-10 is very likely the best hand—but the deduction is wrong. To think you have the best hand isn't sufficient reason to bet. You must ask yourself the question: with what hands that you can beat will your opponent call your bet? In this case, none at all, in which case a value bet at the end is senseless. What about betting as a bluff? Now the question is: what better hands will fold to a bet? The worst hand Barry's opponent can have that beats him is A-J. It's impossible that a player will fold that hand at the end after Barry checked the turn, signaling that he probably doesn't have a flush.

To sum it up: Since betting won't elicit a call from a worse hand and won't force a better hand to fold, the bet can't have a positive expected value.

Betting has the following disadvantages

1) You may be called by a better hand that would not have bet had you checked.

2) You may be raised. If you fold and your opponent had a better hand this is not a problem since you would have called had you checked and your opponent bet behind. However:

3) You may run into a bluff-raise. If you fold to save a bet you may lose the whole pot.

Checking has the one advantage

You may induce a bluff from your opponent, winning you an additional big bet.

Returning to our example, Barry's check at the end looks ordinary at first glance, but is actually quite a sophisticated play.

The second example is from hand 6/75. Mason Malmuth raises from early position. Both blinds call. Three players, pot $180. Flop: A♣-K♥-K♦.

The small blind is a young, loose, Asian guy. In the big blind is an elderly, passive player (see 6/62). Both blinds check and Mason bets. Then the young Asian guy check-raises, the passive player in the big blind folds and Mason calls. Two players, pot $300.

Turn: 6♠. The Asian guy bets and Mason calls (pot $420).

River: 10♦ (board: A♣-K♥-K♦-6♠-10♦). The small blind checks, Mason bets and the small blind calls. Mason turns over A-Q; the Asian guy shows an ace and tosses his hand into the muck.

The hand looks completely unspectacular. Most players will just say that's no feat, everybody would have won with A-Q in that situation. True, but that's not the point. Some average players, especially those who have learned that 'aggressive is right' in poker, would think that Mason should have pushed the hand more, arguing that it was quite obvious that his opponent didn't have a king, since most players don't check-raise the flop with trips in shorthanded pots.

Let's examine Mason's play after he was check-raised on the flop. We must first categorize the type of hand Mason's opponent can hold, and then determine the best course of action in each case. The young Asian player in the small blind can have any of the following hands: a) a king; b) an ace; c) a draw; d) a pocket pair; e) nothing.

Mason is drawing dead or close to it in the first case[42]. So calling is better than raising.

In case b) we assume Mason's opponent holds an ace with a worse kicker[43]. Notice that the pair of kings on board protects Mason. The small blind has to hit his kicker twice to win the pot, or spike a king or queen on the turn or river to split it. As a solid favorite, it can't be wrong to call against an aggressive opponent. But can raising be better?

This depends on the likelihood that the small blind will fold, and on his kicker. A player is probably more prone to fold A-3 than A-J since if he's re-raised on the flop, he must assume that Mason has at least an ace, and then it boils down to who has the better kicker. It's a mistake to assume that a loose, aggressive player won't fold when he thinks he's beat. When way

---

[42] He is drawing dead to A-A, K-K and A-K; otherwise he needs an ace on the turn or river. If Mason's opponent has trip kings, his winning prospects are slim (8.59%).

[43] If his opponent has A-K we have case a); if he has A-Q it probably doesn't matter how he plays.

ahead or way behind against this type of player, it's often correct to cede the initiative rather than play back at him with the risk that you will lose him.

From Mason's point of view it looks like this: Reraising risks two big bets (the turn and river bets he loses if his opponents fold) to win an additional small bet on the flop. In other words, if the small blind folds more than 20% of the time, Mason is better off just calling[44].

But this is only half the story. The folding rate given is not totally accurate since his opponent's fold may save Mason half the pot should a king or queen come off on the turn or river. By playing on, the small blind has a 24.85% chance to split the pot, whereas the probability to win the whole pot is only 0.30%[45]. If Mason reraises on the flop and his opponent folds, then he wins six small bets 100% of the time. If Mason just calls and goes to showdown, he can expect to win 7.3 small bets[46]. And if he reraises and his opponent decides to call him down, Mason's expectation is 8.1 small bets.

Obviously it all depends on how the hand plays out, but from what I have seen the Asian player is more likely to call the flop-raise than to fold. The reason is that this player will interpret a flop-reraise as a clear indication that Mason doesn't have a king. Therefore, he puts Mason on an ace. Now Mason either has an ace with a decent kicker (e.g. A-J or A-10), in which case he thinks his hand may be good or at least tie Mason's hand, or he knows he is in kicker trouble but figures that the pot is already quite big and that he has outs to at least get half of it. In conclusion it appears that reraising in this case is better than just calling.

If Mason's opponent has a draw, case c), it can only be with Q-10 or J-10. By raising, the Asian guy gets pot odds of 11-to-1, just enough to call (assuming Mason doesn't have a full house). It looks like charging the small blind for his draw is superior, assuming he plays according to the pot odds.

Say Mason just calls on the flop. Then an aggressive player like the small

---

[44] This assumes that the small blind calls the turn and the river if Mason just calls. This is very likely, and is what actually happened.
[45] This is true if the small blind doesn't have a suited ace with one of his suit on board; otherwise his win rate increases to 3.94% because he can win by making a backdoor flush.
[46] The assumption is that both hands go to showdown and there are bets on the turn and river. This is realistic, and is what actually happened. In this case, 71.21% of the time Mason scoops the pot, 24.85% of the time he wins 1 small bet (split pot, both players chop the big blind's money) and 0.30% of the time he loses the whole pot.

blind is tempted to bet again. Taking into account Mason's call, he gets 6-to-1 pot odds, but he is 11.5-to-1 against making his hand. He has committed a serious blunder, and he may bluff again at the end if he doesn't make his hand. Calling the flop raise is not risk-free for Mason, but it's usually profitable against a typical aggressive player like the small blind.

In case d), where the Asian guy holds a pocket pair, we have pretty much the same situation as in case c), except the small blind has two outs instead of four. Clearly, letting the small blind do the betting is even better, since there's less danger of being outdrawn.

In case e), Mason's opponent has a busted hand, and calling is clearly superior to raising. If Mason reraises, the Asian guy can only fold and Mason loses a chance to win more money later. By just calling, he may induce one or two bets on subsequent betting rounds.

In summary, calling is clearly better than reraising in cases a) and e), and in the other three situations it depends on how Mason's opponent plays, but from what we know about him, it's clear that calling is usually the superior play, except in case b), when reraising is likely better.

The small blind actually had a pair of aces, in which case reraising would have been almost certainly the correct play. But you have to look at all the possibilities. Therefore, Mason's flop call was not an overly cautious play, but the right play. You can perform the same analysis on the turn; again, calling is better than raising. For instance, if the small blind bets the turn with an ace, as in the actual hand, by reraising, Mason would very likely force his opponent to release his hand. It's much more likely that Mason just wins one big bet instead of three[47].

Session 7: Bellagio, Saturday, September 10, 8:30 a.m.

I enter the Bellagio poker room early on Saturday morning, hoping there are still some overtired tourists desperately trying to get even. There is just one full $30-60 game, with a couple of people on the waiting list. The floorman tells me most names on the list are probably dead. I nod and he puts me on the list. After half an hour I finally get a seat.

---

[47] By the way, it's very unlikely that Mason would bet the river after his opponent called the raise on the turn (unless he fills up on the river) because he had to assume that the small blind called with a king (unless he had a very good read on his opponent).

I take the open 2 seat at table 37. There are three regulars I know: Danny in the 1 seat, Ray (see 2/152) in 3 and J.J. in 8. I haven't seen the other players before and, unfortunately, none looks depressed or overtired.

Session 7: Hands 1-5

I post behind the button and fold **K-2** after an early raise with no callers in front of me. On the next hand I have **7-5**, another quick fold.

I'm dealt A♦-Q♥ in late-middle position. Two players have limped in front of me, I raise, both blinds play and the limpers call. Five players, pot $300.

Flop: 8♠-9♥-3♠. The blinds and the first limper check, then the second limper in the 10 seat bets. I have 11-to-1 pot odds, enough for my two overcards even if the spade outs (A♠, Q♠) should be no good. I call and only the big blind calls behind. Three players, pot $390.

Turn: 8♦. The 10 seat bets. Since the stakes double at the turn, my pot odds have dropped to 7.5-to-1. I'm sure that at least one of my opponents has me beat. I need at least 6.8-to-1 pot odds if—and that's a big if—all aces and queens are live and I'm drawing for the best hand. I have just four outs against a flush draw, three if someone has J-10 (and just two against J♠-10♠), and I'm drawing dead if someone holds an eight. I fold and the big blind calls. Two players, pot $510.

River: 8♠ (board: 8♠-9♥-3♠-8♦-8♠). The 10 seat bets and the big blind calls. J-9 for the 10 seat and A♠-2♠ for the big blind.

I fold **8-6** and **7-6s**.

Session 7: Hands 6-16

Danny limps under the gun and I call right behind him with **K♠-J♠**. Six players, pot $180. Flop: 10-8-5 rainbow. The blinds check, Danny bets and all fold. There was no way I could call with just two overcards and all those players behind me.

Q-3 (UTG), **10-8** (B, RIF), **9-2s** (SB, chop), **J-7s** (B), **9-6** (CO), **10-8**.

Three players are walking. I raise with **K-Qs** from early position and win the blinds.

I lose no time raising with **K-K** under the gun. Only the button calls. Two players, pot $170. The K-6-2 flop is excellent, but unless my opponent has the case king, he has probably missed it completely. I bet and he calls (pot $230). Turn: 4. I bet and the button folds.

5-4 (BB, chop), **6-2** (SB, RIF).

Session 7: Hand 17

It's folded to me on the button. I have an automatic raise with A♣-Q♣.

Only Ray in the small blind calls. Two players, pot $150.

Flop: K♣-4♠-3♥. Ray checks, I bet and he calls (pot $210).

Turn: K♦. Ray bets. This looks highly suspicious. Ray is one of these guys who believes he's the best player in the world, at least at the limit he plays. Consequently, he always tries to play it 'smart'. What does this mean for Ray in this case? He would definitely attempt a check-raise if he held a king, especially because he's played with me enough to know that I will probably bet the turn if he checks.

I'm positive that Ray doesn't have a king, and that he's betting to push me off my hand. Of course, that doesn't necessarily mean that I have the best hand. He could have something like A-4s or a pocket pair. But at least I know that if I'm behind, I'm drawing live. With 4.5-to-1 pot odds, calling with six outs can't be right. It's the combination of outs and the possibility of holding the best hand that makes calling correct. I call (pot $330).

River: 5♦ (board: K♣-4♠-3♥-K♦-5♦). Ray bets and I call. He cheerfully shows 7♥-6♥ for a seven-high straight.

Session 7: Hands 18-19

In the cutoff I pick up K♦-J♠ and open with a raise. Ray makes it three bets on the button; the blinds fold. Another heads-up with Ray, but one thing is certain: I have the worst hand and need help from the board (pot $230).

Flop: K♣-6♠-4♦. I check, Ray bets and I call (pot $290).

Turn: K♥. Looks like I got the help I needed. I bet to keep Ray from taking a free card, and he raises immediately. I feel I've been trapped. Ray calls with a lot of hands. He would have probably called my pre-flop raise with

K-10s, but he wouldn't reraise with it. He probably has A-K or K-Qs, but certainly not a king with a weaker kicker than mine. Unless Ray has a small set, which is unlikely, I still have nine outs: three to win (any jack) and six to split the pot (any six or four). I call, pot $530.

Question 7/1:

Is the turn call correct?

River: 7♦ (board: K♣-6♠-4♦-K♥-7♦). I check and he bets. I have no illusions of having the best hand, but I feel I must call with pot odds of 9.8-to-1 and trip kings with a decent kicker[48]. Ray shows A-K and takes the pot.

I fold **K-3**.

Session 7: Hand 20

Two players are still walking. It's folded to me and I raise with **K-J** in middle position. The button and big blind call. Three players, pot $200.

Flop: K-7-5. The big blind bets. He probably has a semi-strong hand. I would expect him to attempt a check-raise with a big hand because with a raised pot, someone (usually the pre-flop raiser) usually bets. I think my hand is best, so I call with the intention to raise the turn. The button calls behind. Three players, pot $290.

Turn: Q. The big blind bets and I raise as planned. The button folds and the big blind calls. Two players, pot $530.

River: 5 (board: K-7-5-Q-5). The big blind says, "I'm done with the hand," and the action is on me. I check behind. The big blind shows K-2 and we split (we both have kings and fives with a queen). Clearly, I should have bet. My opponent's statement could have been an inducement to check, and if it was, he succeeded. I thought he was either bluffing (with a busted flush draw or a drawing hand like 8-6) or trying to trap me (with a five). In neither case should I bet. I hadn't considered that he might have been try-ing to prevent my betting again. I don't know if he would have folded to a bet. I don't think he would, but if I'm wrong, I just cost myself half the pot.

---

[48] I was deceived by seemingly high pot odds. Calling is correct against a typical opponent. But I've played with Ray enough to know I didn't have a 1-in-11 shot to win the hand.

Session 7: Hands 21-44

Danny raises from under the gun and I fold right behind him with **8-8**.

I pick up another middle pair, **7-7**, under the gun. I call, there is another limper behind me and the blinds play. Four players, pot $120. Flop: 8-8-2. The blinds check; I bet and win the pot.

J-2 (BB, RIF), **K-3** (SB, RIF), **Q-6** (B), **5-4** (CO), **Q-2**, **8-4s**, **10-2**, **10-2**, **8-3** (UTG).

Ray raises from under-the-gun. It's folded to me and I call with **8-8** in the big blind. Two players, pot $140. Flop: A-J-5. I check, Ray bets and I fold. The only hand I can beat is K-Q. Looks like I can't beat Ray today.

A-6s (SB, three bets to me), **7-3** (B), **K-5** (CO), **J-6**.

Ray has left the table and Peter, another regular, has taken the 3 seat. I raise with **A-Q** in early position. Peter makes it three bets and everyone but me folds. I call. Two players, pot $230.

Flop: 2-K-4. I check, Peter bets and I fold. Calling would have been silly. At best I had six outs against a hand like 10-10. If he had a king, then I was drawing slim, and I could have been drawing dead (against K-K) or close to it (against A-A or A-K).

I fold **K-2** in first position.

A middle-position player raises, the button and small blind call, and I call with **A-10** in the big blind. Four players, pot $240. Flop: 2♦-K♦-5♠. The original raiser wins the pot without showing his hand.

K-5 (SB, RIF), **8-3** (B), **J-8** (CO), **9-3s**, **10-8** (UTG).

Session 7: Hand 45

A new player has posted behind the button and raises the pot. The button calls and I call from the big blind with **A-6**. Three players, pot $200.

Flop: 6-7-2. I check, the cutoff bets and the button folds. Holding second pair with no picture on the board, there is a decent chance that I have the best hand. I call. Two players, pot $260.

Turn: Q. I check and my opponent bets. Did the cutoff raise pre-flop because he had a good hand, or did he sense an opportunity to pick up the blinds? I still might be best, and if not, I have probably five outs. I call (pot $380).

River: 8 (board: 6-7-2-Q-8). I check and the cutoff bets. Clearly, I have to call. My opponent shows 10-10 and takes the pot. He played the hand well by not backing off when the queen came on the turn.

Session 7: Hands 46-60

Q-J (SB, three bets to me), **J-7s** (B), **Q-8** (CO), **5-3**, **9-8s** (BB, three bets to me).

I'm down about a grand. There are still some players walking, and a lot of fluctuation at the table. I have moved into the 3 seat. I complete the bet with **Q-2** in the small blind. Three players, pot $90. Flop: K-J-9 and I check-fold.

7-4 (B), **K-10** (CO, RIF), **7-2**, **K-2s**, **6-3**, **8-7s**, **9-4.**

The table is full now. **7-3s** (UTG), **K-10** (BB, chop).

Session 7: Hand 61

Four players limp and I complete the bet from the small blind with **9-6**. The big blind gets a free play. Six players, pot $180.

Flop: 9♠-5♦-2♠. I bet my top pair and get two callers. Three players, pot $270.

Turn: 9♥. I bet and only the button calls. Two players, pot $390.

River: J♠ (board: 9♠-5♦-2♠-9♥-J♠). My opponent appears to have a draw. The only possible draws are a spade-flush draw and a straight draw if he holds 4-3. I risk being raised if I bet into the flush, and if my opponent won't call with 4-3. I check, the button bets and I call. He shows A♠-6♠ for an ace-high flush.

Session 7: Hand 62

A strong Russian female player raises the pot from under the gun and I make it three bets from the button with **Q-Q**. We battle it out heads-up (pot $230).

Flop: 5-3-2. She checks, I bet and she calls (pot $290).

Turn: J. Same action as flop.

River: 7 (board: 5-3-2-J-7). The Russian lady checks, I bet and she flashes me A-K before mucking.

Session 7: Hands 63-67

The under-the-gun player raises and the 2 seat right in front of me calls. I call with **J-J** in the cutoff. The button calls and the blinds fold. Four players, pot $290.

Flop: 8-K-4. The original raiser bets; the 2 seat calls. With this uncoordinated board and two players who are willing to put money in the pot, you can assume that at least one of them has a king (or a better hand). I fold and the button raises (he has 8-8 and wins the pot).

I fold **9-2s**; I raise with **Q-Q** and win the blinds; **7-3s**; **3-2** (UTG).

Session 7: Hand 68

Danny and the Russian lady limp; the small blind completes the bet. I get a free play with **K-J**. Four players, pot $120.

Flop: K♠-3♦-7♠. The small blind checks; I check; Danny bets; the Russian lady and the small blind fold; I raise. Danny immediately reraises, and I make it four bets. That play looks bold with just top pair, medium kicker. But what better hand can Danny hold? He would have raised pre-flop with A-A, K-K, A-K or K-Qs. The only threats are K-Q and 7-7. I assume he has a flush draw and was raising for a free turn card. Danny calls. Two players, pot $360.

Turn: 6♣. I bet and Danny calls (pot $480).

River: 6♦ (board: K♠-3♦-7♠-6-♣6♦). I bet and Danny folds. Looks like he had a flush draw.

Session 7: Hands 69-82

The button opens with a raise. I make it three bets with **A-J** in the small blind. The big blind folds and the button calls. Two players, pot $210. Flop: K-3-3. I bet and the button folds.

I gained some ground on the last two hands, but I'm still down $600.

7-3 (B), **K-7** (CO), **2-2, J-9, 10-3** (UTG), **10-7** (BB, RIF), **J-7s** (SB, RIF), **Q-J** (B, three bets to me), **8-7** (CO), **A-5, Q-4, 10-4, A-9** (UTG).

Session 7: Hand 83

A middle-position player limps and the small blind completes the bet. I knuckle with **8-2** in the big blind. Three players, pot $90.

Flop: 8♠-6♠-5♦. The small blind bets, I call and the limper raises. The small blind and I call (pot $270).

Turn: 3♥. The small blind checks. The limper's flop raise doesn't in itself mean I'm beat. He could have raised with a 7, 4-3, a flush draw or just two overcards. I don't want to give a free card if I'm ahead, so I bet. Both opponents call (pot $450).

River: 4♥ (board: 8♠-6♠-5♦-3♥-4♥). We all check. The limper shows 9-8 and takes the pot.

Session 7: Hands 84-98

J-4 (SB, RIF), **9-5s** (B), **5-3s** (CO), **8-5.** I raise with **A-10** and take the blinds. **A-5, Q-7** (UTG), **10-3s** (BB, RIF).

A late-middle-position player calls. I complete the bet from the small blind with **Q♣-J♣.** The big blind checks. Three players, pot $90.

Flop: J♠-7♦-4♦. I bet out, the big blind folds and the limper calls. Two players, pot $150.

Turn: 6♣. I bet and my opponent raises. A raise on the turn usually means a very strong hand (maybe 7-7 or 4-4), a semi-bluff (such as A♦-5♦) or a hand that your opponent isn't sure is best. Or he might raise with the intention to check down the river (e.g., J-10). In the first case I'm drawing dead; otherwise I'm in pretty good shape. I call (pot $390).

River: 10♥ (board: J♠-7♦-4♦-6♣-10♥). I check and my opponent checks behind. I turn over my hand he shows J-8 and my better kicker takes the pot.

On the next few hands I fold **Q-5** (B), **7-2** (CO), **10-3, A-3s.**

The game is moderately tight and not too aggressive at the moment. I take a chance and call with **Q-10s** under the gun. I get two limpers, and both blinds call. Five players, pot $150. Flop: A-5-9. The small blinds bets, the big blind calls and I let it go.

I fold **3-2** (BB, RIF).

Session 7: Hands 99-111

It's folded to me in the small blind. The big blind doesn't want to chop, so I throw in a $10 chip with **6♣-3♣**. The big blind checks. Two players, pot $60.

Flop: K♣-J♦-J♥. I check and the big blind checks behind (pot $60).

Turn: Q♣. The big blind's check on the flop means he either flopped a monster or has nothing at all. Making a four-flush gives me some insurance, but I'm going to bet in any case, as it's just too likely I can pick up the pot. I bet and my opponent folds.

5-4 (B), **K-5** (CO), **A-6**, **7-6**, **7-4**, **10-9s**, **10-5** (BB, RIF).

Again it's folded to me in the small blind. I complete the bet with **8♠-4♠**. The big blind checks (pot $60). Flop: A♥-9♥-7♣. I check and this time the big blind bets. I'm forced to muck my hand.

I fold **Q-5** (B), **8-4** (CO), **K-7**, **J-4**.

Session 7: Hand 112

There are two limpers in front of me and I call with K♣-3♣.

The player behind me raises and J.J. at the button calls. Both blinds fold and the limpers call. Five players, pot $350.

Flop: A♣-2♣-8♦. The two limpers check, as do I. The original raiser bets, J.J. raises and the two limpers fold. I call with the nut-flush draw, and the player behind me calls. Three players, pot $530.

Turn: A♥. Everyone checks (pot still $530).

River: A♠ (board: A♣-2♣-8♦-A♥-A♠). I missed my draw, but there's a remote chance a bluff might succeed, since no one bet the turn. I bet. Alas, the player behind me raises immediately. J.J. shows 8-8 and tosses the hand into the muck. I fold quickly. I picked the worst possible time to bluff; I ran into the nuts and was already dead on the turn.

I misinterpreted the situation because J.J. played the hand strangely. I figured there was no ace out because everyone checked the turn. But the player behind me held an ace. He bet his pair of aces on the flop and J.J. raised. He must have had a weak kicker and put J.J on an ace with a better kicker, so he just called the raise. He had the same kicker problem on the turn, so he checked his trip aces. I have no idea why J.J. checked behind.

Session 7: Hands 113-134

J-5 (BB, RIF), 6-3 (SB, RIF), 8-3 (B), Q-6 (CO). I raise with K-9s and win the blinds. 5-5, J-10, K-8 (UTG).

Danny limps from the button, the small blind plays and I check with A-J from the big blind. Three players, pot $90. Flop: 3-4-5. The small blind checks, I check, Danny bets and the small blind folds. I instantly fold my two overcards and gutshot. My alarm bells went off when Danny, a usually solid player, just limped from the button. It's too likely he was trying to trap the blinds with a powerhouse like A-A.

Q-5s (SB, RIF), 10-5 (B), K-5 (CO), Q-7, J-4, K-7 (UTG), J-4 (BB, RIF).

Danny is the lone limper again, this time from the cutoff seat. I complete the bet from the small blind with A-7; the big blind checks. Three players, pot $90. Flop: A-A-J. I check to see what happens. Both players check behind. Turn: J. I bet and hope that one of my opponents has a jack (or at least a king). No such luck: both players fold.

5-4 (B), 9-5s (CO), 10-5, 10-6, K-5.

Session 7: Hand 135

Since the game is not overly aggressive, I decide to play A♦-J♣ from under-the-gun. Two players limp behind me, then Willy, another regular, raises in the 8 seat. Blinds and limpers call. Six players, pot $360.

Flop: 5♠-J♥-8♣. The blinds check, I bet, the first limper folds, the second calls, and then Willy in the 8 seat puts in a raise. The two blinds fold, I make it three bets, the last limper folds and Willy calls. I managed to eliminate all but one player. Two players, pot $570.

Turn: 10♣. I bet and Willy calls.

River: 10♦ (board: 5♠-J♥-8♣-10♣-10♦). I bet and Willy calls. I fear he has an overpair and sure enough, he shows me Q-Q.

Had I won that pot I would have been down $500, so I have just left behind $800 of the two grand I brought with me. It's noon, and a new dealer sits down. Time to hit the Bellagio buffet for lunch.

Result Session 7		Total Results	
Hours	3:30	Hours	29:15
Win/Loss	-$1,195	Win/Loss	$2,670

Session 7: Conclusion

Except for losing $1,200, this was a very uneventful session. I wasn't dealt many big hands. No A-A, A-K, A-Qs and K-Qs. Just K-K, Q-Q and J-J once.

I went to the Bellagio poker room early in the morning hoping to catch some losing and steaming tourists that had played all night. That didn't happen. When I sat down, the game was okay, but not really good. Then the weaker players left the table and only regulars were playing. I had dropped a grand quickly and stayed to get even. Not a good decision, so I got what I deserved.

Why do I always have such odd results, such as losing $1195 or winning $697 when we just play with $10 chips at the $30-60 table? First, the casino collects six bucks every half-hour and you have to pay that amount to the dealer in chips. Second, I do tip the dealers, at least if they are doing a good job[49].

Tipping is a frequent topic of debate. Some players say that the house collects money from the players for the privilege to play and that it is there-

---

[49] This restriction is important to me. I don't tip some dealers because they are unfriendly, talk too much or pay no attention to the game. If you tip good and bad dealers alike, there is no incentive for the bad dealers to improve.

fore the house's duty to make sure that the dealers get an adequate salary. Others argue that the dealers provide services to the customers and should therefore be tipped.

The fact is that the dealers only get the minimum wage from the casinos and rely on tips for a decent income. If no one tipped them, the dealers could no longer make a decent living, many would change jobs, and the quality of the dealers would go down.

How much you should tip is of course a matter of opinion. To borrow from Kant's categorical imperative, I would say you should tip in such a manner that if everyone tips the way you do the dealer gets an income you think is adequate. For me a one-dollar tip per pot won in middle-limit games and half-a-dollar at low-limit tables seems fine. That way a dealer can make between $30-40 an hour in middle-limits and $17.50-22.50 in low-limits, depending on the speed of the dealer and the game.

If you play primarily for fun, you can tip any amount you want, but if you play to make money you should give it some thought. A dollar or two per hand may not seem like much, but it can make a huge difference at the year's end.

If you play 1,800 hours per year and win 2.5 pots per hour, pretty typical figures for a professional player, then you have $4,500 less at the year's end if you tip two dollars instead of one. Your hourly win rate goes down $5.00 in the first case and $2.50 in the second.

Some players just feel cheap tipping a dollar when a really big pot is pushed their way. Not long ago, I was playing at a $30-60 table and a player, obviously a tourist, won a huge pot of about $2,000. The dealer pushed him the pot and he tossed her three chips ($30). Then he looked at the large pile of chips in front of him and slid her another three chips. For the dealer it was like Christmas and for the player it looked like not much. However, he simply lost 60 bucks.

There are two things that many players don't understand about tipping. First, since these players only tip when they win a pot, they think it's just a tiny fraction of their winnings. They seem to believe that if they tip, say 2% for every pot won, then they've given up 2% of their overall profit. This can't be right for the simple reason that most players are not winners, and tipping just means that they are losing more. Even if such a player is an overall winner, the assumption that he has tipped away 2% from his winnings can only be true if he wins every pot he plays. Unfortunately nobody bothers to give him back 2% when he loses a hand.

Second, some players believe they won because of the dealer and want to show their gratitude by tipping. This is just nonsense. When the cards are shuffled and the deck is cut, the order of the cards is fixed. Your winning has nothing to do with the dealer (at least if the dealer is honest), who just deals the hands and turns over the board cards. Conversely, you should never blame the dealer if you lose (if s/he did nothing wrong); s/he is just doing his/her job.

I mentioned that you should tip less in low-limit than in middle-limit games. This is because if you tip too generously in low-limit games, you will have a hard time winning at all. In a card room you will often see off-duty dealers play among themselves, typically at low limits. Being dealers themselves, they usually tip liberally. At the Bellagio, where the smallest game is $4-8, this often amounts to $3 or $4 for every pot won, meaning they tip away between $7.50 and $10 per hour. If you tip that much, you have to be a very good player just to break even at that game.

Excessive tipping is not that much of a problem for a good player at middle-limit games, but in the long run it makes a greater difference than most people think.

Session 8: Bellagio, Sunday, September 11, 12:10 a.m.

Shortly after midnight I arrive at the Bellagio poker room. There are four $30-60 games in progress, none full. The floorman sends me to table 19 and I take the 9 seat. My acquaintance Tommy is in the 1 seat, Barry Tanenbaum is in the 2, and there are a couple of Asian players that seem to be quite loose and aggressive.

Session 8: Hands 1-7

I post behind the button. Barry raises from first position, two players call and I fold **9-5**.

On the next hand the Asian player in the 8 seat raises. Peeking at my hand, I see **A-K** and make it three bets. Tommy on the button calls the three bets cold and the blinds fold. Three players, pot $320.

Flop: A-4-2. The 8 seat bets, I raise, Tommy calls and the 8 seat folds. Two players, pot $470.

Turn: 4. I bet and Tommy calls (pot $590).

River: 7 (board: A-4-2-4-7). There's no point trying to figure out what Tommy may hold. He calls with all sorts of hands. I wouldn't be surprised if he had 3-2s. I bet and he calls. I show my hand and it's good (Tommy mucks his hand without showing it).

I fold the next several hands: **Q-8**, **7-3**, **Q-3**, **K-3**, **6-2** (UTG).

Session 8: Hands 8-17

There is a raise with six callers when the action comes to me with **J-8** in the big blind. In a raised pot a weak hand like this is usually a clear fold, but with 15-to-1 pot odds I take a look at the flop. Eight players, pot $480.

Flop: 6♠-Q♥-9♦. The small blind checks, I check, the original raiser bets, one player calls, the button raises and the small blind folds. I have a gut-shot with 10-to-1 pot odds. A call might be reasonable due to implied odds, but my call won't close the action. The original raiser may raise again, and the button could make it four bets. I fold (the button wins with 9-9; the original raiser has K-Qs).

I fold several hands: **K-J** (SB, RIF), **Q-7** (B), **9-4s** (CO), **3-3**, **10-8**, **K-3**, **J-3**, **7-6**. The table is full now, and I fold **Q-2s** (UTG).

Session 8: Hand 18

Three players limp, the small blind completes the bet and I raise from the big blind with **A♥-K♥**. Everyone calls. Five players, pot $300.

Flop: A♠-6♠-3♣. The small blind checks, I bet and only the 3 and the 5 seat call. Three players, pot $390.

Turn: 6♣. I'm first to act and I bet out. The 3 seat calls and the Asian lady in the 5 seat goes all-in for $70. The 5 seat and I put another 10 bucks in the pot.

Question 8/1:

Why haven't I reraised after the lady has gone all-in?

River: 3♥ (board: A♠-6♠-3♣-6♣-3♥). I was afraid of a flush, so this is not a bad card. I bet, the 3 seat calls and the Asian lady angrily mucks two spades. My A-K holds up (the 3 seat doesn't show his hand, but he must have had an ace with a worse kicker).

Session 8: Hands 19-32

K-3 (SB, RIF), **4-3s** (B), **K-Q** (three bets to me), **10-5**, **9-2**, **A-6**, **Q-8**, **8-7** (UTG), **3-2** (BB, RIF).

Tommy in the cutoff seat raises an early-position limper; the button calls. Since the three active players are all pretty weak, I call with **7♦-6♦** from the small blind. The big blind calls. Five players, pot $300.

Flop: K♥-6♠-9♠. I check, the big blind and the early-position limper check, Tommy bets and the button folds. Knowing that Tommy raises with all kind of trash hands, regardless of position, my bottom pair could very well be good and, should he really have a king, 11-to-1 pot odds give me the right price to draw to my five-outer. I call, the big blind calls and the early-position limper folds. Three players, pot $390.

Turn: K♠. The good news: it's less likely that one of my opponents has a king. The bad news: a flush is now possible. I check, the big blind checks and Tommy bets. As usual, I have no idea what Tommy has. He could have a flush, a king, aces or nothing at all. I don't want to be bluffed out of what is already a decent-sized pot, so I call; the big blind folds. Two players, pot $510.

River: 5♣ (board: K♥-6♠-9♠-K♠-5♣). I check.

Question 8/2:

Am I more likely to have the best hand when Tommy bets or when he checks?

Tommy checks behind and wins the pot with 10-9. I had a mandatory river call, so I'm glad Tommy didn't bet.

I fold the next four hands: **K-10** (B, RIF), **8-6** (CO), **A-4s** (RIF), **10-3**.

Session 8: Hands 33-39

A player in front of me limps and I call with **7-7**. Both blinds play. Four players, pot $120. Flop: 8-10-8. The small blind checks, the big blind bets and the limper calls. I would be foolish to call. With two players voluntarily putting money into the pot, at least one of them has an eight or a ten, in which case I'm down to two outs, and my opponents have lots of outs in the unlikely case that my pair of sevens is best. For instance, J-9 has 12 outs and Q-J has 10 outs. I fold my hand (the big blind wins with 10-2).

I fold **A-9** in early position. Then I get a free play in the big blind with **8-6**. Four players, pot $120. Flop: Q♥-2♥-J♥. The small blind bets and, having no heart, I fold.

K-7s (UTG)[50], **Q-9** (SB, RIF), **Q-9** (B), **6-4s** (CO).

Session 8: Hand 40

An early-position player raises and a middle-position player calls. I am dealt A♠-Q♠ two spots from the button. Three-betting is certainly an option here. That would probably shut out the players behind me and give me position for the rest of the hand. But A-Qs plays well in multiway pots, so I don't mind players calling behind me. I call, Tommy calls on the button and the blinds fold. Four players, pot $290.

Flop: 6♦-9♣-7♠. The pre-flop raiser bets and the middle-position player calls. The flop is not much help for my hand. I have two overcards and a backdoor flush draw. But with 11.7-to-1 pot odds, I call, and Tommy calls as well. Still four players, pot $410.

Turn: 2♣. The original raiser bets and the middle-position player folds. My pot odds have decreased to 7.3-to-1, the backdoor flush draw is gone and there is an unpredictable player behind me. I fold and Tommy calls. Two players, pot $530.

River: 8♠ (board: 6♦-9♣-7♠-2♣-8♠). The original raiser now checks, obviously worried about the possible straight. Tommy bets and his opponent calls. Tommy shows K-10 for a straight. The early position raiser has J-J.

---

[50] The player in front of me is buying the button, hence I'm under the gun now, even though I was in the big blind the hand before.

Question 8/3:

Had I known what my opponents were holding, should I have called on the turn?

Session 8: Hands 41-48

9-6s, **8-5**, **7-5**, **7-4** (UTG).

I get a free play in the big blind with **9-6**. Four players, pot $120. Flop: 2-J-2. The small blind bets and I fold.

J-7s (SB, RIF), **A-3s** (B, RIF), **7-3** (CO).

Session 8: Hand 49

Two players limp and I call with A♥-10♦ from middle position. Everyone calls behind, so we have seven players (pot $210).

Flop: A♣-5♦-2♠. It's checked to me and I bet. Only Tommy in the cutoff seat and the under-the-gun player call. Three players, pot $300.

Turn: Q♦. The under-the-gun player checks. Though the queen on the turn is not too dangerous, I can't afford to give a free card. I bet, Tommy mucks his hand and the under-the-gun player calls. Two players, pot $420.

River: 7♥ (board: A♣-5♦-2♠-Q♦-7♥). My opponent checks. Should I bet for value or check behind? There was no draw-out[51], so I assume my opponent holds an ace. He probably would have raised A-K pre-flop; with A-J I'm not sure; if he paired his kicker he would have most likely bet the river. He most likely holds A-3, A-4, A-6 or A-8 through A-J. Against these holdings I lose once, tie once and win five times. Moreover, I'm pretty sure to get a call from any ace. The situation calls for a bet. I bet and my opponent calls. My A-10 wins against his A-8.

Session 8: Hands 50-58

7-4, **A-7**, **10-6** (UTG), **10-7** (BB, RIF).

---

[51] I'm not concerned about 4-3. It's unlikely that my opponent played that hand from first position, and he wouldn't check the nuts three times.

I complete the bet from the small blind with **8-3**. Six players, pot $180. The flop comes 6-10-2 and I give up quickly.

Q-6 (B), **8-6** (CO), **5-4**, **7-3**.

Session 8: Hand 59

The under-the-gun player limps and I call with Q♠-J♥ in early position. This is usually not a good call, but there is a decent chance for a multiway pot in this game. Sure enough, the player behind me, the button and the two blinds call. Six players, pot $180.

Flop: J♦-9♥-6♣. The small blind checks, the big blind bets and the under-the-gun player raises. I don't know where I stand with top pair, decent kicker, but I want to find out quickly, so I make it three bets. The 10 seat behind me and the button fold; both blinds and the under-the-gun player call. Four players, pot $540.

Turn: 8♦. It's checked to me. Either my hand is good or someone is waiting to check-raise me (Q-10 has a straight now, and someone could be slow-playing a set or top two pair). I bet and all three opponents call. Still four players, pot $780.

River: Q♥ (board: J♦-9♥-6♣-8♦-Q♥). The small blind bets out and the two players behind him fold. The queen has made me top two pair, but I'm clearly in second place. Any ten makes a straight. With a big pot and two folds in front of me, I have to make the crying call to keep the small blind honest. I call and he shows K-10 for the nuts.

Question 8/4:

How well did the lucky winner play the hand?

Session 8: Hands 60-67

I fold **J-5**. Then I raise with A♦-J♠ from first position. How I play A-J from early position depends upon the game conditions. In tough, aggressive games I fold without second thoughts, and in average games I usually call. This game is very loose but not too aggressive before the flop. Raising in such games normally results in fewer players, but about the same size pot as I'd get from a call. The risk is that one of the several players behind me might wake up with a better hand. I get calls from the 10 seat, the 2 seat, the button (6 seat) and the big blind (8 seat). Five players, pot $320.

Flop: A♠-J♣-8♦. The big blind checks. My top two pair are strong, but not strong enough to fool around and get fancy. Anyone with 10-9 has an open-ended straight draw, and lots of gutshots are possible. I bet. The 10 seat calls, the 2 seat folds, the button calls and the big blind folds. Three players, pot $410.

Turn: 4♦. An excellent card for me, as I don't have to worry about a straight. I bet, the 10 seat calls and the button folds. Two players, pot $530.

River: 4♥ (board: A♠-J♣-8♦-4♦-4♥). I'm sure I have the best hand. I bet and the 10 seat calls. I show my A-J and my opponent turns over A-10.

I fold **A-3** (BB, RIF), **Q-8** (SB, RIF), **Q-10** (B, RIF), **K-Js** (CO, RIF), **A-8**, **9-3s**.

Session 8: Hand 68

The under-the-gun player in the 7 seat limps and I raise with A♠-A♣.

Sam, a decent player, has replaced Tommy in the 1 seat. He reraises; the small blind, a weak-playing elderly gentleman (the one who beat me with K-10 in hand 8/59), calls; and, surprisingly, the under-the-gun limper folds. Since I have played with Sam for years I know that if I make it four bets my hand is pretty much defined, so I just call. Three players, pot $330.

Flop: 4♥-5♦-K♠. The small blind checks, I bet, Sam raises and the small blind calls the two bets cold. Sam's reraise tells me that he has one of the following hands: A-A (unlikely), A-K, K-K, K-Q or a big pair lower than kings. He's either beating me badly (with K-K) or drawing slim. I take a risk by keeping both of my opponents in with just a call. Three players, pot $510.

Turn: 7♥. The small blind checks, I check, Sam bets and the small blind calls behind. The seven looks harmless enough. I know that by just calling, I will get a sure river call from Sam, and maybe an overcall from the small blind. I call (pot $690).

River: 5♠ (board: 4♥-5♦-K♠-7♥-5♠). The small blind checks, I bet (I don't want to give Sam the opportunity to check it down with a hand like Q-Q) and both opponents call. I show my aces and win the pot (neither opponent shows his hand).

Everything worked as planned. But I questioned my play even as I grabbed the pot. More aggressive play might have made me more money. But if they had folded on the flop or turn I would have lost money. Since neither opponent showed his hand, I will never know.

Question 8/5:

Did I play the turn correctly?

Question 8/6:

How was my river play?

Session 8: Hands 69-81

8-4s, A-2 (UTG), J-9 (BB, RIF), 10-8s (SB, RIF), 10-5 (B), 4-2 (CO), Q-6, Q-10 (RIF), 7-6s, 9-2 (UTG), 7-2 (BB, RIF).

I complete the bet with **Q-6** in the small blind. Six players, pot $180. The flop comes 10-7-10 and I give up quickly.

Three players limp and I call with 8♥-7♥ on the button. Flop: 7♣-Q♠-J♣. I fold to a bet, raise and reraise.

Session 8: Hand 82

It's folded to me in the cutoff seat. I raise with A♠-2♠ and only Dianne, a strong regular, calls in the big blind. Two players, pot $140.

Flop: Q♦-2♦-10♥. Dianne checks, I bet and she calls (pot $200).

Turn: 4♦. Dianne checks again. She called on the flop, so she must have something, most likely a flush, a pair of queens or tens, or K-J for a straight draw. I probably need help, so I check behind (pot $200).

River: 2♣ (board: Q♦-2♦-10♥-4♦-2♣). Dianne bets. I raise, taking the risk that she has a flush.

Question 8/7:

Who is more likely to have a flush in this situation: a bad or a good player?

She calls and is really disgusted to see my trip deuces. She doesn't reveal her hand, which is probably something like K-Q.

Session 8: Hands 83-102

9-8s, 7-3, **K-J** (RIF), **A-5** (UTG), **J-3** (BB, RIF).

I complete the bet again from the small blind, this time with **9-6**. Six players, pot $180. Flop: J-7-7. I've wasted another 10 bucks.

9-8 (B), **Q-5** (CO), **Q-5**, **7-6**, **6-2s**, **K-6s**, **A-3** (UTG).

I get a free play in the big blind with **7-6**. Six players, pot $180. The flop comes A-5-10 and I'm done.

6-6 (SB, three bets to me), **6-6** (B, RIF), **J-5s** (CO), **7-6**, **J-7s**, **K-7s**.

Session 8: Hands 103-111

The game has been excellent, with plenty of loose-passive players. But they've been replaced by much better players. The new lineup looks like this: Sam is in the 1 seat, Dianne in the 2, Ray in the 3, Korean Joe in the 4, a player from a broken game in the 5. In the 7 and 8 seats are two young players who play reasonably well. Only the 6 and 10 seats are still occupied by loose-passive players. The game has changed from excellent to merely okay. But a new dealer just sat down and I paid for my time, so I intend to play for another half-hour.

10-2 (UTG), **7-2s** (BB, RIF).

Sam raises from first position. I call from the small blind with **6-6**. The big blind calls. Three players, pot $200. Flop: 9-K-4. I check, the big blind bets, Sam raises and I fold. (The big blind wins with K-2.)

I fold **9-5** (B). Korean Joe raises from under-the-gun and I fold **A-Q** in the cutoff seat.

The 6 and the 10 seat, the only really weak players, leave the table at the same time. It's no longer worth staying at this table, so I will play until the blinds come around and then walk. **K-3**, **J-2s**, **7-2**, **9-3** (UTG).

Time to go. The game was really good for about three hours, and I've booked another nice win. I head for the Victorian Room at the Barbary Coast for a late-night dinner.

Result Session 8		Total Results	
Hours	3:45	Hours	33:00
Win/Loss	$1,246	Win/Loss	$3,916

Session 8: Conclusion

I've concluded a week recording every hand I played. It was much more taxing and time-consuming than I had anticipated. Before I started I didn't worry much about it. A week ago I sat down at the table with a spiral-bound notebook and started taking notes.

It was easy recording folded hands, of course. It got a lot more difficult when I played a hand. I didn't take notes while the hand was in progress and I was still involved. After the hand was over or I had folded, I wrote down what had happened. This took a lot of time. I had to write down which player limped, bet, raised, reraised, called a raise etc., on every street; who the player was (if I knew him or her); my hand; the board cards; who turned over what hand; anything special that happened during the hand; and my thoughts.

The real trouble started when I played successive hands. Now I had to remember several hands at once, and I was unable to observe the action at hand.

After that first session I resolved to find a way to record a hand efficiently, so that I wouldn't lose valuable information and I could better observe the action. Instead of writing down something like "The under-the-gun player raised, the 5 seat called, Johnny in the 7 seat makes it three bets," etc., I devised a hand chart to which I could quickly add the relevant information.

Here it is[52].

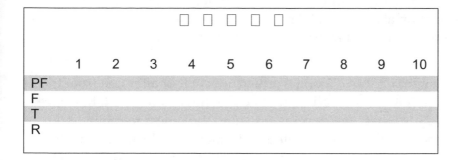

At the end the chart looks like this (example from hand 4/1):

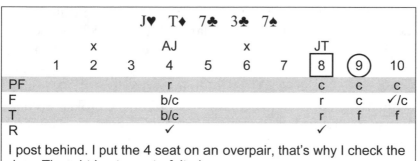

	1	2	3	4	5	6	7	8	9	10
		x		AJ		x		JT		
								8	9	10
PF				r				c	c	c
F				b/c				r	c	✓/c
T				b/c				r	f	f
R				✓				✓		

J♥ T♦ 7♣ 3♣ 7♠

I post behind. I put the 4 seat on an overpair, that's why I check the river. Thought I got counterfeited.

I write the board cards in the top row. The numbers from 1 to 10 correspond to the seats at the table. A square around a number denotes my seat (seat 8 in the example above) and the circle around the number shows the position of the dealer's button (seat 9). The players' hands are visible above the corresponding seats. In the example, the 4 seat had A-J, my hand was J-10, the 9 and 10 seat folded before the river and didn't show their hands. An 'x' denotes an empty seat. There are rows for pre-flop, flop, turn and river play (abbreviations PF, F, T and R). Player actions (✓ = check, c = call, b = bet, f = fold, r = raise, rr = reraise, rrr = rereraise, etc.) are noted in the

---

[52] To my knowledge, the first to illustrate hands in chart form was Mike Caro. He called his chart CASM (Caro action to showdown method, see *Caro's Pro Poker*, Vol. 2 (1994), No. 2, Issue 4, pp. 1ff). A slightly modified version, called an MCU chart, was used by Tony Guerrera in his book *Killer Poker By the Numbers*, 2007. My chart is more compact, easier to read and optimized for limit hold'em (it can easily be adapted to no-limit play).

appropriate cells. At the bottom I write some comments about the hand.

I am showing you the chart because it's an efficient way to record all relevant information about a hand. I now use it regularly. Whenever I play or see an interesting hand, I record it in chart form and review it later at home.

At first I thought my note-taking would draw a lot of attention from the other players, but I was surprised that no one noticed or cared. Ray once wanted to know what I was writing down all the time. I told him I recorded all the mistakes he committed and that's why the book is so thick. He looked at me blankly without saying a word. I guess he didn't find my remark funny.

In the week I kept records I played 33 hours and won $3,916. That looks impressive, but don't draw the wrong conclusions. It doesn't mean that you can make $16,000 per month on a regular basis playing $30-60. So don't sell your house and head to Vegas or Los Angeles to try your fortune as a $30-60 pro. Things are not as they appear . Most of my winnings came from one session when I won $2,700. Had I managed to lose $1,300 in that session, as could easily have happened, then I would have broken even for the week. Then you would probably say, what's this guy doing, playing for a week and not earning a single dime? But it could have been even worse. Instead of winning $4,000, I could have lost $4,000. This has happened to me before, but luckily not too often.

A week seems like a lot of poker, but it's merely a short-term result and lots can happen—good or bad—in the short term. I have seen a truly bad player win $11,000 in four days in a $15-30 game, and I know a pro who lost $15,000 at the same limit over two months. My results from that one week don't tell you if I'm a good or bad player; they just tell you I got lucky. You may be surprised to hear that from me, but it is the truth.

If you want to judge a player's skill, you have to know his long-term results or evaluate his play. If you've studied the hands I've recorded in this book, you may conclude that I do nothing extraordinary, and I would agree. Solid play gets the money in low- and middle-limit play. Fancy play usually costs you money. If you look for so-called 'great plays', you're not going to find many. My only great play—if you want to call it that—was my turn bluff against five opponents (3/65).

But you can't just play ABC poker, at least not in the middle limits. I often vary my play, for instance, mixing folds, calls and raises with the same holdings. Often I delay the flop raise, or I raise the turn when the 'book play' is to call, and vice versa. The key is to balance your play so you're not too predictable, without giving up too much edge.

It's natural to focus on the hands I played and skip over the hands I folded, but there's much to learn from the latter. A good player derives a significant edge from the hands he folds. This is especially true at low limits but also, to a lesser extent, in middle-limit games. Even at the $30-60 limit you will find players who play more hands than they should, granting you a folding edge.

Your folding edge usually decreases at higher limits. Low-limit players tend to be too loose, thus most of your edge comes from folding unprofitable hands that others happily play. Most players at higher limits have a pretty good understanding of what hands to play before the flop, so most of your profit is going to come from post-flop play.

The information I recorded can help us answer some questions. For example, how many hands are you dealt per hour in a casino? I always estimated about 35 hands/hour. Now we can confirm that. During my eight sessions I was dealt 36.2 hands/hour. Though it depends on the conditions and the limits[53], this should be a good approximation for middle-limit hold'em games[54].

We can also calculate my profit per hand. Since I played 1,196 hands and won $3,916, I earned $3.27 on every hand I played or folded. But for reasons we discussed above, this is just a snapshot with little meaning for the long run[55].

We can also answer another question: Was I dealt more than my fair share of big hands before the flop? Take a look at the following table.

---

[53] More hands tend to be dealt in high-limit games because the table is often not full, fewer people enter the pot and the players act more quickly, which results in a faster pace. In low-limit it's just the opposite.

[54] Keep in mind that the Bellagio uses shuffle machines. Fewer hands are dealt per hour at tables without these machines.

[55] See the section "Win rate" in chapter 3 (p.168-172).

Hand	N	+/-	Hand	N	+/-
AA	5	-0.41	AK	13	2.18
KK	9	3.59	AKs	5	1.39
QQ	10	4.59	AQ	15	4.18
JJ	4	-1.41	AQs	3	-0.61
TT	3	-2.41	KQs	4	0.39
Total	31	3.94	Total	40	7.53

N = number of hands dealt   +/- = deviation from the expected value

The table above only shows the big pairs A-A through 10-10, plus A-K, A-Q and K-Qs. The figures show that I got about four big pairs more than I could have expected. I was dealt about the right number of aces, but significantly more kings and queens than jacks and tens. This has a considerable impact, since kings and queens are much stronger than jacks and tens, especially in loose games.

I played a particularly large number of big non-pairs, being dealt a surplus of 7.5 premium hands more than expected. So if we look just at pre-flop hands, there is no doubt that I got lucky in the last eight sessions.

Pre-flop luck is easiest to quantify, but it only tells half the story, as you still have to win the hand. I was dealt a lot of big hands in the first session, but I was in the red when I stepped up from the table.

Let's look now at pocket pairs. If you hold a pocket pair, the odds of flopping a set (or better) are 7.5-to-1[56]. I was dealt 76 pocket pairs, 5.65 more than expected. I should have flopped about 8.9 sets on average, but I only made eight. However, 20 times I didn't see the flop with my pocket pair because I folded, I chopped the blinds or my opponents all folded before

---

[56] There are 19,600 possible flops, 2,304 of which make you at least a set. Therefore the odds are (19,600-2,304):2,304 = 7.51-to-1. See Mike Petriv, *Hold'em Odd(s) Book*, 1996, p. 114f for a more thorough discussion.

the flop. Thus I saw 56 flops with a pocket pair. On average I should have flopped 6.6 sets, which means I made 1.4 more sets than expected. There is no question that flopping sets is a big money maker.

But it's hard to quantify some aspects of luck in poker. After you've gotten your big cards or flopped a set, you have to make it hold up and get paid by one or more opponents. That happened often when I scored my biggest win of the week in the fourth session.

I believe I played reasonably well at the 1,200 hands I recorded this week, but I played somewhat less aggressively than usual, probably because I didn't want to look stupid while recording my play for this book. And I made several mistakes. One was inexcusable (1/19), the others not so serious. I tried to point out my mistakes; perhaps you will see errors that I've overlooked. But remember that you don't have the same information I had, particularly about my opponents, many of whom I've played many times before. I watched the strangers play hands in a certain way that often affected my decisions.

I've tried not to hide my mistakes. Even the best players in the world make mistakes—that's part of playing poker. The key is to make fewer mistakes than your opponents, so you can stay ahead of the competition.

Chapter 2

Answers to Quiz Questions

Answer 1/1

The things to consider are how often the big blind raises and how well you play after the flop.

Calling from the small blind with any two cards when the small blind is two-thirds of the big blind is obviously correct when two conditions are met. First, the big blind should not be a frequent raiser. If he raises often, then you have to tighten up. It's important to understand that you can call for one chip, but if the big blind raises, then you have to release your weak holdings. Don't throw away good money after bad. Second, if you're not a good post-flop player, that single chip might become expensive.

Answer 1/2

I'm about a 33.5-to-1 underdog to win the hand.

If my opponent has a queen, the only card that helps me on the river is a jack for an ace-high straight. With four outs I'm 10.5-to-1 to hit the gutshot. But completing the straight doesn't mean I've won the hand. If a typical player like my opponent plays a hand with a queen in it from under-the-gun, it's probably A-Q, K-Q, Q-J or Q-10.

We can rule out A-Q because most middle-limit players would raise it before the flop. That leaves K-Q, Q-J and Q-10. The last two hands give my opponent a full house, so the only hand I can beat by hitting my four-outer is K-Q. There are six combinations of Q-J, six of Q-10 and six of K-Q (remember I hold a king). Therefore, my straight at the end will only win one-third of the time. My outs decrease from 4 to 1.3, making me a 33.5-to-1 underdog.

Answer 1/3

Barry played the hand correctly and Suzanne misplayed the hand badly.

Suzanne's pre-flop call is too loose, and by just calling on the turn, she fails to protect her hand. The flop call is also questionable. For a more thorough analysis, see the ensuing discussion of hand 1/117.

Answer 2/1

The probability of winning was about 14 % and I should have folded on the flop.

Since we know nine cards, there are 903 two-card combinations [(43x42)/2] that can come on the turn and river.

Hand	Winning combinations	Losing combinations	Ties	Winning probability[1]
A♠-9♠	111	753	39	13.99 %
A♣-10♦	120	744	39	14.99 %
J♥-7♥	633	245	25	71.02 %

1) Two-way ties are counted as a half-win

With 111 winning combinations and 39 ties, A♠-9♠ has a winning probability of 13.99 % on the flop, equivalent to 6.15-to-1 odds. It appears that I had the right odds to call on the flop. However, the odds from the table assume that I can see both the turn and river cards, and my call only enabled me to see the turn card. My flop call was based on the assumption that I very likely had five outs and a backdoor flush draw. The A♣-10♦ killed three of my outs. With just two clean outs, I never had the right odds to continue playing on the flop.

Answer 6/1

Barry's most likely hand is top two pair (or a small set).

We can rule out A-A and K-K because he would have played these hands more aggressively pre-flop and/or on the flop. With J-J, just calling pre-flop would make sense. However on the flop he would have had the nuts and on the turn still the second nuts. That asks for a more aggressive approach. He check-raises me when the queen comes on the turn, so it looks like the queen helped his hand. A-Q makes sense, but I don't think Barry would bet just two overcards in a double-raised pot on the flop, and I doubt that A-Q is strong enough to go for a check-raise. Since Barry bet the flop and check-raised the turn, it looks like he hit his hand twice. So he must have Q-Js.

I normally wouldn't call a double-bet with Q-Js in a three-handed pot, but I know Barry does. With Q-Js he correctly bet his top pair on the flop. After my raise he had to worry that I might have an overpair or a jack with a better kicker, such as A-J, so reraising was too risky. On the turn he made top two pair, a hand that is definitively strong enough to check-raise. Moreover, he could count on me to bet the turn. Since he put me on an overpair or a pair of jacks, he assumed I had to bet because I couldn't afford to give a free card. So Q-Js makes sense. He could also have flopped a set with 6-6 or 3-3. Barry likes to play pocket pairs. My first guess is that Barry had Q-Js; second choice is 6-6 or 3-3.

Answer 7/1

The call is most likely wrong.

I couldn't do the calculations at the table, but I was overoptimistic to think that calling couldn't be wrong by much. If we assume that Ray has a king with a better kicker, there are 45 unknown cards in the deck and $470 in the pot. Three times (if the jack comes on the river) in 45, I will attempt a check-raise and win another $120. Six times (if the board pairs) I will split the pot. And 36 times I will lose a double-bet If I call on the turn and river.

My expected value is

$$\{[3\times(\$470+\$120)] + [6\times(\$470+\$60-\$120)/2] - (36\times\$120)\}/45 = -\$29.33$$

My turn call is only correct if I have the discipline to fold on the river if I don't improve and if I'm correct to do so.

Answer 8/1

The rules don't allow me to reraise in this situation.

After the 3 seat just called my bet and the 5 seat went all-in, I very much wanted to reraise. I obviously had the 3 seat beat at the moment, and wanted to charge him as much as possible for the chance to draw out on me. However, I'm not allowed to reraise because the lady's raise is less than half a bet. Had she gone all-in for $90, I would have the option to just call $30, complete the bet to $120 or raise to $150.

Answer 8/2

The chances are better when Tommy bets.

If Tommy checks behind at the end, he probably has a hand to showdown. The only hands my pair of sixes can beat are things like A-5. Should I have the best hand with my sixes, then that would mean Tommy was bluffing at the flop and turn, and his only way to win the hand would be to bluff the river as well. Of course, a bet by Tommy at the end is not necessarily a bluff. He could have a very strong hand like nines full or trip kings. However, my chances to have the best hand are better when Tommy bets than when he checks.

Answer 8/3

I should have called.

There are 42 unknown cards and I have six clean outs. There are 36 cards that don't help me on the river, so I lose the turn bet (36×$60 = $2,160). Six times I win the whole pot and get an additional bet from the J-J hand (he called when a four-card-straight was on the board, so he would call with a queen or ace at the end as well) for a total of 6×$590 = $3,540. In other words, calling has an EV of $32.86 per hand.

Answer 8/4

He played the hand horribly.

He called three bets cold on the flop with just a gutshot and an overcard. On the turn he picked up an open-ended straight draw, so you can't blame him for calling.

Answer 8/5

I probably played the turn too weakly.

I played the hand too passively, especially on the turn where the right play was to raise. I thought Sam had either A-K or a big pair lower than kings (Q-Q through 9-9). Therefore, the focus of my play was not to lose Sam because with just two outs he never had the right pot odds to play on. I believe I had a good read on Sam, but I still made two mistakes.

I didn't consider that no matter how strongly I played, Sam would never lay down A-K (he would probably fold Q-Q to a turn raise). And I was too fixated on Sam and the pot odds I was laying, neglecting the second player. He most likely had a king—otherwise, how could he have over-called at the end? I had taken that into account and figured that he had four or five outs (depending on Sam's hand). By just calling on the turn I gave him pot odds of 10.5-to-1, just a little short for a four-outer (not considering the possible implied odds).

My thinking on the turn went like this: If I just called, Sam would give me a call at the end for sure. With the second player it was close but I thought there was a good chance he'd overcall with just a king. The prospect of winning two additional big bets on the river led me to conclude that just calling would create a +EV situation for me. But I looked at my opponents' pot odds and outs individually when together they had at least seven outs (e.g., Sam: Q-Q, small blind: K-10) unless they held the same hand. Against seven outs I should have never given 10.5-to-1 pot odds by just calling, hence raising was the proper play.

Answer 8/6

The bet on the river was correct.

Notice that I had just called on the turn to collect two bets on the river. The best way to achieve this is by betting myself. If Sam doesn't have a king, he checks behind and it's very doubtful that the small blind, probably holding a weak king, would bet himself. In this case my (weak) turn play would have been completely ruined. By betting I can at least collect two big bets at the end.

Answer 8/7

A bad player is more likely to have a flush.

There are two reasons for this. First, bad players will nearly always attempt a check-raise in heads-up situations after they complete the flush against an opponent who has shown strength. A good player might also do this, but he sometimes comes out betting so as to avoid being too predictable.

Second, bad players tend to play more suited hands than good players. For a weak player, two suited cards are often all it takes to defend his blind, no matter the circumstances.

Part 2: Theory

Chapter 3

Analyzing the Results

The value of keeping records

It's said in the popular media—and among card players—that at least 90% of all poker players in public card rooms are losers. This doesn't mean that on average you find one winner and nine losers at a poker table. In low-limit games there are often tables with no winner at all because no one can beat the rake. In contrast, you often find four, five and even six winning players at the table in middle-limits. How can this be? The answer is easy.

The winners normally play a lot more than the losers. At the middle-limit games in Las Vegas you see the same faces all the time. These regulars, many of whom win or at least break even, play day in, day out, while the tourists, usually unwilling contributors to the game, come and go. In the course of a year, a regular plays against hundreds of players that come to Vegas to try their luck at the poker table.

If you polled the general public, I believe that about 3/4 of those questioned would claim they are above average as a car driver or as a lover. If you asked poker players if they were winners or losers, the result would be much the same—and equally incorrect. This is curious because it is a matter of fact rather than opinion.

Who are these losers? There is a small group of unhappy players who know that they are losers and admit it. Then there is another small group that know they lose but don't admit it. And finally, there is a large group that believe they are winners when in fact they are not. How can so many players who are objectively losers be so sure that they can beat the game?

There are two basic reasons, and they stem from the following: 1) our almost infinite capacity for self-delusion when the truth isn't comfortable; and 2) short-term luck and its effect on people who play only sporadically.

On the first issue, let's start with a numerical sequence:

189, -143, 611, -26, -263, 576, 213, -860,

449, 21, -30, 509, -1205, -734, 25, 401

These are the results of 16 consecutive $20-40 sessions that I played some years ago at the Mirage in Las Vegas. Did I win or lose? By just looking at the numbers you can't easily tell. Only when you add up the numbers will you see that I lost $300. The occasional player typically plays with money he takes from his wallet, and he doesn't record his results. Sometimes he wins, sometimes he loses. If he doesn't lose excessively, he doesn't know exactly how he is doing, but he assumes he is winning. That's human nature; he wants to win and so he subconsciously places more emphasis on his winning times.

The second reason is that the short-term luck factor is huge in poker, making it easy to deceive yourself. Look at the second session I played (see pp.52-72). I lost $832 in that session. Now look at hand 2/102. I was a big favorite at the turn to win that hand. Had the flush card not come on the river, I would have won an $800+ pot and broken even for the session. Even if you have a devastating losing session, there are usually two or three large pots whose outcomes have a huge effect on your results.

After a losing session a weak player may think, "I had a pocket pair five times and a gutshot seven times but never hit anything. How can I be that unlucky? Had I made two or three of those hands I would have made money." The last statement may be true, but the player wasn't particularly unlucky. Had he hit two or three of his draws, he would have been really lucky. With a pocket pair you flop a set once in about 8.5 attempts and the odds to hit a gutshot are 11-to-1. So nothing unusual really happened, but people often focus on failed attempts without considering the odds of any of the events occurring. That's one of the appeals of poker: If you win you attribute it to skill, if you lose you have been unlucky.

There are two ways to determine beyond doubt if you are a winning player: keeping a separate bankroll and keeping records.

Keeping a separate bankroll for your poker activities is simplest. You don't have to write anything down. Just put a sum of money away for the sole purpose of playing poker. If the bankroll grows then you are a winning player; if it shrinks, you're not. The drawback of this approach is that you only know if you are winning or losing, and how much it is. You don't know how much you make per hour or, if you play different limits, which is more profitable.

If you're really serious about poker, you can't get around keeping records. For any session you have played, you should write down:

- ♠ the date
- ♠ the location
- ♠ the game (e.g., hold'em, Omaha)
- ♠ the structure (limit, no limit, pot limit, spread limit)
- ♠ how long you played (rounded to quarter or half hours)
- ♠ how much you made or lost
- ♠ general comments about the game or play

Then you have all the information you need to answer nearly every question that can come up. A notepad is all you need. However, an electronic spreadsheet is preferable and simplifies the analysis.

Win rate

The win rate[57] is the most important figure in poker, at least if you are se-

---

[57] When I refer to win rate, I always mean on an hourly basis. This is the most common measure used in poker.

rious about the game. It tells you how much you win or lose on an hourly basis. The calculation is easy. You sum up your session results and divide it by the total number of hours.

$$WR = \frac{\sum_{i=1}^{n} R(i)}{\sum_{i=1}^{n} T(i)}$$

where:

WR = Win rate

R(i) = Result of the ith session

T(i) = Length of play of the ith session

n = Total number of sessions

This gives you your overall win rate. If you play at different levels and games, you should calculate separate win rates for every game and limit, so that you know how you are doing at each of them.

It takes a long time to see reliable results, as your win rate converges only slowly on the true rate. This is due to the substantial variance inherent in the game, as seen in the large variation in the 16 session results I posted above. None of these results may be close to the average, but as the number of sessions increases, the average of all the results to date will converge on the true average.

Let's look at the result from the week when I kept records. I played for 33 hours and won $3,916, therefore my win rate for that week is $118.67 per hour. This doesn't tell you much about my true win rate. Instead of winning four grand I could have easily lost $2,000 with a win rate of -$60.60.

Your win rate can vary greatly over short periods of time due to many factors such as number of good players, quality of your play and quality of cards. How many hours must you put in at the tables to reliably determine your win rate?

I created the following table to answer that question. The results in the table depend on your standard deviation (see the next section of this chapter, 'Figuring the Standard Deviation'), and this varies by player. The table below is based on my results.

Win Rate Precision					
	Hours Played				
Limit	250 h	500 h	1,000 h	2,000 h	5,000 h
$4-8	±$7.50	±$5.50	±$4.00	±$2.50	±$1.75
$8-16	±$15.00	±$11.50	±$8.00	±$5.50	±$3.50
$10-20	±$20.00	±$14.00	±$10.50	±$7.00	±$4.50
$15-30	±$25.50	±$18.50	±$14.00	±$10.50	±$7.00
$20-40	±$46.00	±$28.50	±$19.50	±$14.00	±$9.00
$30-60	±$50.00	±$41.00	±$29.00	±$22.50	±$14.00
$40-80	±$89.00	±$60.00	±$43.00	±$29.00	±$18.00

Win rate confidence: 90%

It shows you, with a confidence of 90%, how much your true rate can deviate from the calculated rate.

Example: A player in a $30-60 game calculates a win rate of $40/hour based on 250 hours of play. Using the table we determine that his true rate lies between -$10 and +$90 with 90% confidence of being correct[58]. This player has a pretty good calculated win rate so far, but he could actually be a loser. Given his win rate, a time span of 250 hours is simply too short to know for sure if this player is a winner. At 500 hours there is still a slight chance that he is not beating the game. After 5,000 hours—2.5 years of full-time play—the win rate is precise within $14 either way.

---

[58] $40 - $50 = -$10 (lower bound) and $40 + $50 = $90 (upper bound).

It's tempting to assume that the confidence range in the table is too large. Rest assured that this is not the case. A simple real-life example should make this clear.

Say a $30-60 pro nets $100,000 in a year (2,000 hours) for a win rate of $50/hour. Now, a typical large pot in a $30-60 game has about $2,000 in it. Over the course of a year our pro wins and loses some of these large pots. How would his rate change had he lost instead of won just three of these large pots? Playing 35 hands per hour over 2,000 hours a year, these three hands are just 0.004% of all hands played. But they can dramatically affect his win rate. Losing instead of winning those three hands changes the pro's earnings for the year from $100,000 to $94,000, and his win rate from $50 to $47.

After winning a $2,000+ pot in a $20-40 game at the Mirage, Roy Cooke wrote: "Since I don't play as much poker as I used to, that pot had a big effect on my hourly rate for the year. It contained about 60 big bets, or 60 hours of expectation for a top player. If you are running good or running bad, think of how you are doing in these key situations. Over time, your expectation will always come out correctly. But for any given period, a day ... week ... month ... year ... a card can make quite a difference."[59]

Your calculated win rate never precisely reflects your true rate. In poker everything is in a constant state of flux. Your play changes (hopefully for the better), your opponents change and game conditions change. Nevertheless, it's crucial that a serious player have a realistic idea of his win rate at any given game.

Let's take a look at some of the reasons why the win rate is so important.

♠ The win rate shows if you are a winning or losing player.

♠ The win rate is an objective measure of one's relative playing strength. If two players play under the same conditions, the one with the higher win rate is the better player, at least with regard to the game and the limit[60].

---

[59] Roy Cooke, *Real Poker II: The Play of Hands*, 2001, pp. 200f.
[60] Notice that I said under the same playing conditions. In fact a better player may have a lower win rate than a lesser player because he plays against tougher competition.

♠ The win rate is a reliable indicator of how your game develops. For instance, if your win rate decreases, your game may have deteriorated or the competition may have improved.

♠ Even as a winning player, you need an adequate bankroll to keep from going broke due to normal fluctuations; your win rate has a large impact on the bankroll you need[61]. The lower your win rate, the bigger bankroll you need, and vice versa.

♠ As a pro, you have to know your win rate, so you know what you can expect at the year's end. If you fantasize about turning pro, your win rate will indicate whether you have any shot at all to earn enough to cover your living expenses and even put some money away for a rainy day.

Figuring the standard deviation

Your calculated win rate will fluctuate with each successive session. Behind all this calculation hides a true win rate that represents your skill over a wide range of conditions. There is a way to estimate your true win rate by measuring the variability of your individual sessions. This is known as the standard deviation.

The standard deviation measures the difference between your individual results and your expected value (in statistics this is called the "mean", which in our case is the win rate).

Assume a player has recorded ten one-hour sessions with the following results:

---

[61] See the section on "Bankroll" in chapter 11 (p.308-311).

Session	Result	Squared difference from the mean
1	$93	$3,481
2	$157	$15,129
3	-$51	$7,056
4	$271	$56,169
5	-$151	$34,225
6	-$201	$55,225
7	$17	$289
8	$381	$120,409
9	-$260	$86,436
10	$84	$2,500
Mean	$34.00	
Variance		$38,091.9
Standard deviation		$195.17

The win rate (mean) over ten sessions is $34.00, but individual results vary from the mean. We want to measure the variation that we can expect in session results.

If we simply add up the differences from the mean we always get zero. Instead, we sum up the squared differences from the mean and divide the result by the number of sessions. This way we get $38,091.90, which is called the variance of the distribution. The square root of the variance is called the standard deviation (σ). Since the variance is always positive (it is the sum of squared numbers), there is always a real-number result for the standard deviation.

We can use some basic statistical concepts to make some estimates. A standard deviation is a unit of variability that we can calculate from all the data.

In the normal bell-shaped curve, 95% of all the data are within two standard deviations of the mean and 68% are within one standard deviation.

For example: There are one million sheep on the Isle of Skye, sheep of all sizes, ages and genders. We weigh all of them and find out that the average sheep weighs 100 pounds. The standard deviation is calculated to be 22 pounds. Now we know, according the rules of the normal distribution, that 95% of all sheep weigh between 56 and 144 pounds, and 68% weight between 78 and 122 pounds.

What does all this mean to an aspiring poker player?

Say you play $10-20 limit hold'em, your win rate is $21 and your standard deviation is $233 (reasonable values for a very good player). Then 68% of the time after one hour your result should be within one standard deviation, that is in the range from -$212 ($21 - $233) to $254 ($21 + $233).

The following table shows the confidence intervals corresponding to the first few multiples of the standard deviation.

Range	Confidence interval
σ	0.6826895
2σ	0.9544997
3σ	0.9973002
4σ	0.9999366
5σ	0.9999994

The standard deviation is the square root of the variance, and so it varies in proportion to the square root of the number of hours. In the example above, the standard deviation for two hours is not $233 × 2 = $466, but rather $233 × $\sqrt{2}$ = $330. In other words, 68% of the time after two hours the result should be in the range from -$309 ($21 - $330) to $351 ($21 + $330). For three standard deviations (confidence 99.7%) the results lie between -$969 ($21 - 3×$330) and $1,011 ($21 + 3×$330). This illustrates clearly what can happen at the poker table in a short period of time, even if you are a good player.

Unfortunately hardly anyone records results on an hourly basis. Most people who bother keeping records record the result for the whole session. Since session lengths vary, we must find a way to compute the standard deviation that takes this into account. The formula derived by Mark Weitzman gives a pretty good approximation:

$$\sigma^2 = \frac{1}{n}\sum_{i=1}^{n}\frac{R(i)^2}{T(i)} - \frac{WR^2}{n}\sum_{i=1}^{n}T(i)$$

where:

R(i) = Result of the ith session

T(i) = Length of play of the ith session

N = Total number of sessions

WR = Win rate

σ = Standard deviation

σ^2 = Variance

Compared to the win rate, the standard deviation converges rather quickly. It doesn't require too many samples to get reliable results. The standard deviation for the eight sessions I recorded is $643.33, not too far from the result for all the $30-60 sessions I ever played[62]. Of course, your standard deviation is not set in stone. It reflects your playing style and the game conditions, and both can change.

Ideally, you want a high win rate and a low standard deviation. A loose player normally has a higher standard deviation than a tight player, and it's a well-accepted idea that the key to successful poker is tight, not loose, play[63]. Here we have a situation where considerations of win rate and standard deviation lead us to tight play. But the two goals of high win rate and low standard deviation often conflict. This becomes obvious if we contrast passive and aggressive styles instead of loose and tight.

---

[62] It's about $100 too high. After 20 recorded sessions you should have a pretty good idea of your standard deviation.

[63] I'm talking about full-ring games. Short-handed games are a different story.

An aggressive player puts more money into the pot, thus his standard deviation is higher than that of a passive player. An aggressive player protects his hand better, wins pots by bluffing and semi-bluffing that a passive player wouldn't have won, and gets more free cards (his opponents are afraid their bets may get raised), and consequently enjoys a higher win rate (at least if he knows what he is doing). Hence, aggressive play, applied correctly, leads to a higher win rate, but the standard deviation also increases.

The size of the bankroll a winning player needs to last through the inevitable swings of bad results depends not only on the win rate, but also on the standard deviation. If you insist on playing in loose action games, you must expect your standard deviation to skyrocket. This is no problem if you have a big bankroll. However, if you play on a short bankroll you should avoid these games, as well as high-variance plays with small potential benefits. You give up some edge but keep your standard deviation low—a good tradeoff if you are short on money or don't like large swings.

Understanding your game

Win rate and standard deviation are just two, albeit very important, measures, but they are very broad views of results. You need more details to understand how your style meshes with playing situations and stakes. You can use a paper-based system to analyze your results, but this can be tedious. For instance, you play in two different card rooms and have recorded about 1,000 sessions. Now you want to know: in which card room am I doing better? You must manually sort through all the sessions to answer the question.

For several years I used a computer-based spreadsheet program to analyze my results, but that didn't give me the flexibility and versatility I wanted—and of course the interface was ugly. So, when I had defined the variable set I wanted to track, I created a more-intuitive, query-friendly program, now called Record Keeper, that was much better suited to handle a larger number of session results with ease, and to present the results in a clearly structured and easy-to-understand way. I wrote the program for my own use, but interest from other card-playing friends spurred me to make Record Keeper publicly available[64].

---

[64] You can download a copy at www.poker-soft.com.

The more serious a player is about playing poker, the more intensely s/he should study his/her results. I study my game not merely to satisfy my curiosity, but to find leaks in my play.

We've determined that a player's win rate can vary significantly due to various conditions. Analyzing your results helps you to determine the conditions that have the greatest effect on your win rate.

For example, a player classifies his session results according to session length. He earns 0.85 BB/h in short and medium sessions and 0.4 BB/h in long sessions. From this, he can infer that there may be a problem with stamina. He might work on building emotional stamina to concentrate for longer periods, or avoid playing long sessions.

Clearly, in this example of session length, it's easy to see the reason for the problem. But the causal factor is not always so easy to determine. Sometimes one sees surprising results and it is far from obvious what caused them.

Here is an illustration from my own personal experience. When I first looked at my results for each day of the week, I noticed that my win rate was higher from Monday to Thursday than on weekends. This was somewhat strange because most experienced players, including myself, believed that the games in Vegas are usually more profitable on weekends than during the week. For a while I thought that observation was just a statistical fluctuation that would change over time. But it didn't; I did better on the weekdays against nominally stronger regulars. The difference was not large, but it was noticeable.

I began to think that maybe the profitability of the games on weekends was overrated. Certainly, there are more tourists and drop-ins, but the pros and good regulars know this, so they show up in greater numbers than during the week to take advantage of the good playing conditions. Perhaps, I figured, the greater number of pros and good regulars compensates for the additional numbers of tourists, with the net effect that the games on weekends are not really better.

This seemed plausible but it contradicted what most players thought. I decided to find out if my results were normal or not. I asked several pros if their win rates were indeed higher on weekends than during the week. Unfortunately, most of these players don't analyze their results on a day-by-day basis. Though they actually couldn't prove it, they all said emphatically that they earned more on weekends.

Eventually I spoke to Andrew, a pro who analyzes his results meticulously using my program. His records showed that the weekend games were more profitable for him. Then he added, "Looks like your style of play is more suited to tight and moderately loose games than to the loose and very loose games which are so prevalent on weekends." The same analytical thinking that made him a good pro allowed him to infer a possible cause for my lower win rate.

The points of this example are three-fold: First, only accurate and fairly detailed record-keeping provided enough information to find a leak. More casual records would have glossed over a small but significant difference—and cost me money. Second, until I had information gathered over a long-enough period, I couldn't be certain that what I was seeing was not just a statistical aberration. Third, don't be stubborn. Even if you are a winning player, there is always room for improvement.

Those points reflect some overall concepts:

- ♠ If you are serious and want to win, keep records.
- ♠ Play long and hard enough to be certain that your records have some validity.
- ♠ Use the records to correct your game by thinking analytically about the results and your play.
- ♠ Be willing to alter your play to achieve your ends.

Chapter 4

How to Improve Your Game

Poker is not a simple closed-end game like tic-tac-toe, that one can play perfectly after a while. Playing poker is a continuous learning process. There is always something new to learn. If you don't improve, your opponents will, and you will be left behind. There are a few ways you can improve your game.

Reading about poker

The first, most obvious and least expensive way to improve your game is to study what's available in print about poker. If you are relatively new to poker and don't know much, virtually any poker book will help you, even if it happens to be mediocre or bad, because it's always better to have some idea what you are doing than to be completely clueless. Sure, if you are alert and willing to learn you can improve your game without reading a book, but why sit at a poker table losing money when you can accumulate the basics from a book more quickly and less expensively?

It is certainly preferable to start with a good book because it's always easier to learn something correctly from the beginning than to change bad habits later. Don't make the mistake of assuming that reading a poker book once will do the trick. You just can't absorb all the information a good book provides by reading it once. The better the poker book, the more often you should read it.

The best poker book ever written, in my opinion, is David Sklansky's *The Theory of Poker*. Mason Malmuth, another poker expert, once remarked about it, "I reread my copy every three or four months and always find it helpful to my game."[65] I totally agree. The book is so filled with strategies and useful concepts that one takes a long time to fully understand all the aspects of play that Sklansky discusses. When I started playing poker, I always read one chapter just before I went to play and tried to incorporate what I had read into my game. Even today, every time I fly to Vegas to play poker, I take a copy of *The Theory of Poker* with me and read it on the plane from start to finish.

No matter how good or bad a player you are, studying poker literature is always useful, even if it is only for the simple reason that it forces you to think about the game. Personally, I find good and very bad books the most beneficial and interesting. Mediocre books generally are a rehash of stuff I've read many times before, and I get bored pretty quickly. A good book may teach you something new or present familiar facts in a new and interesting way, giving you new insight into a familiar subject.

I greatly prefer bad poker books to mediocre ones—the worse, the better. Bad books contain many erroneous concepts and statements that compel you to puzzle out which are wrong and why. If you know, or suspect, you are reading a bad book, you should exert some effort to think through the "truths" as presented, and learn for yourself which is correct.

Let's look at an example of bad reasoning that you should be able to figure out. One author wrote: you have "9-6s or similar. Flop comes 7-8-2 with 7, 8 in your suit. You now have 23 outs of 47 to make anything."[66] Then he goes on to explain that you have six outs to pair one of your hole cards, you have eight outs for the straight and nine for the flush, which sums up to 23 outs. The significant flaw here is that the author doesn't realize that, although you have eight outs for the straight and nine for the flush, some of those outs are the same card and he's counting them twice. A straight and a flush draw account for 15 outs, not 17. That reduces the total number of outs to 21.

---

[65] Mason Malmuth, *Gambling Theory and Other Topics*, 1990, p. 250

[66] Bob Turgeon, *Playing Low-limit Hold'em. The 20 – 4 – 50 Way*, 1999, p. 28.

Furthermore, it's highly dubious that a six on the turn really helps you. A nine, giving you top pair, may be better, though it's still questionable that it makes you the best hand. Since the flush draw is not for the nuts, and the nine on the turn may be worth something, I would estimate that you have about 15 outs, and definitely not 23.

Admittedly, this flaw was easy to spot. Being able to count outs is a key skill. However, flaws in thinking are not always so easy to recognize.

Here is an example from another poker book. The author talks about general game conditions and how to adapt your game, and then states, "before the flop the looser your opponents play, the looser you should play, and the tighter they play, the tighter you should play."[67] Here the flaw in reasoning is harder to spot because the first part of the sentence is clearly correct (if the rest of the table is playing loose, you should loosen up your game to take advantage of their slipped standards) and the second part seems just to be the converse. However, it is easily demonstrated that the second part of the sentence cannot be correct in its general form.

Take the extreme case that your opponents only play with pocket aces. According to the author you should now play even tighter, which means that you should play aces every second time you're dealt them or so, an absurd deduction. Obviously, if your opponents play too tight then you should play more hands because it's likely that you can win the pot uncontested.

Of course, your prime goal in studying poker literature is not to find errors, but to improve your knowledge and your game. When you are new to the game and begin reading a poker book, you have no choice but to trust the author. The more you study, the more insight you gain and the more critical you should become.

Don't take anything for granted just because it is in print. Read poker books with an open but critical mind. Always try to determine if the claims an author makes are correct or not, and why this is so. This is the key to getting the maximum benefit from a book; don't just passively consume the content, but get actively involved. Take a book as a stimulus for your own reflections. This way your understanding of the game will deepen and you will see connections you haven't noticed before.

---

[67] Matt Maroon, *Winning Texas Hold'em. Cash Game Poker Strategies for Players of All Skill Levels*, 2005, p. 120

Thinking about the game

When it's your turn to act at the table, you only have a short time to decide what to do. Often the proper play is obvious, but sometimes the decision is tough, and even after you've acted, you may be unsure if your move was sound. Hands like this are optimal candidates to record for later analysis. Don't try to analyze the hand at the table; your judgment might be clouded by emotions, and you won't be able to focus on the game in progress. Doing the analysis later gives you the time and emotional distance to see your play with unbiased eyes.

Here is an example from a $30-60 game at the Bellagio. It was folded to Don, an excellent pro, who raised from the button. In the small blind I held Q♣-J♦. Sandwiched between an expert on the button and a loose aggressive Asian player in the big blind, it wasn't obvious what to do, but I decided to call. The loose player in the big blind called behind as expected. Three players, pot $180.

Flop: K♦-J♠-10♦. Being first to act after the flop I bet my second pair and open-ended straight draw. The big blind and Don called. Three players, pot $270.

Turn: 9♦. The nine gave me a straight. However, it made a flush possible as well. I bet, the big blind raised and Don folded. I called. Two players, pot $510.

River: A♦ (board: K♦-J♠-10♦-9♦-A♦). I now had the second nuts but my hand didn't play by itself. All I knew was that my river bet would be correct if I had the best hand two times out of three. I figured I'm probably better than a 2-to-1 favorite, and I bet my hand. The big blind raised, I called and he showed me Q♦-4♣ for the nut flush. Being unsure if I had played the hand correctly, I did what I always do in such a situation: I recorded that hand using my hand chart (see. p.153) and reviewed the hand later at home. Let's do that now.

What do we know about Don's hand? Remember, he is an excellent player. He knows that the big blind is extremely loose, therefore he is not trying to steal the blinds with air. He doesn't necessarily have a premium hand, but he is definitely not playing trash like 7-4s. So we conclude that he has a medium to very strong hand.

Now, what should I do in the small blind with Q♣-J♦? The small blind usually either raises or folds to a late-position raiser Normally I would raise, bet out no matter what comes on the flop and hope that Don has missed completely. But here the presence of the big blind poses a problem. He is so loose that if he would call a bet, he would call two bets as well. So, I must decide if I'm willing to play Q-J for two or three bets against two players along with being out of position for the rest of the hand. Suddenly raising no longer looks that good. It's a close call between folding, calling and raising. I like calling here best, followed by folding and lastly raising, but it's close to a coin flip.

I called and the big blind called behind, as expected. The flop was very favorable for me, giving me second pair and an open-ended straight draw. I had the choice of betting out and checking with the intention to check-raise. For three reasons, betting out is my preferred play. First, I don't want to give a free card. Second, I may have the best hand. And third, I'm not afraid of a raise. Trying for a check-raise is not a bad play either, though it has the drawback that both players may check behind and it makes it less likely that I can make Don fold[68].

Both players called my flop bet. Neither raised, causing me to believe I had the best hand at the moment (an assumption that proved to be wrong). The turn card made things interesting. Not only did it complete my straight draw, but with three diamonds on the board a flush was possible. Though I didn't have the nut straight, the only real threat was a flush. It was unlikely that Don had a flush because he would probably have raised on the flop with his draw.

At this point, I had no idea what the big blind had. In this situation I simply have to assume that I have the best hand and bet out because if none of my opponents holds a queen, they will probably check, and a queen on the end would counterfeit my hand.

The big blind responded to my bet by raising, and Don folded quickly. The big blind couldn't have a better straight than me (this player would have three-bet an A-Q before the flop), so he either had the same hand or a flush. The jack of diamonds in my hand gave me some hope that I might have a redraw. There was a slight chance that I was drawing dead (against

---

[68] Don is more likely to fold if I bet and the big blind calls than if I check and the big blind bets. The reason is that a loose aggressive player like the big blind often interprets a check as an invitation to bluff or to bet a weak hand, and of course Don knows this.

A♦-x♦ or Q♦-x♦), but my call on the turn was clearly correct in my eyes.

The A♦ on the river put four diamonds on the board and gave me the second nuts. I had to be a 2-to-1 favorite to justify betting. This is because the big blind would raise if he had me beat, but would not lay down a smaller flush or a straight if I bet, so I would lose two bets if I was behind and win one bet if my hand was best. In the heat of battle I couldn't go through all the combinations my opponent could hold, but I estimated I was a little better than 2-to-1 since there were three queens left, one of them the queen of diamonds, and if he had a flush on the turn, there were a lot of combinations that didn't contain the queen of diamonds.

If the big blind had a queen there were 27 combinations that gave him the nuts and 54 combinations that lost to my hand[69]. If we further assume that he called before the flop with any two diamonds (a realistic assumption since he called with any queen) that adds another 21 combinations that gave him the second-best hand. All in all there were 75 combinations I could beat and 27 where my opponent had the best of it, meaning I was a 3.6-to-1 favorite and my bet at the end was sound. In fact I was a bigger favorite than I had thought.

If you perform a hand analysis like this, don't focus just on your own hand; study your opponents' play as well. Notice that the big blind made an extremely bad call before the flop with Q♦-4♣, but then played the hand flawlessly. More interesting is how Don played his hand. He later told me that he had K-10. Such a holding is definitely strong enough to raise the blinds, even if one of them is so loose that he will nearly always call.

What is remarkable is how Don played the flop. He had top and bottom pair. Why did he just call my bet? Was he afraid his hand was no good? Don had to know he almost certainly had the best hand. Look at the hands that would beat him: A-Q, K-K, J-J and 10-10. With any of these hands both I and the big blind would have made it three bets pre-flop. What about K-J and Q-9? Don knew I wouldn't call him with Q-9, and the big blind would have raised with the made straight on the flop. The only hand Don had to worry about was K-J. But only I could have it since I would bet the flop with it, but the big blind would not just call with top two pair.

---

[69] I have excluded A-Q, K-Q and Don's hand. With A-Q the big blind would have raised pre-flop, with K-Q he would have raised on the flop, and Don's hand is unknown so far.

Now you can see that Don played the hand superbly. He knew it was very likely that at least one of his opponents had a straight- or flush-draw. By just calling on the flop, he wanted to take a cheap look at the turn; he intended to raise if no straight or flush card showed up. Playing that way has two advantages: by delaying the raise he gets more money into the pot when he is a big favorite, which decreases his risk since he has only to survive one more card, and he can save money when things go wrong for him on the turn. The latter is exactly what happened, and Don lost the absolute minimum. For a player of Don's caliber, the fold on the turn was a no-brainer. He was a 10.5-to-1 underdog to fill up, and the pot odds were only 7.5-to-1.

Usually, when you do a hand analysis you want to know if you played correctly. Sometimes, however, even if you have all the information about a hand, it is difficult to reach a definitive conclusion. Here is an example.

This hand was played many years ago in the $20-40 game at the Mirage, at a time when I was pretty new to that limit. I had just sat down and in the second round it was folded to me in the cutoff seat. I raised with 9♠-9♣.

The button and the small blind folded. The big blind, a young player I had never seen before, reraised and I called.

Flop: J♥-5♣-2♥. The big blind bet, I raised, he reraised and I called.

Turn: 9♥. The big blind apparently wasn't worried by the third heart on board and bet out. I raised with my set of nines, he reraised and I called.

River: 5♠ (board: J♥-5♣-2♥-9♥-5♠). Again, the big blind bet out, I raised, he made it three bets and I called. Pause for a moment and try to figure out what my opponent had[70].

This was one of the most interesting hands I have ever played. Not only did I manage to lose $360 in a $20-40 heads-up confrontation, but I raised on every street and was reraised every time. For years I have thought about that hand but haven't formed a final opinion. I tend to think that I played the hand correctly, but I leave it to the reader to reach his own conclusion[71].

---

[70] He had J-J.

[71] Hint: the crucial point is my call on the flop after I was reraised; all my other actions are impeccable in my opinion.

Analyzing a hand at home is much more detailed and time-consuming than what you can do at the table—that's why you are doing it at home. I often go through all combinations my opponent could have, try to determine the optimal play against every possible combination, run hot-and-cold computer calculations against my opponent's probable holdings and contemplate the results. You can't do anything like that at the table, but that doesn't mean that after-game analysis is worthless.

First, a thorough analysis helps you to understand the situation better and makes you aware of the key elements you should consider. Second, you learn about your opponent's motivation and method of play. Third, if your analysis shows that you played the hand correctly, you gain confidence in your game, and if you see that you misplayed the hand, you now know your mistake and you can correct it in the future. Finally, no two situations are completely alike, but similar situations arise and when they do, you will have a better idea of how to play.

Take the time to study hands away from the table. I do this frequently, and have always found that is time well spent. There is no doubt in my mind that my game benefits from it.

Learning from others

Reading and thinking about poker while you are away from the table are extremely helpful, but you limit yourself to only your own resources.

The good news is that all it takes to beat low-limit games is to read a good book and stick to its advice. If you are disciplined enough to do that, success will come.

But even the best book can't answer all your questions, and if you perform your own hand analysis, you can make mistakes or overlook key factors. You can gain a lot from exchanging thoughts with a competent and knowledgeable player.

If you play low-limit, many players at the table are typically more than happy to give you advice and offer their opinions on a variety of topics. But what is that worth? Truthfully, if you have read even a single poker book, you already know more than most players at the table. That doesn't mean that there are no good and knowledgeable players in low-limit games but, speaking from my own experience, most players at these games have little clue what they are doing.

This changes dramatically as you step up to mid-limit games. These games are much tougher and, unlike low-limit games, the presence of pros at the table is not the exception but the norm.

But don't expect a pro to discuss poker seriously with you. To a pro, you are just a customer. If he wises you up by discussing poker hands with you, he is costing himself money, and that's bad business. Of course, most pros are willing to discuss poker, but only if you are at or close to their level, so that the information exchange is mutual. Before you can seriously discuss poker with a pro, you have to gain his respect.

Don't make the mistake of bragging about your poker skills, hoping to impress the pro. You can't fool a pro. If he has seen you play, he knows how good you are, and if hasn't, then he won't take you seriously anyway.

Many, if not most, pros don't like to discuss poker at the table. If you intend to talk to a pro, it's best to approach him when he's not in a game. One day I was playing in a $30-60 game at the Bellagio with Roy Cooke on my left. Roy's policy is never to discuss hands at the table. There was a raise, followed by a call and a reraise before the action came to me. I looked at my hand in the big blind. Just for the fun of it, I showed my hand, K♠-J♠ if I remember correctly, to Roy, who had already folded. "Roy, what should I do?" As expected he started stumbling, saying, "Oh … well … I don't know."

I agree with Roy's policy to keep your mouth shut in such situations. If you start discussing hands at the table, you are no longer focused on the game, and other people might hear what you say.

There is an old poker axiom, "Don't tap on the glass." The unspoken second sentence is, "You'll scare the fish." If, because of your need to talk, a weak player realizes that there is more to poker than he had thought and thinks, "Boy, these guys know a lot more about poker than I do. I'd better switch to a lower limit where the players are not as sophisticated," or if it causes a weak player to play tighter because he doesn't want to be regarded as a fish, then you have done yourself and all the other players at the table a disservice.

If you are really lucky, you'll find an excellent player who likes you and takes you under his wing. Twice I was fortunate enough to meet such a player who was way ahead of me in playing skills, yet was willing to share knowledge with me. I would sit behind them at the table and I could see every hand they played. Afterwards they would answer all my questions about why they had played a certain hand in a certain way. We would analyze my play on hands I had recorded and, from them, I learned which part of my game needed the most attention.

Even if you don't have a mentor, just watching a pro can be helpful. Most people look at a pro simply as someone who plays few hands, doesn't give much action when he doesn't have the best of it, and is difficult to play against. All this is true.

A pro usually costs you money when you play against him just because he is better than you. But that's not just money lost. Watching a pro can improve your game. A good pro knows every type of "regular" player inside and out. His play can give you lessons on what to do against a certain player, what to look for and how to exploit players' weaknesses.

Study what a pro is doing. When he shows down a hand, replay that hand in your head. Try to understand the play and think about how you would have played it differently. Record or memorize that hand and analyze it later. Chances are that he is right and you are wrong. Your task is to determine why he made that play, and to identify the factors that led you to a different conclusion. If you do that for a while, you will start thinking and playing like a pro. You may never reach a pro's level of perfection, but your game (and your win rate) will increase significantly.

Practice

Many years ago I was playing in a $6-12 game at the Mirage. I was dragging in a nice pot when an elderly, grey-haired gentleman to my right said, "We could all take lessons from this kid." A very flattering remark indeed but it didn't go unnoticed. Another older player at the table said, in an irritated tone: "What are you talking about? I have forgotten more about poker than this kid will ever learn in his whole life!"

Both of them were right. Though I was pretty new to the game, there was no doubt (at least in my mind) that I was the best player at the table. The second gentleman was right to point out that I wasn't yet much of a player, that I still had to learn a lot. I could beat the $6-12 game, but the $10-20 game was still way over my head, and it took me a while to make the transition to middle-limit games.

Ironically, the player who bragged about his experience was actually a very bad player. He called raises with all sorts of junk hands, bluffed too much and called without regard to pot odds. Later he informed the whole table that he had been playing poker for fifty years and nobody could teach him anything more about the game.

There is a common fallacy among certain, usually weaker players that the more hands you have played the better you will become. The lesson is that experience without reflection only improves your game minimally. It doesn't take much experience to recognize that A-A is the best starting hand, that Q-Js is a better hand than Q-J and that you can call more liberally if there is more money in the pot.

Look around at your local card room. Who has seen the most hands in his life? Very likely it's not a player—it's a dealer!

A dealer usually works eight hours a day, five days a week and, if the card room is busy, he may work overtime. If he is employed in one of the major card rooms he deals in low- and high-limit games, in pot-limit, no-limit and limit games, in cash and tournament games, he knows even rarely-played game variations such as triple draw, razz and badugi. He deals to drunks, maniacs, idiots, pros, local champions and, maybe, to the best players in the world on a regular basis.

When it comes to experience, who could be better suited than a dealer to be a successful player? However, the reality is different. Many try, but only a very few succeed. More common is the player who tried to make a living at poker and ended up a dealer.

There are two problems with basing your playing decisions only on experience. First, the brain is not really suited to make good probabilistic decisions. If the two outcomes of an event are very close in likelihood, your memory is not much help. For example, assume a call at the end has a 47% chance to succeed and a 53% chance to fail. Even if you have been in a similar situation many times, relying on your experience is not better than using a coin flip to reach a conclusion. If you don't believe that, tell a friend to generate a random 0/1 sequence about 1,000 digits long containing 47% of one number and 53% of the other. You can look at the numerical sequence for hours without being sure if it contains more 0s or 1s. The only way to find out is to actually count the numbers.

Second, your memory is often unreliable because the data saved is not unbiased. For instance, should you call a raise pre-flop with A-J? If you think you should, every time your play works you get a positive reinforcement, which has a stronger impact on your memory than the times it fails. Therefore you will continue calling with A-J, convinced that the play is sound. This will happen as long as the likelihoods of the two outcomes are not too far apart.

This doesn't mean that experience is worthless. Quite the contrary. Experience is a remarkable reinforcement to knowledge. You can read poker books until the cows come home, but only experience tells you how to put what you have read into practice. A good book conveys many valuable concepts and strategies, but learning them is just the first step. It is crucial to recognize opportunities to apply your book knowledge, and only experience can tell you that.

A book cannot cover all possible playing situations. Take hand 3/35 where I bluff-raised Pizza Mike. No book can tell you what to do. The situation was unique, it has probably never happened before and will probably never happen again. Experience at playing in general and playing against Pizza Mike specifically enabled me to recognize the situation. I knew how he played, how he thought and how he would very likely respond to my action, and knew that my strategy would likely work in that situation.

Experience is helpful not just against players you know, but against strangers as well. No two people play exactly alike, but most players fit into one category or another. Hence, after even a short time observing a complete stranger, an experienced player can often anticipate with a high degree of certainty how the player will react in a certain situation.

Neither knowledge nor experience is everything, but knowledge is nothing without experience, especially in higher-limit games. In low-limit games your book knowledge may overcome your opponents' experience, but at the higher limits the knowledge gap between players narrows, and experience becomes paramount.

Chapter 5

Playing Tight

Playing tight means being selective about the hands one plays. It is an accepted fact that the key to becoming a successful limit hold'em player is to be tight and aggressive (see the next chapter). However, playing tight on an expert level doesn't mean that you just play a fixed set of starting hands. Let's look at this in more detail.

Things to consider

Most struggling players can easily improve their win rate by just playing fewer hands. The most frequent and serious mistake these players make is simply playing too loosely. There are many supposedly good starting hands that are, in certain situations, simply not profitable, even for the best players in the world, and if an expert can't win with a hand, it belongs in the muck.

Most people do not understand what it means to play tight. Some believe that all you have to do is to play only quality hands, which to them usually means any two cards ten or higher. I have seen many of these players, and they can never win beyond low limits. They don't realize that a hand like K-Q may be strong in some situations but weak in others. It will do you no good in the long run to stubbornly insist on playing K-Q because it is a quality hand, totally ignoring the situation.

Some believe that it will do the trick to religiously follow one of the many starting-hand charts found in beginners' hold'em books. The authors of these books usually understand that position matters a great deal in poker, so they distinguish between early, middle and late position, telling you what hands to play in each case. There is no doubt that these charts can be extremely helpful to new players, but you must understand that these are just general guidelines, and that to become successful at higher-limit games you must often deviate from the chart.

Here is a true story to illustrate my point. It happened several years ago at the Mirage. A new player, Pizza Mike (we've already met him in hand 2/66), had arrived at the $20-40 game. He had thought about what to do for a living and decided that playing poker would be an easy way to make some bucks. He had obviously read at least one book, from which he had taken away two things: First rule, he thought, was that you had to play middle-limit to make enough money as a pro. That's why he jumped right into the $20-40 game. Second rule: if you know how to play before the flop, that's enough for most games. He had printed and laminated a starting hand chart that he had found on the internet. At the table he tried to conceal the chart under a pack of cigarettes; it was his secret weapon.

One day the following happened: A tough pro had raised under the gun and our hero on the button was the only caller. The flop came ten-high. The pro bet and Pizza Mike called. The same thing happened when blanks fell on the turn and river. The pro turned over K-K for a pair of kings and our hero produced 10-8 for a pair of tens. It was clear to me what had happened. I was sitting next to Pizza Mike and I grabbed the laminated chart; sure enough, the chart read, "call with 10-8 in late position".

Playing 10-8 on the button might be okay under certain conditions, which obviously wasn't the case here. Playing heads-up with the worst hand against an experienced pro is a sure way to lose money.

Playing more or less correctly before the flop is not too difficult, but it's not so easy that you can just follow a simple starting-hand chart. Poker is a dynamic game. The strength of your hand changes constantly depending on the other players' actions. It obviously makes a big difference whether an early-position raiser is tough or loose-aggressive.

Players often pay little attention to the game. They may talk to a friend and, when they are told it's their turn, they look at their hand and act immediately, not paying attention to the circumstances. By playing like that, you are prone to make mistakes, because you are treating hold'em like a static game and following the starting-hand chart in your head[72].

Your pre-flop decision should be based not just on the strength of your hand, but on what's going on at the table. Even in the same position with the same hand, the proper play can vary depending on the specific playing conditions. Let's say you are dealt J-10s, a good but not great hand, in late position. What should you do? There is no right or wrong answer as long as the whole picture isn't known.

If there is an early-position raise from a good player, J-10s belongs in the muck; it's not strong enough to call a raise cold or reraise. But, if there are four callers in front of you, you definitely have a call[73]. With the same hand, if everyone folds to you or there is just one middle- or late-position limper, then your best option is to raise.

As you can see from this simple example, though the starting hand and the position is always the same, every action—to fold, call or raise—is possible, and no starting-hand chart can cover all situations. As useful as they may be for a beginner, if you want to successfully attack middle limit games, you must free yourself from these charts and understand the intrinsic value of a hand in a specific situation.

I have already stressed the importance of position, and if you have ever read a poker book, you know that position is paramount. Therefore, you should understand how you will do financially from various positions. This will help you to understand why you must adjust your play according to position. The following graph shows how position affects the win rate of a very good player in a ring game.

---

[72] Admittedly, there are a few hands where the play is automatic, no matter what the circumstances. E.g., if you hold 7-2 and are not in the blinds a fold can't be wrong, or if you pick up A-A a raise can't be faulted.

[73] Raising is certainly an option here to exploit your positional advantage. I tend to call because I don't want to shut out the blinds. J-10s plays well in multiway pots, so I welcome additional players. I sometimes raise to mix it up.

Position and Win Rate

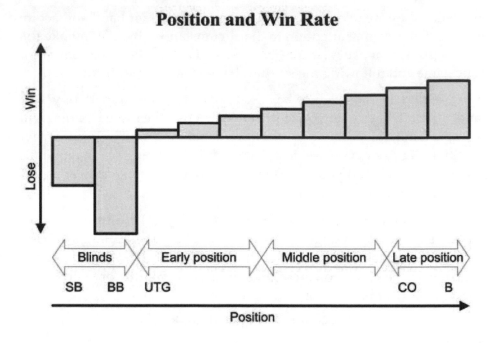

Notice first that the y-axis contains no numbers. The actual numbers depend on the limit, how tough the opponents are and how well you play. What really matters is how results vary by position. Several essential conclusions can be drawn from this graph.

♠ You must accept that you will lose money in the blinds. The better you play, the less you lose, but even the best players lose money from the blind positions. The double handicaps of being forced to put money in the pot with two random cards and play out of position for the rest of the hand are simply insurmountable.

♠ The blind structure is the prime determinant of the amount you lose in the small blind. The smaller the small blind is relative to the big blind, the less you will lose, at least if you are a skilled player[74].

---

[74] This statement may not hold for weak players. In my experience, weak players play the small blind not much differently if it is half or 2/3 of the big blind—they simply play too

- ♠ According to the graph, the loss in the blinds is less than the sum of the small and the big blind. This is easy to understand. You can limit your loss to the sum of the small and big blinds by never playing in the blinds. You can cut your losses ever further by only playing aces and kings from the blinds, since both hands are long-term winners even from the blind positions[75].

- ♠ You should show a profit from all other positions. One poker author once wrote: "Throughout their poker careers most players, even the most successful pros, lose money on *any* hands they enter the pot with from the first three positions."[76] I hope that you realize immediately that this is pure nonsense. I can refute this assertion with the same argument I used in relation to the the blinds. By never playing a hand from early position, you can't lose anything, and you will certainly profit by simply exempting pocket aces from the always-fold-strategy.

- ♠ A position's profitability increases with proximity to the button. The closer your position is to the button, the better.

- ♠ Here is a concept that seems counterintuitive. The closer you are to first position, the higher the win rate of the hands you do play—if you are playing correctly. How can this be and, if true, shouldn't you earn more money from early position? The explanation is actually quite straightforward. From early position you can only play a few hands, mostly high pairs, profitably, and big hands win big pots. Of course, hands that are profitable from early position are even more profitable from later positions. This ex-

---

many hands. However, the higher the small blind is in relation to the big blind, the looser you should play, which means weak players by pure chance play correctly more often in this case. Thus, it could be that weak players lose, at least relatively, less in a 2:3 than in a 1:2 structured limit hold'em game.

[75] This doesn't mean of course that you should only play aces and kings in the blinds. It only serves the purpose to demonstrate that every player can do better than losing the full amount of the small and big blind.

[76] T. J. Cloutier/Tom McEvoy, *Championship Hold'em. Limit Hold'em Cash Game Strategies*, Las Vegas 2000, p. 85 (emphasis by the author).

plains why you win more money from the later positions, but not why your win rate per hand played upfront is higher. Here, another factor comes into play.

♠ The later your position, the more hands you can play profitably. Many hands that are big losers in early positions can be played profitably in later positions. For example, K-9s is a weak hand that is rarely correct to play from early position, but can be profitable in a multiway pot or as a blind-stealing hand. Even if the situation is right, it will only show a modest long-term profit, and if you never play K-9s, you won't hurt your win rate much. But many such hands are playable in later positions, showing small profits. Thus, the win rate for the later positions increases substantially while the win rate per hand goes down.

♠ The graph clearly shows what it takes to be a winning player. The cumulative total from first to last position has to exceed the losses in the blinds plus any time fee or rake the house charges you. Your goal is to minimize the losses from the blind positions and to maximize the winnings from the non-blind positions. Unfortunately, this is easier said than done.

It is said that in a full-ring game the best limit hold'em players play about 15% of the hands dealt, sometimes a little more, sometimes a little less, depending on the game conditions, the playing style and the player's skill. This does not mean that you can just run a hot-and-cold computer simulation of starting hands and play the top 15%, thinking that your pre-flop play is on a par with the best players. By doing that you play too many hands from early position and far too few from late position.

Though I advocate tight play, I hope it has become clear that tight play isn't the same as just waiting for A-A, K-K and A-K before putting any money into the pot. Nothing could be further from the truth. Yes, in early position you have to be very selective about the hands you play, but in later positions you can (and should) loosen up a lot. Otherwise you are just leaving money on the table.

Tight play has a bad image. For many players, the very words conjure up the image of an unimaginative rock who waits patiently for big hands. Many players don't regard themselves as tight, and don't like to be termed as such. Try viewing it from another perspective: you only play hands that have long-term profitability in a given situation. Actually, that is the same as (correct) tight play, but doesn't it sound a lot better?

Tristan's three golden pre-flop rules

Playing before the flop in hold'em is a lot easier than afterwards, because the number of possible playing situations is a lot less and the correct play is, at least for the good player, generally obvious. The following three rules do not treat every possible situation, but they are simple and basic rules that should form a solid foundation for your pre-flop decisions and keep you out of trouble.

> Rule #1: Every starting hand except pocket aces is potentially a folding hand. You should have a well-founded reason for continuing to play, taking into account not just the strength of your own hand, but the situation as a whole.

You will probably say, "This guy is nuts, K-K a folding hand?"

Imagine you have found a very predictable player who only raises pre-flop with A-A. If this player raises and you sit behind with K-K, the proper play is simply to muck the hand. Granted, I have never seen a player so timid and predictable that he only raised with aces (though I have seen players that never raised pre-flop), and I don't want you to routinely fold K-K. But realize that the strength of your hand is not absolute, but relative to the holdings of your opponents. Even a seemingly very strong hand becomes unplayable against an even better hand.

Let's look at a more realistic example. A player in front of you raises. You have watched him for a while and only seen him raise with A-A, K-K and A-K. You hold Q-Q. Pocket queens are usually strong enough to make it three bets. You correctly figure that there are 28 combinations the raiser can hold. Twelve times you are behind (against A-A and K-K) and 16 times you are ahead (against A-K). Since you have the better hand more often than not, you should raise. Right? Wrong! Twelve times you are in pretty bad shape (about a 4-to-1 dog) and 16 times you are only a little better than even money[77]. Hence, playing the queens can't be profitable.

You may say that having the best hand pre-flop is just the first act of this play, that there are still five cards to come that can change the value of the hands drastically, that the queens have position and that outplaying your opponent gives you another way to win without the best hand. This is true, but the fact remains that a better starting hand tends to make the better hand at the end. If it's heads-up, your opponent holds Q-Q and you have J-J, neither the cards to come nor position help you enough to make the situation profitable.

In a nutshell, pre-flop strategy is easy; you want either the best starting hand or the right odds to draw. This statement leads us to the second part of the first rule; if you don't have aces, you need a well-founded reason to play. Frankly, I have never found a player who couldn't explain why he played a hand. Ask a player who has played Q-10 and he will likely say something like this: "Queen-ten is a strong hand. I can make a big pair or a straight." With 5-3s, that player will say: "This is a nice deceptive hand with flush and straight potential."

If you listen to table talk, you have heard justifications like that many times. These explanations express a lack of understanding because they only refer to the holding, absent the context in which the play was made. This is fundamentally different from the the play of a good and experienced player. He always thinks: "Can it be profitable to play my hand under these circumstances?" If the answer is "no", he folds his hand. If the answer is "yes", he thinks about calling or raising.

Hand strength is only one factor (though an important one) that a good player considers. He might fold a seemingly strong hand when he would have played a much weaker hand in a different situation. For instance, K♥-J♥ is certainly a much better hand than 6♥-5♥. But a good player would quickly fold K♥-J♥ from the button if an excellent player had raised from early position with no callers, whereas he would gladly call from the button with 6♥-5♥ with five limpers in front.

---

[77] Pocket queens are a 4.42-to-1 underdog against A-A, a 4.51-to-1 dog versus K-K, a 1.17-to-1 favorite against A-Ks, a 1.31-to-1 favorite against A-K. All in all, Q-Q is a 1.51-to-1 dog.

Though K♥-J♥ wins more often than 6♥-5♥, pot odds of probably 1.75-to-1 (if the blinds don't play) are not enough to call against a lone early-position raiser. With 6♥-5♥ and five limpers, the pot odds are probably 7-to-1 (if the small blind calls). You will not win often eight-handed with 6♥-5♥, but when you do, you are rewarded with a big pot, which makes the pre-flop call profitable.

To sum up: You need a well-founded reason to play a hand if you don't have aces. A well-founded reason can never just be the two cards you have in your hand. Statements such as, "King-ten is a strong hand," "It's my favorite hand," "I have never folded two big cards," or "I always do well with that hand," are not sufficient reason (at least if you are serious about poker) to play a hand. Always look at the situation as a whole. If you conclude that the situation is profitable, then go ahead and play the hand. Otherwise, just let it go.

Rule #2: Never call a raise. Either reraise or fold.

There will be exceptions to this rule but I have intentionally formulated it in this strict form because most players call raises far too often. This is one of the most obvious leaks that most players have. When I observe a poker table, I always watch how people react to a raise. If players tend to call, I know it's a good game.

It's easy to show that this rule holds for heads-up play. Imagine the following: Before the flop you can see your opponent's hand and after the flop your opponent can also see your hand. If your opponent raises, what should you do? You simply raise if you have the better hand, fold a worse hand and if both of you have the same hand it doesn't matter what you do[78]. Of course, poker is not played like that. Usually you don't play heads-up, and dead money gives you better pot odds, so you don't have to win at least half the hands to show a profit, and if you call behind you have position on the raiser, which is worth something. Nonetheless, the simple fact remains: if there is a raiser, no one has called and it's up to you,

---

[78] To keep the argument simple, we neglect the blinds. E.g., if there are blinds and you have the same hand, it doesn't matter if you call or raise, but you should definitely not fold because you would forfeit your part of the blinds.

your hand is either profitable or not, meaning you should either raise or fold[79].

In the first part of this book, I sometimes violated this rule by being the first to call a raise (e.g., hand 1/3). I do this only if two conditions are met:

- ♠ I don't have much information about the raiser yet.
- ♠ I hold a middle pair.

The first condition is more or less self-explanatory. If you have sufficient information about the raiser, you should know whether your hand is strong enough to raise. The second condition requires a more detailed explanation. I never call with two unsuited high cards, only with middle pairs, usually pocket nines (with tens I tend to raise and with eights I usually fold). The reason is that middle pairs are much easier to play post-flop than a couple of high cards.

Let's compare A-Q to 9-9. Since you just called pre-flop, the raiser keeps the initiative and will most likely bet the flop, no matter what comes. With A-Q about one-third of the time you flop an ace or a queen. With this flop you will tend to either win a small pot or lose a big one. For instance, if an ace flops and your opponent doesn't have an ace, it's tough to get much money. On the other hand, if an ace flops and you get a lot of action, there is a good chance that you are running into A-K or a set.

Two-thirds of the time you don't flop anything with A-Q. For instance, the flop comes J-5-3 and the original raiser bets into you. What are you going to do? You can take the safe route and fold, reasoning ,"I don't have anything and my opponent probably has me beat." A less conservative move is to call, thinking, "I still have probably six outs. Let's see what my opponent does on the turn." The bold approach is to raise, figuring, "If my opponent doesn't have a big pair then it's unlikely that the flop has helped him."

---

[79] Just to set the record straight: The strength of your hand against your opponent's range is not the sole criterion. Other important factors are: how well your opponent plays post-flop, how well you play post-flop, how well you can read him, how predictably he plays, whether you have control over him (e.g., can he be bluffed easily?), etc.

All these considerations have merits, and each may be correct in a given situation, but it's difficult to make the right decision. You want to avoid tough decisions because it's easy to make costly errors.

Things change a lot if you hold 9-9 instead of A-Q. You muck your hand if a couple of high cards fall on the flop, you assume your hand is best if the flop is all low, and you're in the driver's seat if you flop a nine. If a single overcard falls then you have to go with your feel. But 9-9 is certainly much easier than A-Q to play post-flop against a single raiser.

There is another reason why I prefer to call a raise with 9-9 but not with A-Q. By calling instead of raising, you offer the player behind you better pot odds, which makes it more likely that the pot becomes multiway. If the pot is five-handed, you are in pretty good shape with your nines. You play them strictly for the set value. You flop a set or you're gone. With A-Q you don't welcome additional players because in multiway pots A-Q loses a lot of its value, and it's extremely difficult to play out of position.

Though I gave you some reasons why I occasionally call a raiser, don't draw the wrong conclusion. I call because I know I don't make much of a mistake one way or the other. That makes calling reasonable, but it doesn't make it correct! I would never call if I knew the raiser better or knew what he might hold.

That you should never call a raise is only true if you are the first one to do so. If there are callers between you and the raiser, the enhanced pot odds give you an incentive to play, but the value of some hands changes drastically. For example, A-J is much better than J-10s in a shorthanded pot, but in a raised, multiway pot this is no longer true. If there is a raise with four callers, you should gladly call with J-10s, but you should fold A-J. In a multi-way pot you want cards with the potential to make a big hand (like J-10s), not second-best (like A-J).

Look at it this way: With one raiser and four callers, if the raiser has aces, then J-10s is not going to win with a pair of jacks or tens; you have to make a hand that beats an overpair. Now, look at A-J. How can you win? You can make a straight, aces full of jacks or three jacks, but all of these hands are extreme long shots.

One last argument. Previously I said that you want either the best hand or, given the pot odds, a drawing hand with the potential to make something big. Clearly, in a raised multiway pot neither J-10s nor A-J will be the best hand[80], thus both must be treated as drawing hands. Whereas J-10s has maximum straight potential and good flush potential, A-J is a poor drawing hand that often comes up second-best.

Another exception occurs when you are in the blinds. You have already put some money into the pot, and that improves your pot odds. If there is a single raiser and the small blind has folded, you get pot odds of about 3.5-to-1, depending on the blind structure[81].

Many people always defend their blinds because they have already put money in the pot. This is complete nonsense. That money is no longer yours; it belongs to the pot and it doesn't matter who put it there. Instead of desperately trying to defend money that is no longer yours, you must think both in terms of pot odds and the overall situation.

Imagine that a very good player raises from early position and everyone folds to you in the big blind. How would you play A-J compared to 9-8s?

A-J is very delicate to play in this situation. Pot odds of 3.5-to-1 seem attractive. However, 2/3 of the time you won't hit anything. Since it's obvious that in all likelihood you don't have the best hand, the action will go check-bet-fold in this case. One time in three you hit your hand. The problem then is to extract some money if your hand is best and avoid losing too much if you are second-best. You will usually win a small pot or lose a big one. All in all, that doesn't look like a paying proposition to me.

Similarly, with 9-8s you can't expect to have the best hand pre-flop. If you flop a pair, you have to worry about an overpair, but not about being out-kicked. The real difference is that if you hit your hand, you stand a good chance to win a big pot. Let's say the first-position raiser has pocket kings. If you have A-J and flop an ace, the best you can hope for is that the raiser will call you down; if you flop a jack, well then you will lose a bundle. If you flop two pair, trips or a straight with 9-8s, then you can expect to get plenty of action from the kings. Thus, I'm more inclined to call with 9-8s than with A-J.

Say the raiser made his play from late instead of early position. Does that

---

[80] This is why A-J is much better short-handed then J-10s. A-J is much more likely to be the best hand than J-10s.

[81] The pot odds are 3.33-to-1 if the small blind is 1/3 of the big blind, 3.5-to-1 if the small blind is half the big blind and 3.67-to-1 if the small blind is 2/3 of the big blind.

change anything? Now I would raise with A-J but just call with 9-8s because there is an excellent chance that A-J is the best hand. A good player will raise from late position with many hands that A-J can beat, such as K-J, J-10s, A-xs or even 7-6s. You're still unlikely to have the best hand with 9-8s, but given the pot odds and the potential of the hand, a call is in order.

Besides playing too many hands and calling raises too often, calling too liberally from the blinds is the most frequent mistake players make before the flop. Don't fall into the trap of throwing good money after bad.

A raise in front of you means two things. The raiser is telling you he has a big hand (given his playing standards), hence you must tighten up considerably. Your task is to compare the strength of your hand to the range of hands the raiser can have, and to carefully assess whether playing can be profitable. If so, then go ahead and raise; otherwise just muck your hand. You will often throw away hands you would otherwise have raised.

Example: A tough player raises from early position and you hold A-10s in middle position. This is a clear fold against a solid player since there is no way you can have the best hand. However, had everyone folded to you in middle position, then you would have raised.

If there are callers between the raiser and you, the raise-or-fold rule is no longer valid. Generally speaking, the more callers, the more liberally you can call. But don't get carried away. Even if there are a lot of players, don't call with 7-4s. A hand like that doesn't win enough to make calling worthwhile. And keep in mind that hand values change in multiway pots. Unsuited high cards lose value and suited connectors gain value. In raised, multiway pots it's much better to hold 10-9s than Q-10.

Be careful when the pot is raised and you are in the blinds. You get better pot odds, but that doesn't justify imprudence. If there is a single raiser, always notice the character and position of the raiser. Most players have markedly different raising standards between early and late position. Play very tightly if the raise came from early position and the raiser knows what he is doing. But if the raise came from late position and you think you could have the best hand, don't be afraid to play aggressively.

Things change considerably in raised pots when there are callers involved and you are in one of the blinds. Now your pot odds are so favorable that you can call with many hands. One of the biggest pots (in terms of big blinds) I ever won was in a $30-60 game when there was a family pot, I called the first-position raise with 5-2s from the big blind and was fortunate enough to make the flush at the end.

Though I just talked about the 'blinds', it obviously makes a difference if you are in the small or big blind. The crucial point is the blind structure. You can call more freely in the small blind if it is 2/3 of the big blind, since you get better pot odds compared to when the small blind is half or 1/3 of the big blind.

> Rule #3: If you are the first one in from late position, always raise the pot.

Many weak and inexperienced players just call from late position when no one has opened the pot. They see a hand they like to play, such as 10-9s, but think it's not strong enough to raise, so they call. This is wrong for two reasons. First, you give the small blind great odds to play, and the big blind plays for free. Second, if you raise with good hands and call with average hands, you give away the strength of your hand and set yourself up to be outplayed by the blinds after the flop.

By always raising from late position you have three ways to win:

- ♠ You can win the blinds instantly and without risk if the players behind you fold.
- ♠ You can out-flop the competition.
- ♠ You can outplay your opponents.

If you call instead of raise, you voluntarily give up one way to win. Sure, you have to invest twice the amount of money for an additional way to win, but that is well worth it. In a game where the small blind is half the big blind, you risk two bets to win 1.5 bets. That means if your opponents fold more than 57 % of the time you show an immediate profit. Of course, your opponents don't have to fold that often to make the play correct. If one or both of the blinds calls, you can still out-flop or outplay them.

Some people carry the play too far, interpreting late position as a free license to steal. They think that the combination of folding equity and positional advantage means the play is always correct, no matter what they are holding. But even an average player will quickly catch on. If the late-position player always raises when he gets the chance, he may just have two random cards, so the blinds will always call or, even worse for the raiser, start playing back at him. Thus, the late-position player should not automatically raise. He should throw away his weaker hands to give his raises more credibility and, consequently, increase his folding equity. How often you should raise from late position depends largely on how often the players behind you tend to fold and how well they play. The more prone they are to fold, the more often you should raise, and the better they play, the less often you should raise.

What should you do if one or both of the blinds never folds to a raise? You find such players quite frequently even in middle-limit games. Since one of your ways to win is gone, the situation looks similar to just calling, and you will have to out-flop or outplay the competition. Should you call in this case? I don't think so. Calling in this situation is not consistent with the tight-aggressive style I prefer, and in any case you still give away too much information if there is a correlation between your raising standards and the strength of your hand.

When it's obvious that I will be called, I tighten up my opening range, but I still raise. For example: I would not raise with 9-6s in this case. Why should I put money into the pot with a hand that is an underdog against two random cards? And, if my opponent re-raises, I've been caught with my pants down. But I'm still going to raise with a hand like J-10s. Admittedly, J-10s is not a big money maker, but it's a solid holding and I have position. Even if one of the blinds wakes up with a big hand and reraises, I still have a reasonable chance to win.

Another interesting case emerges when you open with pocket aces in late position. An acknowledged poker theorist has recommended just calling, arguing that pocket aces are worth more than the 1.5 small bets you can win from the blinds by raising. I don't like this advice for several reasons:

- ♠ Collecting the blinds is always a good result. Though I agree that pocket aces have a greater expectation than 1.5 bets, this does not mean that you actually make more money by calling. That your opponents fold to a raise is a strong indication of weakness, and it's by no means sure that they'll flop a hand worth putting money in the pot.

♠ The blinds often have enough of a hand to call a raise but not enough to raise[82]. For instance, if the big blind has 10-8s, he will probably call a late-position raise but will not raise himself. In these cases you lose money by calling instead of raising your aces before the flop.

♠ The tricky play can backfire. This occurs in two ways. In the first, an opponent (usually the big blind) who would have folded to your raise flops a hand that beats your aces. For example, the big blind holds 7-3 and the flop comes J-7-3.

♠ In the second situation, you just call with your aces against an experienced player who has seen you raise from late position with, say A-3, K-9 or 8-6s. What do you think he puts you on if suddenly you just call from steal position: a weaker hand or a monster? An experienced player will happily take a free look at the flop, but you'll get no action if he can't beat aces or he doesn't get the right price to draw.

♠ Even below-average players understand that an open raise from last position could be a steal attempt, so they call more often than otherwise. Of course, you're delighted to see action with your rockets. But you usually don't have a big hand. Say you raise with 9-7s and everyone folds. This is an excellent result; you don't figure to make 1.5 bets if you're called, and your EV is most likely negative if you're reraised. Therefore, to give your raises credibility, you not only have to fold weak holdings but to show some big hands now and then. What bigger hand can you show than a pair of aces?

---

[82] Don't confuse this statement with the general advice that you need a stronger hand to call a raise then to raise yourself. The latter assumes that you don't have any money in the pot. In the blinds you have a hand that warrants a call but isn't worth raising.

Open-calling with aces from late position is the superior play if: 1) your opponent would not have called a raise; and 2) he puts money in the pot after the flop with the worse hand.

If you really want to slowplay aces from late position, then do it only against obviously weak players that you haven't played before. Even if you pick your spots carefully, it doesn't have enough impact on your win rate to worry about it. I always raise with the aces and if I just pick up the blinds, so be it.

A corollary to the third rule is that you should raise when you have posted behind the button and it's folded to you. The odds are such that you should make this play with virtually no regard to your holding. You risk one bet to win 2.5 bets, showing an immediate profit if your opponents fold more than 28.6 % of the time[83].

These three simple rules cover the vast majority of situations that occur before the flop. Some readers may be disappointed that they didn't get some easy-to-memorize rules such as "fold hand x from early position, call with it from middle position and raise with it from late position". But the point of these rules is to make you aware that poker is a dynamic game. To improve your pre-flop game, you must free yourself from slavishly following a fixed set of starting-hand recommendations and understand that every situation is unique. You must determine the best course of action in each situation, given the information available. This is much more difficult than following a chart, but the reward is well worth the effort.

Getting action

Many players, especially loose players, believe that you don't get enough action if you play too tight. You have to give action to get action, as the saying goes. Strictly speaking, this statement contains two assertions: that you can play too tight and that a tight player doesn't get enough action.

It's theoretically possible to play too tightly. If you only play aces, kings and queens, you are playing too tight; you will never win enough to cover your expense in the blinds. I have seen a lot of tight players over the years, but never one that played too tight. If a tight player could not beat the

---

[83] For a more in-depth discussion of the play see p. 105

game, it was because he played too passively and/or predictably.

The second question is whether you get enough action when playing tight. One day in a $30-60 game I simply couldn't get any playable hands. Finally, under the gun, I was dealt two black aces. Not having played a single hand for one-and-a-half hours, I thought that if I raised, everyone would fall from their chair. Nonetheless, I raised. What happened? I got six callers! How can that be?

The common explanation is that many players don't pay much attention to the game, so they don't realize that you are very selective about your starting hands. I don't think this is true. Look at it from the habitual caller's point of view. Because he is loose, he plays a lot of hands and usually faces the same opponents contesting the pot, namely the other loose players at the table. Suddenly he sees a new face putting money into the pot. Do you think he won't notice that? Of course he will. As a matter of fact when I raised with the two black aces, the first player said, "You finally found a hand?" But this didn't keep him from calling.

These guys don't call with obviously inferior hands due to a lack of awareness. The reason is that weak players only play their own hand. They peek at their starting hand and see, for example, Q-10. Their thinking is: "Two high cards. I'm going to play that hand." They make up their mind regardless of what's going on at the table. They may reconsider if it's three or four bets to them, but if someone has limped in front, they will limp behind (or raise) and if the pot is raised, they will call. In middle-limit hold'em, most pots are raised, so that's nothing unusual, at least nothing that will prevent their calling.

Notice that someone who only plays his own two cards violates Tristan's first golden rule. You should evaluate the whole situation before forming a decision. Of course Q-10 can be a profitable hand in the right situation, but imagine that a player who hasn't played a single hand in an hour opens from early position with a raise, everyone folds to you and you hold Q-10. It doesn't take a rocket engineer to realize that calling can't be profitable. Yes, you have position, but you have by far the worst hand. There is no legitimate hand your opponent can hold that you can beat. You are usually a 2-to-1 underdog and if your opponent happens to have one of the top three pairs your odds are even worse.

Some people will mark you as a good player and give you action with inferior hands because they want to play you—and beat you. I remember an Iranian player that would nearly always call me when I entered the pot. Here is an example of his play.

In a $30-60 game I raised from middle position with K-K. It was folded to my friend in the cutoff seat. He was clearly ready to fold until he noticed that I was in the hand. He promptly called me and everyone else folded. I knew he had zilch and he was hoping for a miracle. The flop came 10-2-8. I bet and he called. Turn: 6. I bet and he called again. River: 5 (board: 10-2-8-6-5). The board looked harmless enough, so I bet the river. My Iranian friend lost no time raising. I didn't know what he had, but I was certain that he had me beat because he wouldn't raise me without being able to beat an overpair. I called and he showed me 7-4!

It's easy to see what had happened. Even for him, 7-4 just barely warranted a call. He wouldn't usually call me with 9-2 but with 7-4 he had straight potential. On the flop he had nothing, so why didn't he fold? Easy, he put me on two big cards, and since no high cards were showing, he figured a seven or four on the turn would give him the best hand. The turn gave him a gutshot, so he apparently had ten outs, though I'm pretty sure he'd have gone with the gutshot even if he knew I had a big pair. The river gave him the pleasure of raising me with the second nuts.

If I was certain that I was beaten, why did I call the river raise? I don't want to play a guessing game against a highly unpredictable player. I always bet until my Iranian friend either folds or raises[84]. If he raises, I call him down. My play is based on simple statistics. Since I usually start with the better hand, I win the majority of the pots. I give him the advantage of winning an occasional extra bet by not folding, but I never lose a pot I'm entitled to win. In other words, he can't bluff me off the pot.

Now, back to the question of why I didn't fold at the end. I could only be sure that I was beaten because I had trained him not to bluff. You can only achieve this if you always call a raise. If I'd folded at the end, I would have saved sixty bucks. The next time he raises, I can fold again and save another sixty bucks. But he'll eventually see what I'm doing and he'll start raising with nothing. And if I fold then, I don't lose an extra bet but the whole pot. Since I'm usually a big favorite, I don't want to be bluffed out.

---

[84] Of course, I don't bet two unimproved high cards at the end, and I'm only playing that way when we are heads-up.

Ironically, we're both satisfied with our situation. Me, because I'm the net winner in our private duel, and him, because it gives him deep satisfaction to beat me. My Iranian friend is not an idiot. He knows full well that he is losing money to me. He is a successful businessman, so winning money in a middle-limit hold'em game is not his principal concern. Usually his wife is sitting behind him when he plays poker, and he wants to show her that he can beat me.

A tight player will get action, but not as much as a loose player. The good players will quickly notice that you are very selective about your starting hands, and they won't play you without a strong hand. Not to worry. These types of players are usually tough opponents, so at best, your advantage will be slim. You want to face players that grant you an advantage right from the start by playing substandard hands. These loose players don't care how many hands you play; they came to the card room to play, not to fold.

Deception

Another objection to tight play is that a tight player's range is so narrow that his opponents have a good idea of his holding, and therefore the tight player doesn't get full value from his hands. Thus you should play more hands to better disguise your strength and make yourself more difficult to read.

Years ago in the old MGM poker room there was a player in the $10-20 game who always put in the last raise pre-flop (if it wasn't capped in front of him, in which case he would call). On the flop he didn't raise, but he didn't fold either. This was the most deceptive player I ever saw. Not only because he played every hand (I have seen that many times, even in mid-limit games), but because he never looked at his hand before the turn. He was completely unreadable. You can't read a player who doesn't know what he has[85]. Alas, this ultra-deceptive approach was not a winner. He lost rack after rack, and the waiting list for his table was a mile long.

What can we learn from this little anecdote? First, being selective about

---

[85] By the way, this is a good argument for not looking at your hand pre-flop before it's your turn to act.

starting hands is more important than deception. The players that beat the 'no-peak' player all played fewer hands than he did. He was deceptive to the extreme, but this did not overcome the disadvantage that came from playing too many hands.

Second, in general, the fewer hands you play, the more readable you become. Let's assume that the loose player from the example above thinks over his strategy and comes to the conclusion that playing 3-2 is unprofitable. Does this make a difference to his opponents? Usually not, but there are exceptions. If you are heads-up at the end with this player, you have A-A and the board is 4♦-10♣-A♠-9♥-5♦, then it makes a difference.

Being selective with the hands you play is clearly more important than deception, but this doesn't mean that you should neglect the latter. Here is a simple example from pre-flop play. When in first position and no one has opened the pot so far, which hands should you play? This is a common situation, so it's important to give it some thought.

Let's say a player decides to play the following hands:

Hand	Action	Hand	Action
A-A to 7-7	r	A-Js	r (75%), c (25%)
A-Ks	r (50%), c (50%)	A-J	r (83%), c (17%)
A-K	r	K-Qs	r (50%), c (50%)
A-Qs	r (75%), c (25%)	K-Q	r (83%), c (17%)
A-Q	r		

r = raise, c = call

The hand selection is very reasonable. Nearly all pros play along these lines with only small modifications. But keep in mind that although the situation is always the same, your play should vary. A lot depends on the game conditions (more on that later). Notice further that the player with the above starting-hand list already gave the subject of deception same thought. He doesn't always do the same thing with the same hand. With A-Ks he limps half the time and raises the other half[86]. That makes it more difficult to put him on a hand. Nonetheless, there is something wrong with the starting hand selection chart. Can you see what it is?

Our player raises 76.8 % and limps 23.2 % of the hands he plays. If he raises, he either has a pair or two high cards. However, a limp always means two high cards. This gives an attentive opponent the chance to out-play the limper if the flop comes all low, because the limper can have no piece of it.

How does one correct that problem? There are two possibilities: You can either raise every time you open or, if you like to limp as well, you have to mix it up in such a way that a limp doesn't automatically mean that you don't have a pair. Both strategies are possible in middle-limit hold'em.

Alan, one of the best middle-limit players I know (see p. 311), always brings it in for a raise. This is the high-limit approach. All the good high-limit players usually either raise or fold when they enter the pot. If you intend to play $100-200 or higher, that's the course of action you should take.

In middle-limit you can find many excellent players, such as Roy Cooke, who like to limp from early position. I use that approach because it gives me more flexibility than always raising. Keep in mind that the array of hands you can play from early position is not static, but depends on the game conditions. If the game is soft, meaning that a lot of players like to see the flop and the game is not overly aggressive, you can play more hands than usual; in a tough game you have to fold some hands you would normally play.

If you always raise from early position, you can adjust to tough playing conditions by folding some of your weaker hands, such as 7-7, 8-8, A-J and K-Q, but you lose the opportunity to take advantage of good playing conditions. When the game is soft, hands like Q-Js, J-10s and small pairs become playable even from early position, but you don't want to raise with

---

[86] It may seem odd to always raise with A-K and to either raise or call with A-Ks, since A-Ks is undoubtedly the stronger hand. But the mixed strategy makes sense. A-K doesn't play well against many opponents, so you want to raise with it to keep the pot short-handed. But A-Ks plays well short-handed and in multiway pots, therefore it's sound strategy to sometimes just call to attract more players.

them. If you call with J-10s and get five or six callers, you have put yourself in a profitable situation. If you raise that hand and because of your raise there are only two callers behind, you are out of position with probably the worst hand, a situation that can't be profitable. If you usually raise from early position, you can't suddenly start limping, because this gives your hand away. This is the advantage of having a mixed raising/limping strategy from early position. You can reduce the number of hands you play in tough games, and you can take advantage of soft games by playing more hands, and it still looks natural.

The following hand came up in a $15-30 game. I limped from early position, two players behind me called, the cutoff raised and the big blind called. The two limpers and I called the raise. The flop came Q-7-2 rainbow. Everyone checked to the raiser. He bet and only the big blind and I called. On the turn another deuce fell. Again it was checked to the raiser. He bet, the big blind check-raised and I made it three bets. The original raiser folded and the big blind called reluctantly. On the river a brick came, my sole remaining opponent checked, I bet and, after some deliberation, he folded.

While I dragged in the nice sized pot Kim, a Korean girl to my right, whispered to me, "You had pocket sevens." I turned around to her: "You're sure?" She said, "Absolutely! With queens or ace-queen you would have raised before the flop, you don't play pocket deuces from early position, and king-queen is not strong enough to make it three bets on the turn." A perfect analysis and, of course, she hit the nail on the head. I had played with Kim for many years at the Mirage and she probably knew my game better than anyone else. If you have observant opponents like that, from time to time, it's appropriate to do something unusual to throw them off.

Not long after this incident we were playing at the same table. Kim was sitting in the 10 seat and I was in the 3 seat. Two times in a row when she had the big blind, there was no action and she chopped the blinds. Both times she showed her hand, K-K and A-Ks, complaining that she never gets action when she holds a big hand. On the next round when Kim was in the big blind again, the two players in front of me folded and I raised with K♠-7♠.

Since the table was pretty tight and I hadn't played a lot of hands, I thought I had a good chance to win the pot uncontested. In that case my intention was to show my hand to give a false impression about my game, to hopefully loosen up the table and to tease Kim a little bit (I know, men often do silly things in the presence of a nice girl). My plan nearly worked. Everyone folded to Kim. She looked at her hand, looked at me and finally called. Though I didn't have much, I felt confident. I was hoping Kim would miss the flop and that I could pick up the pot by betting. The dealer turned over 2♦-K♥-7♠.

I hadn't expect to flop top two pair with my weak hand, but now I had to make the best of it. Kim checked, I bet, she check-raised me, I three-bet, she raised again and I made it five bets. She shook her head in disbelief and reluctantly called. What is her hand and what did she put me on?

From my point of view the hand looked like this: Pre-flop she called my raise from the big blind. She wouldn't do so with nothing, so I knew she had some sort of hand, but I didn't know how strong it was. Kim check-raised me on the flop, giving me a much clearer picture. Since there was no draw out, her check-raise meant one of three things:

- ♠ a pair below kings (e.g., 9-9 or A-7s). By raising, she was trying to find out if her pair was good.

- ♠ a pair of kings (e. g., K-Q)

- ♠ a hand that could beat kings

Because I could beat most of those hands, I raised again. Her four-bet narrowed her range even further. Now we could exclude the first two cases. Kim would never make it four bets if she couldn't beat A-K. That meant she had a hand better than kings. This left only A-A, K-K, 7-7 and 2-2. Since I had a king and a seven in my hand, there was one combination for K-K and 7-7, three for 2-2 and six for A-A. I decided to raise again for two reasons. First, I was a 6-to-5 favorite to have the best hand, therefore putting more money into the pot had a positive expectation. Second, by raising again I could find out if my hand was good. My guess was that Kim would definitely reraise with K-K (notice that K-K was the best hand at that time and that heads-up, the number of raises is unlimited) and in all likelihood with 7-7 and 2-2, but absolutely not with A-A.

From Kim's point of view, the hand developed like this: She picked up A-A in the big blind after a tight player had raised from early position. The natural play is to raise. However, she knew that if she raised I would put her immediately on A-A, K-K, Q-Q or A-K. So she smooth-called to disguise her hand, a very reasonable play.

The flop was very good for Kim. She could hope that I had a piece of it and that she was still best. Her check-raise was automatic[87]. That I made it three bets was no disaster for Kim. My most likely hand was A-K, and she could beat that. Hence, she was still confident when she made it four bets. But all this changed when I raised again, as I must have had a hand that could beat A-K. She knew that I don't play 2-2 from early position and that I most likely would just call with 7-7 before the flop, so it looked to her like I had K-K.

She knew she was beat (albeit putting me on the wrong hand) but she called me down[88]. Since the board didn't pair, I won the hand. When I turned over my hand she looked flabbergasted: "You play this?!"

My unusual loose play worked, but don't draw the wrong conclusion. To play a substandard hand in this way, the situation has to be right and you must proceed with extreme caution.

♠ Make unusual plays only if several players at the table know your play pretty well. Against strangers, players you will never see again or opponents who don't care what hands you play from what position, the play is wasted and will only cost you money.

♠ Don't make the play with complete trash. You want a hand that can make something big. Best candidates are suited connectors or at least K-xs as in the example above.

---

[87] She knows that as an aggressive player I will bet the flop no matter what comes. So she gets at least the bet she forfeited pre-flop should I fold to the check-raise. Waiting for the turn to check-raise is an option, though not without risk. Notice that there is no draw out. If she calls the flop I have to assume that she has something, which makes it tough for me to bet the turn with nothing.

[88] Which was, by the way, correct. Kim had a 25.5 % chance to win and pot odds of 13.7-to-1. But since she put me on K-K this would mean that she only had two outs and consequently she should have folded. However, I can't fault her for not folding pocket aces heads-up.

- ♠ Don't get stubborn. Give up quickly if things don't go your way. For instance, had Kim check-raised me with a flop of J-5-3, I would have folded immediately.

- ♠ And the single most important point: Make the play only occasionally. The benefits are twofold. It helps to conceal your starting-hand strategy (at least it puts doubt in the minds of your more attentive opponents) and you have the surprise factor on your side should you hit anything big. But playing such a hand is by itself –EV. You can't do it often without significantly hurting your win rate.

While suited connectors are good candidates for such a play, there are many such combinations and you can easily overdo it. Here is a reasonable piece of advice: If you decide the time is right for a disguise play, choose in advance the hand you will play. Select, for example 7-6 suited, all black. These are only two of the 1,326 combinations of suited connectors you can be dealt.

One further remark: Playing a hand for deception is one of the rare cases where you should consider showing your hand even if it's not required. For instance, at the end your opponent shows the winner. Turn over your hand and make sure it doesn't go unnoticed. Remember, you paid for the play to disguise you starting hand strategy. If nobody sees your hand, you haven't achieved anything.

So far we've discussed playing a weak hand strongly for deception. The other possibility is to play a strong hand weakly, and by that I mean one of the top three pairs. This is usually not a good idea because it costs you more money than raising once in a while with a substandard hand. Nonetheless, you often see players that just limp from early position with K-K or Q-Q. If you have K-K, you don't want to allow a player to sneak in cheaply (or get a free play in the big blind) with a weak ace. If somebody wants to draw out on you with a weak ace, make him pay for it.

There is another oft-overlooked reason why calling with kings can't be good. By just limping, you give the players behind you better pot odds, which tends to increase the number of active players. Assume you've raised with your kings and the flop comes Q-7-3 rainbow. If you don't have completely loose opponents, you're nearly certain to have the best hand. There is a remote chance that someone has a set of sevens or treys (pocket queens would normally have raised pre-flop).

In an unraised pot with the same flop, you are no longer sure where you stand. The blinds have more or less random cards, and the players in late position will (correctly) call with all sorts of hands. You can easily run into hands like Q-7, Q-3 or 7-3, hands which would normally fold to a raise, and which could now cost you the pot. Look at it this way: Whether you raise or not, you often see about the same amount of money in the pot. But when you limp you have to beat about twice as many opponents!

Limping with queens is even worse because you are not only vulnerable to the dreaded ace on the flop, but to the king as well. With pocket aces the situation is different inasmuch as there are no potential overcards that can hurt you. In no-limit, just calling with aces is a reasonable and often-employed strategy. You hope that somebody will raise and then you can come over the top. That way you either win some money without risk or you can play a large pot as a big favorite.

That play is not so effective in limit hold'em. Because you can only raise one small bet, there is no chance to win the pot immediately, and you pretty much give away your hand. If you see somebody who makes it three or four bets after limping from early position and is not a complete maniac, this usually means A-A, or sometimes K-K or A-Ks.

Though limping with aces is worse than raising in limit hold'em, if done sparingly it can have its merits. You send out a strong message that limping doesn't mean you don't have a big hand. If the game is good or excellent, or even normal, I will never limp with aces. But I will occasionally make that play in a tough game with several good players who know me well. Then I choose a combination in advance (usually two black or red aces) with which I will limp. In that case, I am only limping with 1/6 of all dealt aces. Again, don't make this play carelessly and regularly. It's a strong play that your observant opponents will remember for a long time.

Don't be seduced into constantly looking for reasons to make deception plays. It's generally neither necessary nor appropriate. Against not-so-observant opponents, just playing your regular pre-flop game, which means playing extremely tight from early position and often quite loose from late position, gives your game enough deception. These players will see you turn over the same weak hands they always like to play, like J-10,

A-3s or 6-5s, without noticing that you only play these hands in favorable situations (which means from late position and/or against many players). Many players just look at the hand you turn over, paying no attention to your position.

Deception can extend to post-flop play. Let me say it again: the fewer hands you play, the easier you are to read. The tight player must play in a way that makes it tough for an attentive opponent to put him on a specific hand. The key is not to always play the same way in a given situation. If you play in a rigid style, you are what is called a weak-tight player. It's easy to play against weak-tight players because they always respond in the same way. They never get full value for their hands because you always have a good idea what they hold, and you can act accordingly.

It's not a bad idea to start as a weak-tight player, since this type of player is usually a winner at low limits. But this approach will not make you a winner in higher-limit games, and it's tough to make the transition to middle-limit games because you have to change your playing style[89].

Ironically, average players often play in a predictable way, thus conceding the deception advantage they have against a tight player. Here is a simple example: In a multiway hand the flop comes 7-3-3. A player calls two or three bets cold on the flop and turn, then suddenly springs to life and starts raising. This player almost certainly has either a trey or pocket sevens. Nearly all weak and average players follow this course of action when they flop three of a kind or a full house. They don't want to win a small pot on the flop, so they wait until the stakes double on the turn to become active. This strategy has even been recommended in print:

> "If you flop a beautiful set, hopefully there will be a big card or two also. Your hand is so well disguised that if you're in early position you should go ahead and bet. If you're in late position and the pot is opened before it gets to you, don't raise until the turn when the bet doubles."[90]

---

[89] I can tell you this from experience, since I started as a weak-tight player, had quick success in low-limit games and then struggled for quite a while before beating the higher limits (see pp. 288ff).

[90] Susie Isaacs, *1000 Best Poker Strategies and Secrets. Tips and Strategies to Help You Walk Away a Winner*, Naperville 2006, p. 29

That's exactly how amateurs play the hand. To them it looks like this play is deceptive and makes more money.

Let's take the author's scenario: You are on the button and you have flopped a set. First player bets; there are four callers before the action comes to you. It's clear that you should raise now and not just call. Why? Because you have to anticipate what's going to happen. The most likely scenario is that everyone will call, putting an additional five small bets into the pot. To do better than that, you have to entice three additional bets on the turn by not raising on the flop. That's very unlikely.

I'm not saying that you never should wait until the turn before you force the action. As the author points out, there are situations where this course of action makes sense. But the book from which this quotation originates is about strategy, and the correct strategy is not to play passively on third street if you flop big. On the contrary, if you flop a hand that's very likely to be the best at the end, you should do everything possible to maximize the number of bets that go into the pot.

It's often correct to wait for the turn before becoming active with a big hand. The author's advice could be correct as a general guideline if this were a unique situation, in which case it could make you more money.

Giving a free or cheap turn card increases the chance that someone will draw out on you, but usually it's well worth that risk. But this situation is not unique. Paired flops come up all the time. If you treat each situation individually, not thinking about future consequences, you tend to act predictably, needlessly giving away your hand and making it easy for opponents to play correctly against you.

If you always do exactly the same thing in similar situations, such as slowplaying the flop with a big hand, then this play, even if best in a concrete situation, loses much of its power, to the point where it becomes suboptimal. Look at the resulting drawbacks:

♠   You give away your hand at the turn. You will only get action from a good opponent if he has a superior hand or the right odds to draw.

♠   Most people realize that a paired flop, especially if it contains no drawing possibility, presents a good bluffing op-

portunity. If you always wait for the turn to bet trips or
better, you can't seize that opportunity. If you bet the flop,
an observant opponent will immediately realize that you
can't have trips. If he has a hand himself, he will let you
bluff away your money, or he can bluff-raise you with air.

♠ It becomes tough to protect your legitimate hands. Say the
flop is 7-3-3 as above, and you hold Q-7 in the big blind.
There is a good chance you have the best hand, so you
want to bet your top pair to protect it (a free card could
easily be a disaster if an overcard falls on the turn). Again,
a good opponent recognizes that you don't have trips and
may put you to the test by raising. Now you are in a tough
spot. There is no draw-out and you can be beaten badly.
You have maneuvered yourself into a position where you
can easily make a disastrous decision (calling and running
into a big hand or folding the best hand).

Now it becomes obvious how a good player handles a situation like that.
He will frequently bet or raise with a big hand on the flop. By playing that
way, he effectively conceals his hand. Is he betting the flop to pick up the
pot, is he trying to protect his hand, or is he looking for action with a monster hand? By varying your play, even a sharp hand reader will be left in
the dark.

This is a very important concept. You sometimes have to play a weak hand
strongly or a strong hand weakly. You give away too much information if
you only check, call, bet and raise according to your own hand strength.
Simple, straightforward play is usually enough to get the money in low-
limit games because the players lack sophistication, but the better players
at the higher limits will read you like an open book. It's of utmost importance to employ a mixed strategy so that you keep your opponents guessing about your holdings as much as possible.

Chapter 6

Being Aggressive

Nearly all hold'em books agree that besides playing tight, you must be aggressive. There are some good reasons for this:

- ♠ You will win more when you have the best hand.
- ♠ You can take down pots without the best hand.
- ♠ You don't give many free cards, making it expensive for players to draw against you.
- ♠ Your opponents give you a lot of free cards and/or let you draw cheaply.
- ♠ You often decrease the number of players contesting the pot, increasing your chances to win the hand.
- ♠ The other players fear you.

There are some drawbacks as well, such as:

- ♠ being check-raised more often

- ♠ losing more when holding the second-best hand
- ♠ larger swings (your standard deviation goes up)

But it's clear that aggressively play is vastly superior to passive play.

The value of aggression

Let's look at an interesting example. In a $40-80 game the under-the-gun player raises, two middle-position players call and it's up to me. As a new player at the table, I've posted behind the button and see J♣-10♣. I'm already halfway in, so I call. The big blind calls as well, and we see the flop five-handed: 6♦-5♣-2♣.

The big blind checks, the original raiser bets, one middle-position player calls and the other folds. I think about raising. The most likely scenario is that the big blind folds and the remaining two players call. That means I get 2-to-1 for my money as a 2-to-1 underdog to make my flush. But if the original raiser reraises, I will likely have to play heads-up with the worst hand. With my drawing hand, I want to keep the players in so that I get paid off if I make my flush. I call and hope the big blind will call behind me, which he does.

The turn is the 9♠. Everyone checks to me. With just one card to come, my chances to complete the flush have dropped considerably. No one seems to have much, but a bet on my part would offer them 8-to-1 pot odds, which means even two overcards could draw profitably. The original raiser has two overcards for sure; the others might have overcards, or perhaps a small split pair or pocket pair. They would probably call with any pair. Betting wouldn't accomplish much, except to make the pot bigger while I hold the worst hand. I check for the free card and hope the river will improve my hand. No luck for me, as the 5♠ comes off.

Again, everyone checks to me. I briefly consider betting. How likely is it that all three players will fold with 8-to-1 pot odds? Not very. How would my bet look to the other players? I would bet in last position after three players had checked; I called the flop and checked the turn, and now I bet after a blank has fallen at the end? That smells like a desperation bluff. I check behind and surrender the pot. The original raiser shows A-Q and takes it down.

I have made it a habit to think about every hand I play at the table, won or lost. When analyzing this hand I was shocked at my poor play! Everyone makes mistakes, and I am of course no exception. But in this hand I didn't make just one mistake; I misplayed every single street! It was one of the worst hands I ever played, and that's why it stuck in my mind. I played the hand like a low-limit player, and in low-limit it might be okay[91] but that doesn't cut it in higher-limit games.

Holding nothing back, I've shown the thought process behind my play. I had rational reasons for everything I did—I might even have convinced you that I played the hand correctly!

But having good reasons is not enough to be a winner. Every player—even the worst player you know—has reasons. The question is: do the reasons behind your decisions take into account the whole situation? In other words, do your decisions likely maximize your expectation?

In the example above, I was fixated on my flush draw and didn't consider using my position to put pressure on my opponents, possibly winning the hand without improving. I was playing only my cards and not my opponents. Keeping this in mind, let's take a more thorough look at the hand.

The play before the flop is straightforward. J♣-10♣ is a pretty good hand there. I would have called with much worse hands with a raise and two callers. Though I had position, I think reraising would be overplaying the hand. You don't want to three-bet with J-10s. It plays well multiway, so you actually welcome additional players. So, calling pre-flop was correct.

The flop (6♦-5♣-2♣) was very good for me. With a flush draw and two overcards, I had a strong hand. Just calling was a reasonable play. With my flush draw, it paid to keep players in the pot to maximize my return in case I hit my hand. But there was a better course of action with this raggedy board. No one had shown any strength, and the original raiser's bet could mean he had a big pocket pair or just a couple of high cards. Having just checked or called the two remaining players seems weak. Perhaps one of them was slowplaying a big hand, but this is unlikely, given the board[92],

---

[91] With the exception of the flop play. You should raise for value because you can usually expect to get more than two players in low-limit.

[92] Keep in mind that the pot was raised before the flop, seriously reducing the chances that the board had hit some of the players really hard.

and I still had a flush draw.

This brings raising into play. By raising, you no longer solely rely on your flush draw; you try to exploit your opponents' weaknesses. As I mentioned, raising had the drawback that if the original raiser had an overpair, he would reraise and we would likely play the hand out heads-up. But that was no catastrophe. First, I had a 1-in-3 shot to win the hand and with 16-to-1 pot odds, I had an easy call on the flop and sufficient pot odds to call on the turn. Second, play would become easy on the river. I hit my flush or I was gone. A typical under-the-gun raiser is more likely to have two high cards than a pocket pair[93]. You don't win immediately if you reraise him, of course. But that's not your aim.

You are trying to set yourself up to steal the pot on the turn or river. You have to think ahead, to anticipate the future action. Your raise will probably cause the big blind to fold and the original raiser and the middle-position player to call (it would be nice, albeit unlikely, if the middle-position player were to fold). That means you will see the turn three-handed. Of the 47 cards that can show up, only 9 are bad for you: any ace, king or queen that is not a club. With a jack or ten you might or might not have the best hand. In that case betting is mandatory if it's checked to you. What you are hoping for (besides a club) is a small card (2-9) that is very unlikely to hit one of your remaining opponents. A bet on your part has a very high chance to make the other players fold if the turn card is a brick. Should one of the two other players be stubborn and call, he is a big underdog to improve on the river and you will bluff again should you not complete your flush. Your turn bet looks strong to your opponents, not only because you raised on the flop but because you posted behind the button. People know that you would call in this situation with a wide range of hands, with the consequence that the flop and/or turn might have hit you.

There is another reason why raising on the flop might be beneficial. Your raise could make the big blind lay down a jack or ten with a better kicker. The chance to gain three additional outs is well worth the investment of an extra small bet. Conclusion of the flop play: Calling is reasonable and raising is the superior play, but nothing is lost yet.

All three players checked to me on the turn (board: 6♦-5♣-2♣-9♠) – a strong

---

[93] This is just a matter of combinatorics. E.g., there are 18 combinations for A-A, K-K, Q-Q and 32 combinations for A-K, A-Q.

indication that they're weak. I figured that betting can't be good because two overcards get the correct odds to draw. That's true, but it's only half the story. It assumes that my opponents know that their hand is good if they make a pair, but that's quite dubious. Let's look at the big blind first. We don't know what he had, it was likely he had two overcards such as K-Q. Even if he thinks a king or queen at the end would beat me, the pot odds don't justify his call. There is still the original raiser behind him, and this player likely has A-K or A-Q. If this player calls as well, then the big blind is drawing with three outs and nowhere near sufficient pot odds. Most players would (correctly) fold. If the big blind folds, the under-the-gun raiser has no easy decision either. He still has to worry about the player behind him.

Pot odds of 8-to-1 are seductive even for just two overcards, but hitting an ace or king on the river may not make the best hand. I could have a set or two pair, in which case the overcards are drawing dead. Or I might have a pair with a side card that duplicates one of the players' hole cards, like A-6 for example. Then the original raiser is down to three outs.

The original raiser faces a tough decision. He neither knows where he stands nor what he should do. Most players would routinely fold. That leaves the middle-position player. He's shown no strength. Chances are he's got nothing and will fold to a bet.

It's true that it is seldom a good idea to bluff several opponents. This is an exception for several reasons. First, no one has shown they have a piece of the board. Second, it's a raised pot and it's possible that everyone missed this board. Third, you posted behind the button, giving your bet credibility despite the low flop. Fourth, technically you're not bluffing but semi-bluffing because you can still make the best hand. You prefer that every one fold, but if some of your opponents decide to take a shot with over-cards or someone calls with a small pair, so be it. That's the risk you take. You can still make your flush or, depending on what comes on the river, run another bluff. A (semi-)bluff doesn't have to work every time to show a profit. Let's do the math for the turn bet. You risk $80 to win $580[94]:

---

[94] $420 (before the flop) + $160 (on the flop) = $580 ($20 from the small blind). Explanation of the following equation: You will win the $580 pot a proportion x of the time, and therefore lose your $80 investment a proportion (1-x) of the time. If we equate the two expressions, we can calculate the point where the two plays (raising and winning the pot, raising and losing a double bet) are neutral.

$$580x = 80(1-x)$$

$$580x = 80 - 80x$$

$$660x = 80$$

$$x = 0.12$$

You show an immediate profit if the bluff succeeds more than 12% of the time. The actual figure is even lower because you could win on the river.

Conclusion of the turn play: Betting is mandatory, checking is horrible.

The river paired the five and didn't complete my flush (board: 6♦-5♣-2♣-9♠-5♠). It's human nature to be disappointed when you miss your draw. But you shouldn't just give up. You have to evaluate the situation carefully and try to determine if a bluff might work.

You shouldn't just bet automatically when you miss your draw. A player who is prone to make such a play will say, "That was the only way I could win!" That appears to be plausible, but a bluff only makes sense if it has a positive expectation. Often that misguided player bets when a complete blank has fallen. This play looks so strange that he'll almost certainly get a call.

When I played the hand I feared I would make that mistake. The bet looked too suspicious. I had played passively all the way, and then I bet when the five paired the board? That didn't look right to me. But is the bet really that suspicious? Could I have any hand that would explain my bet on the river? Absolutely! I could very well have a five in my hand. Hands like A-5, K-5 or even 5-3s are not unusual for a player posting behind the button, and these hands would be consistent with my play.

I was hasty to think bluffing would be hopeless. If you look at the math, nothing had changed compared to the turn. My bluff would be profitable if my opponents folded more than 12% of the time. In this case that's absolutely realistic. Granted, the success rate of the river bet is significantly lower than for the bet on the turn, because it would (probably) only cost my opponents one big bet, and there was no further action. Even if they suspected a bluff, the decision was far from easy. The big blind and the under-the-gun player had to consider that someone behind them might overcall—or worse—raise. If both players folded it was up to the middle-position player. He couldn't beat A-Q, and so would fear that he couldn't even beat a bluff. Say he had K-Js. Even if I was bluffing, I might have a weak ace and beat him with ace-high.

Conclusion for the river play: Bluffing has positive expectation, checking it down is weak.

This example shows you impressively the value of aggression. Had I played the hand more aggressively, I almost certainly would have won it. This was a $580 pot; you have to play a long time to win that back. One reason why I misplayed that hand so badly was that I wasn't accustomed to playing stakes that high. At that time I was primarily playing $20-40 at the Mirage. When I saw that juicy $40-80 game, I couldn't resist taking a seat, though I wasn't ready yet. It's something you can observe quite often: If a player plays higher than he is used to, he plays more passively because the money involved bothers him.

Over-aggression

It's commonly accepted that you must be aggressive to win in higher-limit poker games. Even most of the passive players know that. If you lay down hand after hand because you haven't flopped anything and your opponents keeps betting into you, you start to wonder how they can hit the flop nearly every time while you do so rarely. It usually doesn't take too long until you realize that your opponent isn't luckier than you; he just bets more often.

If both players miss, the more aggressive player usually wins the pot. Though the passive player realizes that he is outplayed, he doesn't draw the correct conclusion. Instead of playing more aggressively himself, he starts calling more. That leads to even tougher decisions. If the flop missed you and you have two big cards, chances are the turn is a blank and your aggressive opponent will bet again. Now it will cost you (probably) two big bets to find out if your opponent has anything. To sum it up, the aggressive player is betting and the passive player is guessing. It goes against the nature of the passive player to turn the tables. Many players are just not able to bet or raise without having a hand they think might be best. Well, that's why they are passive players.

As important as aggression is in higher-limit games, it is not an end in itself. More aggression is not necessarily better. Aristotle says virtue is the middle between two extremes. This is true for aggression in poker, too. On one end of the spectrum is overly passive play; on the other end is over-aggression. Both are bad. You have to balance your play so that you are not too passive and not overly aggressive. If you play too passively your opponents will run over you; if you play too aggressively your opponents can profitably call you down.

A lot of players are too aggressive, especially at the higher-limit games. They have concluded that poker is all about aggression, the more the better. These players usually do well against passive opposition, but they fail against good and attentive players.

Here is a type of hand that comes up quite often in higher-limit games. A middle-position player raises and everyone folds around to the big blind, who calls. The flop comes something like A-5-2 rainbow. The big blind bets, the original raiser raises again, the big blind reraises and the opponent makes it four bets. The big blind folds, turning over A-J. The winner proudly shows his A-K. Now, who played the hand better? The big blind flopped top pair but he had to worry about being out-kicked. It cost him three small bets to find out that his hand was no good. He got away from it quite cheaply. On the other hand the pre-flop raiser had gotten the best situation he could hope for: both players flopped top pair but he had the better kicker. In this case a good, balanced player should make more than three small bets.

Let's see how the hand likely progresses when the pre-flop raiser plays differently. On the flop he just calls instead of raising. Now the big blind, thinking his hand might be best, bets the turn. The middle-position player calls again. On the river the big blind will get suspicious because the pre-flop raiser called the flop and turn bets, so he checks. Time for the A-K to collect another big bet. The big blind will most likely not fold to his raise because he showed weakness by checking, he can now close the action by calling and he has good pot odds.

This time the A-K made five small bets instead of three by playing the hand less aggressively. Of course, that's not the only way the pre-flop raiser can play the hand. If he knows the big blind is the kind of player who likes to find out where he stands on the flop, he can take advantage of that knowledge. In this case he raises the big blind on the flop but only calls the reraise. This way he denies the big blind the information he was looking for, namely whether his hand is any good. The big blind now knows that his opponent has some hand, but he can't be sure if he is behind or not. Being cautious, he will probably check the turn and river but most likely not fold to a bet. In this case the player holding A-K can even win seven small bets.

Some people might object that by playing aggressively on the flop you win three small bets for sure whereas by keeping the big blind in the pot you risk being outdrawn. That's not the correct way to judge the situation, for two reasons. First, taking risks is part of playing poker. As long as the risk-reward ratio is positive, you should go for it. The out-kicked player has only three outs to win. The chance to gain two (or more) small bets is well worth the risk of being outdrawn. Second, the big blind might actually have the best hand. He could have a set or two pair with a hand like A-5s. In this case the big blind will cap the flop and bet the turn and river. It's very unlikely that A-K can get away from his top pair, top kicker, resulting in a loss of nine big bets!

The conclusion here is obvious. By playing too aggressively, you win less if your hand is best and you lose more if it's not. That means you should not play aggressively when you are either way ahead or way behind. You don't want to lose your opponent if you're ahead, and you want to limit your losses if you're behind.

Aggressive play is also wrong when you suspect your opponent is bluffing. A classic example where both of these cases came together was the hand Mason Malmuth played (hand 6/75, p. 128). His opponent was either way ahead, way behind or bluffing. In neither case is aggressive play appropriate. That's why Mason just check-called the hand.

Here is another variation of overly aggressive play that you see all the time these days, at least in middle-limit games. A player open-raises in early position with a solid hand and a player behind him makes it three bets with a small pair. This play is quite common because every player immediately sees the logic behind it. The reasoning goes like this: A typical raiser is more likely to have two high cards than a pocket pair. A pair, however, is a favorite against any two overcards, even A-K[95]. By raising, you stand an excellent chance to isolate the original raiser and play the

---

[95] This statement is not totally accurate. E.g., J♦-10♦ is a slight favorite against 3♣-3♠.

hand heads-up. If this succeeds, the player with the small pair must have the best of it because he is a favorite, and has position as well.

It's easy to see the fallacy behind this concept[96]. The player who makes the bold three-betting play is either a very small favorite (pair vs. two over-cards) or a big underdog (pair vs. overpair). Having position is not enough to overcome that disadvantage, and the post-flop play can get rather tricky. So the proper play is to muck the small pair.

Let me reiterate what I said at the beginning of this chapter. Aggression is an important tool in the arsenal of a successful player. If you want to excel in middle-limit poker games, you have to be aggressive. But always consider all possibilities. In the long run, it's not the most aggressive player who wins the most money, but the player who makes the best decisions.

---

[96] The assumption is that the original raiser opens with solid holdings. If this is not true, then three-betting with middle or small pairs can be reasonable. For instance, the cutoff opens the pot with a raise. You pick up 6-6 on the button. There is nothing wrong with reraising here. Given the wide range of hands the raiser might hold, you could be a significant favorite, e. g., if he holds A♦-3♦ or 7♥-6♥.

Chapter 7

Bluffing

Most people who know poker primarily from the movies think poker is all about bluffing. The TV coverage of the World Poker Tour and World Series of Poker reinforces that impression. The sessions aired are usually at the end of the tournament when the blinds and antes are high and many players are short-stacked. That (correctly) leads to looser play and more bluffing. And of course, the episodes are heavily edited, and tend to show the most interesting hands, and bluffs are what the viewers love. But bluffing is just one aspect of the game, and most often not the most important one. Nonetheless, bluffing is what makes poker unique. There is no other game where you can win with the worst hand without your opponent knowing it.

Bluffing and game type

An entire book has been written on the subject of bluffing[97]. The author's examples are quite good, but I was disappointed that he didn't discuss the effect of the game type on the value of bluffing. There are at least three dimensions that alter the value of bluffing dramatically: game form, game structure and limit.

---

[97] Matt Lessinger, *The Book of Bluffs: How to Bluff and Win at Poker*, 2005.

The importance of bluffing is not the same in all forms of poker. For instance, bluffing has more value in hold'em and in stud than in Omaha hi-low. The value of bluffing in Omaha hi-low is much less because the two-way nature of the game makes it more difficult to put a player on a hand. Additionally, each player has four cards that make six hand combinations compared to one in hold'em. The effect of these multiple combinations is that if the board doesn't help you, it's likely to have helped your opponent(s), hence a bluff might not be effective. That doesn't mean you can't bluff in Omaha hi-low, but it's just not as important as in hold'em or stud.

The structure of each game plays an important role, too. You are limited to a fixed bet size in limit poker, so the pot odds your opponent gets if you bluff are only affected by the pot size. If the pot contains nine big bets and you bluff, then your opponent gets 10-to-1 pot odds. With pot odds like that, your opponent can sensibly call with a lot of hands. In pot-limit you can significantly decrease the pot odds you give your opponents. If you raise the maximum (the pot), your opponent has pot odds of 2-to-1 regardless of the original pot size. In no-limit you can decrease the pot odds even further as long as you and your opponents have enough money on the table. The ability to bet more in relation to the pot increases your risk, with the benefit that your success rate goes up. Take an extreme example: First hand at the World Series of Poker main event. The blinds are $25-50, you are dealt 7-2 offsuit and go all-in for $10,000. If nobody has A-A, you will most likely win the pot. Who wants to chance elimination on the first hand?

Another factor that influences the value of bluffing is the limit[98]. Low-limit players tend to play too many hands and go too far with them. Pots are contested by multiple players and the best hand usually wins at the showdown. Obviously, if you usually have to come up with the best hand there is not much room to bluff. Indeed, I think most low-limit players would do better if they never bluffed. A game like $3-6 can be beaten easily without ever bluffing, simply by employing good, solid play. Bluffing opportunities may arise in low-limit games, but these are rare. I remember betting the river in a $3-6 hold'em game and one player called who could barely beat the board. He was fully aware that he couldn't win; he just wanted to

---

[98] Actually it's not the limit but the way the players typically play at the different limits. But because the play in low-limit games is usually quite different from middle- and high-limit, it makes sense for reasons of simplicity to stick to that term.

see what I had! When people are calling even out of curiosity, it's obvious that bluffing is not a productive tactic.

Are you really bluffing?

Most middle-limit players bluff less often than they think. Let's look at two examples that arise in middle-limit hold'em play all the time:

- ♠ Example 1: You raise in middle position with 9-9 and only the big blind calls. The flop comes K-Q-4 rainbow. The big blind checks, you bet and the big blind folds.

- ♠ Example 2: All hands fold to the button, who raises. The small blind folds and you hold A♥-J♥ in the big blind. You assume your hand is a favorite against the range of hands the button might be holding, so you raise. The button calls and the flop is 8-6-8 rainbow. You bet and the button folds.

In the first example it looked like a pretty bad flop because the two overcards appeared to be very dangerous. A typical low-limit player might have checked here, but even a below-average middle-limit player would bet. Without a doubt, the bet is mandatory. So the question is not what to do but why you are doing it.

To say that with this ugly board you bet as a bluff exhibits a serious lack of understanding. Bluffing means that you bet to make a better hand fold. What better hand could you make fold in this situation? With a set or two pair, the big blind would raise or slowplay. There is no way he would lay down top pair, even with a bad kicker like K-2, and it's highly unlikely he would fold a pair of queens heads-up. But these are the only hands that could beat your pair of nines. In the example, the big blind folded to your flop bet and the only logical deduction is that you had him beat. Any bet here was a value bet, and the idea to bluff makes absolutely no sense. When the big blind checked on the flop, you had to assume you had the best hand, and you had to bet because you couldn't afford to give a free card. You bet to protect your hand.

Now, the second example should be clear, too. You reraised pre-flop because you thought you had the best hand. There is nothing wrong with that. You can't know for sure, but your opponent just called, which would tend to confirm your assumption. Why should you change your mind with a flop of 8-6-8 rainbow? Not many hands trailed you before the flop and then beat you afterwards. You bet the flop because you thought you still had the best hand and didn't want to give a free card. Your opponent's fold confirmed your assumption. As in the first example, you almost certainly didn't make a better hand fold. With this board every button player would have called with a pocket pair, even a small one. The only non-pair hands that beat you were A-K and A-Q. Heads-up, most players with these hands would take at least another card off.

You were relieved in both cases when your opponent folded because the flop was not favorable for your hand, but that doesn't mean you were bluffing. You were actually betting for value.

In the above examples my intention was only to show that players often think they are bluffing when they are not. You might ask what difference it makes if you are bluffing or value-betting when the outcome is the same. If you don't have a clear understanding about bluffing, then this confusion can lead to disaster in other situations. You often observe this when someone without a proper understanding of bluffing plays A-K. A typical hand might go like this: The player with A-K raises and gets one caller. He bets the flop and the turn, though his hand hasn't improved, and his opponent calls both times. Another blank comes on the river. Now the player with A-K is very frustrated. He waited so long for a premium hand, and now he can't hit anything. He figures that having been called all the way to the river, he's probably second-best. So he makes a desperation bet, thinking he has to bluff to win the hand. If his opponent folds, this player thinks he's pulled off a successful bluff; otherwise he bemoans his bad luck.

What kind of bet is the player with A-K making at the end? He thinks he is bluffing (what else can he be thinking?) but what better hands can he make fold? If someone called with one pair on the turn, he will call at the end as well. Everyone knows that one pair heads-up is a decent holding, especially if there is no ace or king out. The most likely hand a raiser is put on is A-K. That means the river bet can't be a bluff because the chances a better hand will fold are close to nil. Contrary to the two flop examples above, it can't be a value bet either. What worse hand can call? Once in a blue moon someone with A-Q or A-J may call, but usually when A-K gets called it's by a better hand. The bet at the end is neither a bluff nor a value bet; it's just a bad bet. Most players don't understand that an unimproved A-K heads-up at the end is a bad bluffing hand but a good bluff-catching hand!

Successful bluffing

Most people bluff because they were drawing at something, couldn't make their hand, look at the big pot and bet, thinking this is the only way they can win. Plays like this only rarely succeed because it looks odd when someone who only check-called suddenly bets the river after a blank has fallen.

For example, a player with J♠-10♠ calls in the big blind after a middle-position player has raised. The flop comes K♠-7♦-2♠.

The big blind checks, the raiser bets and the big blind calls. The turn is Q♣. The big blind check-calls again. The river brings 3♥. The big blind had high hopes. The flop gave him a flush draw, and the turn added another six outs before the river card shattered his hopes.

He looks at the pot. There is no way his jack-high can win the 5.25 big bets in the middle, and it would only cost a big bet to take a shot at the pot. The risk-reward ratio looks reasonable, so he bets. But what is the big blind trying to represent? Pocket treys? Possible (if you play long enough you've seen it all) but highly unlikely. K-3? Looks more logical, but the problem remains that not many hands make sense. As a matter of fact, the bet looks suspicious enough that the original raiser will call with a lot of hands, even hands like 9-9 or 7-7 that he would have folded on the turn had the big blind played better.

The bluff in this spot is doomed because it doesn't look plausible. On the other hand, a bluff that tells a believable story has a good chance of success. Here is an example.

I was playing in a $30-60 game at the Bellagio. A loose-aggressive player raised the pot in second position. It was folded to me. I held K♠-Q♠ in the cutoff seat. It's not my habit to call a raise with K-Qs, but folding was out of the question, given the wide range of hands my opponent could hold.

Raising looked attractive. In all likelihood that would make the pot heads-up, ensuring me position, and I might even have the best hand. This would have given me the initiative, something you usually want to have. But this player was not afraid to splash his chips around, and the last thing you want is to be check-raised with K-Q when you don't have anything. So I planned to just call and let him bet. If I got help from the board I would just call and let him bluff his money off. Otherwise I would turn the tables and raise him with air on the turn.

That left the players behind me. All of them were pretty tight, so I took the risk and called. The button and the small blind folded, but the big blind called. The player in the big blind was Alan, probably the best middle-limit player in Vegas and usually not one you want to have involved in a hand with you. I would have preferred that he fold, but his call wasn't a disaster. I still had position and probably the best hand, and the presence of such a strong player would prevent the loose-aggressive player from getting too fancy. The flop came 8♣-J♠-3♣.

Alan checked and the other player bet as expected. The flop was no help, but a lot of good cards could come on the turn. A king or queen would give me top pair and probably the best hand, any spade would give me a flush draw, any ten an open-ended straight draw and any nine or ace at least a gutshot. If Alan called on the flop, I intended to raise if I got help on the turn. I called and Alan called as well. The turn was 10♦. Interestingly, Alan now bet out. The loose-aggressive player looked confused, and then called. My original plan was to raise when the ten came, but that was based on the assumption that Alan checked and the other player bet. In that case Alan would probably be forced to fold and the other player would have a tough call.

Now, with two players already in for one bet it was very unlikely that both of them would fold. Without the chance to win immediately, raising lost most of its value. Time to reassess. I had six nut outs, two outs that would very likely make me a winner, and six outs that might or might not be good[99]. With pot odds of 6.75-to-1, I had a call.

The river brought 5♣. Alan checked. The loose aggressive player grabbed six chips, intending to bet, then looked at me and finally checked. When

---

[99] Nut outs: A♠, A♦, A♥, 9♠, 9♦, 9♥; likely winners: A♣, 9♣; additional outs: K♣, K♥, K♦, Q♣, Q♥, Q♦.

the 5♣ came I was done with the hand, but the two checks opened new prospects. I had to act fast, and fortunately the situation was easy to analyze.

Alan had bet on the turn when the 10♦ came, which makes it likely that he had a pair of tens. He knew it was unlikely that the original raiser had a jack, and I couldn't have one because I would have raised the flop to protect my hand. He figured his pair of tens might be good, and so he bet it. That nobody raised reinforced his suspicion. He would have bet again at the end had a blank fallen, but the flush card forced him to check. So I believed that Alan had a pair of tens and the other player had a hand that couldn't beat second pair.

But could I represent a flush? I had played the hand passively all the way to the river, just as most players would play a flush draw. A bet would be consistent with that. Would Alan fold? If we were heads-up, probably not, but here he had to deal with an unpredictable player behind him. This player had threatened to bet the river and then recoiled from it. My read was that this player was weak, intended to bluff and then realized that he couldn't bluff both of us, but I wasn't sure how Alan judged the situation. I thought a bluff might work, so I bet the river. Alan thought for about three seconds (which is long for him, as he usually acts extremely quickly) and then folded. The loose aggressive player pondered for a while. If he wasn't putting on an act worthy of Hollywood, he wasn't as weak as I thought. He had something, though probably not much. I put him on a small pair or ace-high. Weak, but enough to take down the pot. Finally, he folded.

The art of bluffing has nothing to do with shoving in your chips thinking you have no other way of winning, holding your breath, crossing your fingers and hoping for the best. Successful bluffing is a two-step process. First, you have to determine your opponent's strength. If it's obvious he has a relatively strong hand, then your chances to pull off a bluff drop close to nothing.

Let's say in a multiway pot a player is calling all the way. At the turn, after a third flush card has fallen, he suddenly bets into the whole field. Everyone folds to you. You have the ace of the possible flush suit and call, hoping for another flush card. At the end the board pairs. Bluffing to represent a full house is completely pointless. Your opponent will fear that you have filled up, but he will never fold. In limit you can only bet one big bet at the end, and that's not enough to make your opponent lay down a flush. Second, you have to consider how your bluff looks to your opponent. You have to replay the hand in your mind and see if any hands that threaten your opponent are consistent with the play of the hand. A bluff must be believable; nobody likes to lay down a hand at the end. Most people look for a reason to call; give them a reason to fold!

In the example above, I had a plan for the hand before I saw the board. I couldn't act on that plan because Alan's call changed the situation. But sometimes you know you will play your hand in a certain fashion even before you have seen your hole cards. The prerequisite is that you know exactly how the hand will develop. This is rare, but it happens. Here is an example. We were playing in a shorthanded $30-60 game when a former world champion, obviously short on money, sat down. When players who usually play high-limit sit down in a middle-limit game, they like short-handed games, because they think that middle-limit players have no clue about shorthanded play and are therefore easy pickings.

I was sitting two spots to the left of "Chuck", as we will call the world champion, which meant every time he had the button I was in the big blind. The first time this scenario came up it was folded to Chuck, who lost no time raising. The small blind reraised and I folded. The small blind bet all the way and the button called him down. At the showdown the small blind showed A-Q and Chuck, holding 10-4, took down the pot with a pair of fours. The next time it was folded to Chuck on the button, he raised again, the small blind folded and I called. I checked the flop, he bet and I called. I bet the turn and Chuck folded. This scenario played out five times in a row. You might have noticed that I didn't identify any of the cards. This is because I knew in advance what I would do, regardless of the cards.

The first hand Chuck had played from the button gave me all the information I needed. If he raised with 10-4, he would raise with any two cards. To me that meant that I would never give up the big blind. I was getting odds of 11-to-3, and no hand is that much of an underdog against random cards.

I had to devise a way to exploit his loose play. First is the math aspect. Two-thirds of the time he hits nothing. The figures are even worse because if you play any two cards, even if you hit your hand, it is often so weak that you have a hard time calling if someone puts pressure on you. Would you really call with J-3 when the board shows Q-3-9-A and your opponent bets into you? Second, how could I exploit the fact that he holds nothing most of the time? An aggressive player like Chuck would bet the flop and turn every time I showed weakness by checking.

My first idea was to raise him on the flop and then to bet the turn. To an average player this looks like a powerful play that puts a lot of pressure on your opponent, but a high-limit player interprets this move more as a sign that a weak opponent is trying to move him off the pot. Without a doubt, a player of Chuck's caliber was capable of reraising me on the flop or turn with nothing, which would put me in an awkward position.

My second idea was to call the flop and check-raise the turn. This is more likely to succeed and is a lot easier to play. If he folds to the turn check-raise, I take the pot, if he reraises, I fold (unless by pure chance I hold a strong hand). It could only get tricky if he called the reraise. The drawback is that it costs me 2.5 big bets (not counting my initial call before the flop) to find out if it works, maybe even more, because if he calls my turn raise I might be tempted to bluff on the end.

I finally decided to check-call the flop and bet the turn. It was a somewhat unusual play, which could confuse him. The beauty is that weak players play exactly like that. They call when drawing or when they are unsure if they are ahead. Then, when their hand has significantly improved, they start betting. I hoped that mimicking that play would make it appear that I'd made a strong hand at the turn. Take any flop at all: J-5-3 rainbow. I check, he bets, I call. The turn is a king. What does my turn bet look like to my opponent? He most likely assumes that I hit the king or made two pair, holding K-5, for example. That play looks even stronger than the check-raise on the turn, and it only costs me 1.5 big bets!

It worked, but some words of caution are in order. First, pulling off that play five times straight was just pure luck. Obviously, Chuck never hit any-thing. Second, I was facing an excellent player who, sooner or later, would realize what I was doing and would start to bluff-reraise me on the turn. Fortunately, the game broke up before that happened. Third, I was willing to milk the cow as long as I could, because this guy rarely plays as low as $30-60. I would use the same strategy against a regular player in my game, but I would disguise it by playing differently about half the time. You have to mix up your play to protect yourself from counterstrategies.

Catching bluffs

Bluffing and bluff-catching are two sides of the same coin. If you bluff, you hope your bet convinces your opponent to fold. If you have a mediocre hand and someone bets into you, you must try to find out if your opponent has the strong hand he represents, or if he might be bluffing. Let's look at an example.

In a $30-60 game Nadine, a solid regular, opened the pot with a raise from under the gun. Sitting right behind her, I made it three bets, everyone else folded and Nadine called. The flop came 9♥-2♥-9♣. Surprisingly Nadine bet out and I called. Turn: Q♦. She bet again and I called. River: Q♠ (board: 9♥-2♥-9♣-Q♦-Q♠). With little hesitation, Nadine bet out.

Question: What is my play?

I haven't identified my hand, but it's of no importance. Unless Nadine has quad nines or has backed fortuitously into a full house, her bet must be a bluff, and therefore raising is generally the preferred response[100]. Say I hold A-K. The correct play is to raise. Raising is superior to calling because it prevents splitting the pot should Nadine have a hand like A♥-10♥.

Let's take a closer look at the hand. When Nadine didn't reraise me before the flop, I knew she didn't have aces or kings. She is quite straightforward in this regard, and would have promptly reraised with either of these hands. The flop bet was quite unusual. Basically she was telling me one of three things:

a) I have a nine

b) I have a pair

c) I have a flush draw

Case a) is very unlikely. With trip nines you know you have the best hand, and if you check with this flop, it's nearly certain that a player who made it three bets pre-flop will bet. Most players would check-raise the flop or wait for the turn here.

---

[100] The exception is if you have something to show down like 10-10. In this case you achieve nothing by raising. If Nadine is bluffing, she will fold to your raise, if she has a nine or queen, she will call or raise, in which case you lose an additional big bet.

Much more likely is case b). Say Nadine has 10-10 or 8-8. There is a decent chance her hand is best. Her bet is not meant to make me fold. Nadine knows that I'm not going to fold after I made it three bets with a flop like this. The bet is first for value (chances are she has the best hand) and second, to set herself up to win the pot on the turn. In case I don't have a pair and don't improve on the turn, a turn bet will most likely take it down.

Pushing the flush draw, case c), is the third possibility. Nadine knows that if she plays the flush draw passively, she can only win if her hand improves. However, if she plays aggressively, especially with a flop like that, there is a good chance that she can win the pot on the turn without making her hand. Again, in this case the flop bet is in preparation to win the pot on the turn.

Now we take these three possible cases to the river and examine how the last two board cards affect them. The board was 9♥-2♥-9♣-Q♦-Q♠.

In case a) we assume Nadine has trip nines. Would she bet at the end knowing that every queen beats her? Perhaps. But even good players are usually not prepared for every scenario when a new board card arrives. Certainly, someone who bets this turn with trip nines intends to bet the river as well. But the queen affects her hand considerably.

A solid player like Nadine might now think: "There was a queen on the turn but my opponent didn't raise me, therefore it's unlikely that the second queen hurts me," leading her to conclude that her hand is probably still best. The second queen on the end would prompt most players with a nine to reassess the situation, and that takes time. But Nadine bet without hesitation. The only hand that would explain this would be quad nines. If we look at our flop and river analysis for case a) then, it is extremely unlikely that Nadine has nines full (or quad nines).

In case b) we must differentiate between a pair that actually plays and a pair below the two pair on board. In the first case Nadine holds J-J or 10-10[101]. With any of these pairs there is a good chance to have the best hand, which doesn't mean that you want to bet the hand. First, what lesser hands can call your bet? Maybe nines or tens if you have J-J but then it gets tough to find additional hands. Second, you are in an awkward position if

---

[101] We have already excluded A-A and K-K. Q-Q is not possible because I had a queen in my hands; see below.

raised. Third, if you check and your opponent bets, you have a good calling hand. A solid player like Nadine is not going to bet J-J or 10-10 here.

Things get interesting if Nadine holds a pair lower than nines. In this case the second queen on the end counterfeited her hand. Now, from her perspective, betting makes sense because that's the only way she can win.

In case c), the flush hasn't come. Again, betting makes sense because only a bet gives her a chance to win the hand.

Notice two things here. A bet most likely means a counterfeited pair or a busted flush draw. Conclusion: With a high degree of certainty, Nadine is bluffing. Second, bluffing seems natural from her perspective, since she was betting all the way. Of course, there is a small possibility that Nadine holds a queen and backed into the top full house by pure chance.

It's time to reveal the hands. I had A♦-Q♥. The queen of hearts is not unimportant because it prevented Nadine from making a full house with a flush draw (with a hand like K♥-Q♥). Most readers will probably find my plays (I called the flop and the turn and raised the river) quite unusual and would have either raised on the flop or the turn, therefore I will give you the reasons behind my plays.

When Nadine bet into me on the flop, I immediately put her on a pair, probably J-J to 6-6. Having played countless hours with this nice, elderly lady helped me to understand her game. With trips or even quads she would not lead out, but would instead try to trap me. I have seen her play flush draws strongly, but only against a raiser, not a reraiser. That led me to believe she had a pocket pair.

Now the question was how to proceed. The standard play is to raise on the flop, hoping to see the turn and river cards cheaply. I didn't like that play for two reasons. First, there was no way Nadine would fold to my raise. She knew that my raise was far more likely to indicate two high cards than A-A or K-K. Second, I would likely need to improve to win. The idea behind the flop raise is that your opponent will check the turn, giving you a free look at the river card if you don't improve. But if the play works, which means Nadine checks the turn, then I'm conceding the pot if the river card doesn't help me. The only card that gave me a realistic bluffing opportunity was a king at the end. And I wasn't even sure I'd get a free river card. Nadine would surely bet again on the turn if a blank fell, in which case I had just paid double for the turn card.

Since I had a pretty good idea what she had, I wanted to win the hand even without improvement. My plan was to call her flop bet and raise her on the turn (I knew Nadine would bet again on the turn if no ace showed up), representing a big pair.

I had to change the plan after I hit one of my hole cards on the turn. The original idea was to win the pot without improvement. With a queen on the board I was certain that I had the best hand, and my priority changed from winning the pot to extracting as much money as possible from Nadine.

This is an important concept. Limit hold'em is not about winning pots but minimizing losses when you are beat and maximizing winnings when you're on top.

Nadine bet out as expected. Again, the obvious play was to raise. Let's compare raising to calling, assuming Nadine had a flush draw. (I didn't put her on a flush draw, but you have to consider the possibilities.) If I raised, she would call with her draw. If she didn't make her flush, she was done with the hand and I would win no more. If the flush card came on the end, she would bet and I would call (the pot is too big to take any chances). So, by raising I would either win two or lose three big bets. If I just called the turn bet, Nadine would bet the river no matter what came (as either a bluff or a value bet), so I would either win or lose two big bets.

Conclusion: I was better off calling than raising against a flush draw.

If Nadine held a pair and I raised the turn, there was a high probability that she would fold. The queen was an overcard to her pair and it would now cost her two big bets to find out if I was (semi-)bluffing. If she folded, then I would win the pot immediately and she couldn't draw out on me on the river. But I wouldn't win any more money. That's why it's better to just call.

If I called the turn, Nadine wouldn't bet the river but she would call a river bet, because the pot was too big and there were some legitimate hands she could beat, such as A-K. But there were two exceptions. She would bet out on the river if she hit her hand (two outs) or if her hand was counter-feited[102]. In the first case she had to bet because she couldn't count on me to bet the river and give her a chance to check-raise. In the second case she had to bluff because that was the only way that she could win the hand.

---

[102] This is not possible if she has J-J or T-T. Any queen counterfeits her hand if she has a pair lower than nines.

Just calling the turn involves some risk, but it's well worth it. Two times I lose the whole pot and 44 times I win an additional big bet.

Here is what really happened. The queen at the end gave me queens full. Nadine bet, I raised and she showed me pocket sevens.

Unfortunately, it's not always so easy to determine if someone is bluffing. First you must look at your opponent's past action to see if his bet makes sense; can he have what he is trying to represent? Usually that is the case. The next step is to see if there are any missed hands (straight or flush draws, high cards like A-K) that your opponent would have played the same way. If this is the case, you have to ask yourself how often your opponent bluffs. Most players bluff either too often or too seldom. If your opponent likes to bluff, then this should tip you toward calling, and vice versa.

The next thing to consider is the size of the pot. The smaller the pot, the more often you have to be correct to make calling worthwhile. The strength of your hand also plays a role. You don't want to make a seemingly great call, only to realize that your opponent's bluff beats your calling hand. I once saw a player inform the whole table that his opponent was bluffing, which was why he called with queen-high. That was a great read. Unfortunately, his opponent won the pot with king-high!

Let's say you have 6♥-5♥ and missed your flush draw. Your lone opponent bets into you on the river. You suspect a bluff, but with six-high you can't even beat that. Your play here is to raise. But don't make these moves routinely. It costs you twice as much as a call, so you should be fairly confident that your opponent is weak. There is one exception. Some players immediately muck their cards when they're caught bluffing. Against this type of player you can even call with six-high. If he was bluffing, he'll throw his hand away. If he shows his hand, you will muck your hand without showing.

Though you use objective criteria to find out if your opponent is bluffing, in the end your decision is mostly subjective. You have to develop a feel for the situation, and the better your feel, the better you will do.

Bluff-raising

Many years ago I was playing in a $20-40 game at the Mirage. At the end the board was K-Q-7-2-K. I had been betting all the way. I bet again and my lone opponent raised. I reraised him, he made it four bets and I raised again. My opponent folded quickly. That was the only time someone bluff-raised me not only once but twice. It was bad timing by my opponent because I was holding the nuts (K-Q) and would have never laid down my hand at the end against this overly aggressive player in any case.

My opponent had marked me as a tight player and thought I would be an easy target for a bluff. This is a common misconception that you even see in print. Tight just means that a player is selective about the hands he plays; it does not imply anything about how often he would fold to a bluff. This is true for loose players as well. You might ask how you can bluff a player who calls too much. Well, even most loose players eventually give up if they don't hit their hand. These players call to make a certain hand, and they often give up if they don't make it. And some loose players have pretty high calling standards at the end.

Back to bluff-raising. Though my opponent above carried it too far, bluff-raising is a valid play if employed sparingly; appropriate opportunities rarely arise. You have to be pretty sure your opponent is bluffing, because most people who bet for value habitually call for just one extra bet, especially heads-up. It's a high-risk play; you invest two bets while your opponent only has to call one bet to see the showdown. Knowing your opponent is critical, as is having a solid image.

I don't bluff much on the river; I prefer to do my bluffing on the turn. This puts more pressure on my opponent than waiting for the river to make my play. If you bet or raise as a bluff at the river, it only costs your opponent one big bet to see if he's the winner. When you bluff at the turn your opponent knows it will very likely cost him two big bets before it's over. It's even possible to bluff-raise at the turn, as demonstrated in the hand I played against Pizza Mike (3/35). Again, these opportunities don't come up often.

A lot more important than pure bluffs is bluffing when you have outs. David Sklansky coined the term semi-bluffing for that. Semi-bluffing simply means that you are betting or raising in the hope that your opponent(s) will fold immediately. If they call, you have outs so that your hand can improve to win the pot. Obviously, this is only possible if there are cards to come.

Let's look at an example we've already discussed. A middle-position player raises and the big blind calls with J♠-10♠. The flop is K♠-7♦-2♠. The big blind check-calls. The turn is the Q♣. In our example the big blind check-called again. This is a poor play. With that many outs, the big blind should bet himself or, if he is reasonably sure the other player will bet, raise to give the original raiser a chance to fold. The way the big blind plays, he can only win if he makes his hand, but he's an underdog to do so.

How often does the original raiser have to fold to make that play profitable? If the big blind bets the turn, he invests $60 to win $200.

$$200x = 60(1-x)$$
$$200x = 60-60x$$
$$260x = 60$$
$$x = 0.23$$

The big blind shows an immediate profit if the original raiser folds more than 23% of the time. The numbers change slightly if the big blind check-raises on the turn.

$$260x = 120(1-x)$$
$$260x = 120-120x$$
$$380x = 120$$
$$x = 0.32$$

At first it appears that betting out is the better play because you invest less and it takes fewer folds to see a profit. But your opponent will fold more often to a check-raise, which can make up for the play's higher cost[103]. I would go for the check-raise if I were reasonably sure my opponent would

---

[103] Don't confuse this statement with what I said about my play against the former world champion above. I stated that a bet at the turn might look stronger to him than a check-raise. That was a completely different situation. Basically it was two random hands against each other and my opponent was an experienced short-handed high-limit player.

bet regardless of what he had. Remember that the calculated numbers are for an immediate profit, and are therefore too high. In our example the big blind has up to 15 outs, should his opponent call.

How a player reacts to a raise is an important piece of information. I always observe what a player does when he's raised. I'm not talking about tells, but simply whether he folds or not. Some players never fold to a raise. It's crucial to identify them because it's futile to (semi-)bluff-raise them. In the above example you should definitely bet because he might fold, whereas check-raising is counterproductive.

Semi-bluffing becomes even more important at higher limits. The value of bluffing and semi-bluffing goes down in low-limit games in which many players see the flop and call often. Contrast this to middle- and high-limit games that are often shorthanded after the flop, and you can see how important semi-bluffing becomes. The ability to semi-bluff effectively is one of the prime differences between winners and losers or break-even players at the middle limits.

Showing your hand

Should you show your hand after you've run a successful bluff? Many pros won't show their hand. You could hold a pistol to Alan's head and he would tell you, "You have to pay to see my hand." This way you never give away information about your hand for free. I'm not as rigid. I usually don't show my hand if I don't have to, but there are two exceptions. If a bad player is at the table who just wants to have a good time and shows me his hands all the time, I will satisfy his curiosity should he ask to see my hand. I'm doing this as a courtesy, and quite frankly I think it's good business. You want the contributors to be happy. Of course, I would only expose my hand if I was pretty sure I had the best hand anyway. Never would I show a bluff. I have never done so, nor would I in that case.

The second exception is when I think I might achieve something by showing my hand. For example, if I raised three times from the button and the big blind folded every time, and then I ran the same play with A-K, I might show him my hand to encourage him to keep folding. This is not the most sophisticated move, and it only works against occasional players. Don't do it against good and attentive opponents, because they will see through it.

The following hand occurred long ago in a $10-20 game at the Mirage. It was folded to the button who raised. The small blind folded and I had J♥-9♥ in the big blind, no hand to brag about, but strong enough to call a button raise. The flop came A-K-J rainbow. I didn't like the overcards, but since I had a piece of the flop, I bet. The button raised me instantly. Now I was in a tough spot. Should my opponent have an ace or king my five-outer wasn't enough to make calling profitable. The button seemed to be loose-aggressive, so I wasn't convinced he had me beat. I took another card off. The turn was the worst card I could get, a queen (board: A-K-J-Q). Now I couldn't beat any ace, king, queen or ten. I checked, and folded to his bet. Without saying a word, the button threw his hand, face-up, in the middle of the table. He had 3♣-2♦.

Some players seek respect. He had completely outplayed me but nobody would see his great play. By showing his hand he was saying, "Hey, look how good I am!" I didn't take it personally. He had played the hand fearlessly. I thought he'd made a mistake to show his cards because it would affect his future play and I might take advantage of that.

The same thing happened on the very next round. It was folded to him on the button. He looked at his hand, looked at me, hesitated and finally called. The small blind folded and I looked at my hand: K-Q. How should I react to the button's call, a strange play, especially from a loose-aggressive player? I figured he was either trying to trap with a monster hand like A-A or K-K, or he had a hand that he thought was just good enough to play. He didn't raise because he thought after the last hand that I would call anyway. That would mean he wasn't very strong. I opted for the latter, which was mathematically more likely.

What should I do with my K-Q? I decided to raise for two reasons. I was probably ahead and I wouldn't give away information about my hand because he expected me to raise. The flop came king-high. I bet. My opponent looked to be unsure about what to do. After pondering, he finally called. To make a long story short, nothing special came on the turn and river. I bet both times and he called me down. My pair of kings was good and I was rewarded with the pot. I didn't see his hand, but assumed it was a small pocket pair, a small split pair or ace-high. He couldn't get away from his hand because he thought I was trying to turn the tables on him. Showing his bluff had indeed influenced his play. First, he just called from the button instead of raising, which would have been the proper play. Second, he couldn't get away from his hand when it was pretty obvious it wasn't good.

The conclusion is clear. If your play is on the loose-aggressive side, you should never show your bluffs. It might affect your play, and people will call you down more often, which is not good, given your playing style. On the other hand, if you only bluff rarely and don't get enough action, then showing a bluff occasionally could prove advantageous.

Should you lose money on bluffing?

Let me close this chapter with a discussion of the theory that you should actually lose money by bluffing. Some poker theorists advocate that you should look at your bluffs as necessary expenses to create a loose and wild image, which enables you to cash in by playing solid hands. The idea is to make some crazy bluffs at the beginning of a session so that you get paid off for your solid hands later. Basically this means that you lose money on your bluffs but are overcompensated by the fact that you win more with your legitimate hands. I believe Mike Caro was the first to state that theory, and it still haunts poker literature.

Assuming the concept is valid, it could only work against complete strangers. But if you play regularly in a casino, half the players at the table are probably common faces, and you're not going to fool them for long. The other half of the table might be tourists or drop-ins. These players often don't play very long, and after an hour you might be looking at some new faces, and they didn't see your reckless bluffs. All they see is a tight player, which means you spent your money without getting the desired effect.

Furthermore, you never know if the loose image you have created is really beneficial later. Playing solid starting hands doesn't guarantee you'll make any big hands after the flop. A (semi-)bluff might succeed with a tight image, which makes your loose image counterproductive. The loose-early-tight-later concept might have some value in no-limit where you can bluff for less money and possibly win the whole stack of an occasional player, but it doesn't work in limit play where the costs of your loose play are simply too high and the benefits too uncertain.

Instead of trying to create a certain image, you should let the flow of the hands dictate how to proceed. For example, if you're caught bluffing several times at the beginning of a session, cut back on your bluffs and value-bet more. Or, if you haven't played many hands for some time, start bluffing more to exploit your extremely tight image.

My position is clear: Bluffing, like any other play, should yield a long-term profit. If you don't make money by bluffing, you either bluff too much or choose the wrong spots.

Chapter 8

Tells

If a player faces a tough decision in a televised game, the commentator will often mention the he's looking for a tell, i.e., a mannerism that might indicate the strength of a player's hand. In my opinion, tells are grossly overrated. Here's why.

The reference work on tells is by Mike Caro[104]. I still remember, shortly after I read that book, playing in a $3-6 hold'em game at the Mirage. In first position I raised with A♠-A♦ and got six callers. By the turn I had eliminated all but one player. The board was 9♠-A♥-4♥-7♦, giving me a set of aces.

The river was the Q♥. I was worried about the possible flush, but the body language and sigh of disappointment of my opponent led me to believe he was looking for a different card. Caro's book had said that someone who appears to be weak is actually holding a strong hand. That would mean my opponent had made his flush. I looked at him. He was obviously new to the game, handled the cards clumsily and had trouble handling the chips. Would this newbie try to fool me? I decided that his disappointment was real, and bet the river. The chips had hardly touched the felt when

---

[104] Mike Caro, *The Body Language of Poker*. The book was originally published in 1984. Since then several editions have been printed. A DVD edition is available.

that player sprang to life and raised. I made the crying call, wishing I had listened to Caro. My opponent showed me 3♥-2♥ and happily grabbed a big pot.

You might assume this little story demonstrates convincingly the usefulness of tells. Quite the contrary, I didn't lose that double bet on the end because I ignored the obvious tells of my opponent, but because I played that hand badly, plain and simple. As the hand developed, it became clearer and clearer that he was drawing. When the river card came and he showed signs of disappointment, this well-founded suspicion hardened into certainty. My opponent's tell, real or faked, had absolutely no bearing on the correct play of the hand.

If he hit his draw, I should not have bet. The only draw the Q♥ could have completed was a flush, and my set of aces couldn't beat that. If he missed his draw, then my bet didn't matter, because he most likely wouldn't call. In that case I should have checked in order to give him a chance to bluff at the pot. There was no need to interpret any tells; the correct play was to check in any case. And that's my main criticism of tells: there are usually better things than tells to inform your play.

The problems with tells

I know some players, even pros, who say that the most important skill is the ability to read tells. But if you ask him to pick a player at the table and identify one of his tells, he comes up empty. You can argue that nobody likes to give away secrets for free, but that's not the case. I know some of these players pretty well, and they would tell me or at least confirm that they had a tell on that player. Instead, they admit that they are pretty bad at reading tells, and that's why they concentrate on that aspect of the game. Why they think tells are so important is beyond me. I suspect it has something to do with human nature; perhaps it's the inability to admit that someone else just plays better.

You observe that some players make more money than you do. Being successful yourself, it would never cross your mind that they are superior players, so you look for other reasons that explain their results. Being better at reading opponents is a natural reason. That way you can explain why someone makes more money without conceding that he actually plays better. But the fact is that a guy like Alan doesn't make more money than you do because he is a better tell-spotter[105] but because he plays better[106] technically.

There are several reasons why I am critical when it comes to tells:

- ♠ Exploitable tells are hard to spot
- ♠ It's difficult to verify tells
- ♠ Tells are unreliable
- ♠ Tells are often useless

Let's take a closer look at these objections.

It's extremely hard to find exploitable tells. Many years ago I was playing draw poker in a private game. One of the regulars was a pretty strong player. Every time he held a monster hand he unconsciously leaned forward in such a way that his belly touched the table edge. If that happened, I laid down any hand that wasn't the nuts or close to it. That was the only totally accurate tell I've ever seen.

Over the years I came across other players who had some tendencies when they were bluffing or holding a strong hand. Based on their body language, you could predict with probability greater then 50% whether they were weak or strong, but it wasn't close to 100%. That's better than nothing, but in limit poker it's usually not worth much (see p. 256).

If you want to find out if it's hard to spot a tell, you can do it yourself without even sitting down at a poker table. Today, when poker is aired nearly around the clock on various channels, pick one player and try to spot some tells. You even have the advantage of seeing their hole cards. Many might argue that you only see the best players on television and they don't have easy-to-spot tells. That's true for top players like Doyle Brunson, the late Chip Reese or Bobby Baldwin, but in tournament poker you see lots of weak players even at the final table.

---

[105] Well, he probably is, but that's not a prime factor in my opinion.
[106] Another reason might be that he reads other players better. More on that topic later.

In 2003 Chris Moneymaker, someone who had never played a live tournament in his life, won the World Series of Poker main event. His road to success is well documented on DVD. He ran some well-timed bluffs even against sharp players like Johnny Chan. Look for yourself and see if you can spot any bluffing tells. At least Sammy Farha, a top professional, couldn't when they were heads-up at the end and Moneymaker bluffed him in one hand at the turn and the river, a spectacular hand that was decisive in the outcome of the match[107].

Imagine seeing that a player has been caught bluffing and you remember that he scratched his nose before betting. Have you found a tell? Actually it doesn't mean anything. All you have is the observation of two isolated events. A chronological sequence of events doesn't imply mutual dependence. It's your task to determine if the scratching of the nose is significant. Unfortunately, the verification process is tedious, and you can easily be misguided.

In middle-limit, a lot fewer hands go to showdown than in low-limit. Several times you might see a player scratch his nose and then bet, but no one calls, or he folds to a raise. Not being able to see his hole cards, you lose a lot of valuable information. Even if you can confirm the tell, he may not show it in the future.

Maybe in the next session he'll bet into you heads-up at the end without scratching his nose, you'll throw away top pair, top kicker and he'll smilingly show you a stone-cold bluff. Later you'll learn that he had a cold three days ago, which is why he was scratching his nose, and that he couldn't catch any cards so that he bluffed more often than usual.

To confirm a tell takes time—usually too much time, because the player you are observing has already left the table before you can even think about taking advantage of a possible tell. I can tell you from experience that the best

---

[107] Moneymaker raised with K♠-7♥ to 100,000. Farha called with Q♠-9♥. The flop came 9♠-2♦-6♠ and both checked. Turn: 8♠. Farha bet 300,000 with top pair and a flush draw. Moneymaker, having the better flush draw and an open-ended straight draw, raised 500,000 more. Farha called. The river brought a blank: 3♥. Farha checked and Moneymaker went all-in. Tough decision for Farha. He had some feeling that Moneymaker might be bluffing (He said, "You must have missed your flush, eh?"), but he didn't trust his read enough to risk losing the tournament with top pair, mediocre kicker. After studying Moneymaker for a long time, Farha finally folded. Shortly thereafter it was all over and Moneymaker was the new world champion.

candidates for tells are players that play infrequently. Unfortunately, you usually play only one session with such a player. Regular players, the ones you play against most often, only rarely exhibit exploitable tells.

Clearly, the more often you observe a possible tell in connection with a certain play, the more reliable your observation becomes. Let's say you observe that a player sometimes cuts his chips when betting, and other times splashes them. You suspect this might relate to the strength of his hand. You notice that he turns over a very strong hand after having bet by cutting the chips neatly. But you discard the hypothesis when he shows a big hand after splashing the chips.

But your conclusion might be premature.

Had you taken meticulous records of this player over the next ten sessions you might have noticed the following: 23 times when he was cutting the chips he showed a strong hand and six times he was bluffing; five times when he splashed the chips he was holding a big hand and four times he was bluffing. What you would have found in this case is what I call a tendency. It's a tell, but it's not totally accurate. This is the norm and not the exception. To find a tell that is absolutely reliable is extremely rare. As I said, in the many years I have played poker I only once saw a tell that was totally accurate[108].

After betting at the end, a player starts shuffling his chips. That's not unusual, as many players are doing that. But he's shuffling at a lower speed than usual. He gets caught by his opponent and throws his hand away without showing his cards. He was obviously bluffing. The next three times you observe him betting at the end and shuffling at his normal speed, and he shows a legitimate hand each time. You have found a subtle tell. When this player holds a strong hand he is relaxed and confident; he needn't worry about anything because he expects to win the pot. The effect is that he shuffles at his normal speed. When bluffing, he is under pressure, hoping no one will call so he can pull off the bluff. The tension he

---

[108] When it comes to tells, by far the best book is John Fox, *Play Poker, Quit Work and Sleep Till Noon!* Don't be fooled by the strange title, the fact that it is quite old (originally published in 1977) and that it mostly deals with draw poker. It's still the most extensive, thorough and knowledgeable account of the subject of tells I have read. Fox claims there is a technique to induce a tell if someone is bluffing that is totally accurate. Unfortunately, he doesn't want to give away the only reliable tell "in a book that costs less than $20".

feels is passed on to the shuffling process, thus he unconsciously gets slower[109].

The speed variation of the shuffling process can be a useful tell but, like nearly all tells, it's not foolproof. The tell is based on the stress someone feels when he bluffing. However, that doesn't mean the player is under pressure each time he bluffs. For example, a player is running really good. When he bluffs he might not feel any tension because, win or lose, he is still nicely ahead. Or for whatever reason, he is quite confident that his bluff will succeed. The result is that he will shuffle at his normal speed, even though he is bluffing.

The opposite might also occur. He might be focused on something other than the game and the hand he is holding. He might have argued with his girlfriend before coming to the poker room. The consideration of his relationship leads to mental stain. In this state of mind he might shuffle slower than usual while betting a strong hand. Such factors make tells unreliable. That doesn't mean tells are useless, but you should be careful.

There is another factor that makes tells unreliable: Most tells can easily be faked. You, as an avid student of the game, are not the only one who takes a close look at tells. There are few successful players—and hardly any pros—who haven't read Caro's book of tells. These players are familiar with the content of the book. For example, Caro states that a player who bets and looks right into your face is less of a threat than a player who looks away. Now, let's say a good player bets at the end, fixes your eyes and you have a hand that can beat a bluff but not much more. You have to guess if this player falls in Caro's act-strong-means-weak category or if he is double-faking[110] a tell. It's a cat-and-mouse game. You might be better at outguessing your opponent than he is at trying to fool you, but that doesn't change the fact that tells are unreliable. Often there is a better option than trying to figure out tells, as we will see shortly.

Consider the following scenario: The first-position player opens with a raise and one player calls behind, as does the small blind. You call in the

---

[109] Sometimes it's just the opposite. Bluffing creates stress, which increases your heart beat. As a result, some players actually shuffle faster.

[110] Notice that the classic act-strong-means-weak tell is actually a faked tell because the player acts in the opposite way of what he really has. If you double-fake this tell, you act weak when you are weak and strong when you are strong.

big blind with 10♥-9♥.

The pot contains eight small bets. The flop comes Q♥-6♣-2♥

The small blind and you check, the original raiser bets, and the player behind and the small blind both fold. You think about raising. That would be a good play if you had position and could hope for a free turn card. You call (pot: 10 small bets). The 2♠ comes on the turn. You check, the first-position player bets and you call, hoping to complete your flush on the river (pot: 7 big bets). Alas, no such luck. The river brings the 10♦. Again, you check and your sole opponent bets (pot: 8 big bets). You have a tell on that player that's 80% accurate and it indicates that the player is strong. What should you do?

It's a simple question of math. If you fold, your EV is $0. If you call and play out the hand 100 times you will lose on average 80 times. That's a loss of 80 big bets. The other 20 times you will win 8 big bets, for a net win of 0.8 big bets per hand[111]. As you can see, trusting the tell would result in a whopping loss of nearly one big bet per hand on average. In limit poker, the pots often get so big that you may make a serious mistake by blindly basing your decisions on tells, as reliable as they may be, and an 80%-accurate tell is a pretty good tell. Let's calculate how accurate the tell must be in this case to show a profit, so that you don't lose money by following it.

$$x = (1 - x)\, 8$$
$$x = 8 - 8x$$
$$9x = 8$$
$$x = 0.89$$

The result is about 90%, and that for a pot that is not really big. That is what I mean when I say that in limit poker tells are often useless: The pot is usually too large for tells to be profitable. Keep in mind that I talk about limit poker. In pot- and no-limit, the picture can change drastically. Here you often get pot odds at the end that are a lot lower, therefore increasing the value of tells.

---

[111] (20×8 big blinds - 80 big blinds) /100 = 0.8 big blinds

Situational tells

When we talk about tells we usually mean what I call repeatable tells, or you can call them classic tells: A particular body movement or behavior, usually unconscious, is connected to a particular action. For example, a player makes a forceful bet or starts joking because he is bluffing, or a player's hand starts shaking because he is betting an extremely strong hand. In contrast, situational tells are characterized as strange behavior in a specific situation. Unlike repeatable tells, situational tells are not hard to spot, but they're just as difficult to interpret.

I was playing in a $15-30 game and raised in second position with A♦-A♠. Only the big blind called. The flop came J♦-J♥-J♣. The big blind, a weak and inexperienced player, checked. I bet. My opponent stared at the flop for a while, then grabbed three chips as if he intended to call, but instead of putting the money in the pot, he started thinking again.

That was very strange. I mean, no matter what you have, a flop with three jacks is not too difficult to play, at least heads-up. I said to him: "If you have a jack, you got the nuts!" He looked at me, smiled in embarrassment and softly said, "I know." Now, another strange thing happened. Though he already had three chips in his hand, he went back to his stack and raised me. I had never seen such odd behavior, and wondered how to re-act. Why did my remark induce him to raise instead of call? Could it have made him aware that I feared quads, and that he was trying to take advantage of that?

That was a possibility, and it would mean he was representing a jack he didn't have. But I thought that was very unlikely because the strange behavior started before I said anything to him, and he appeared to have had no intention of folding. My guess was that he had planned to check-raise me on the turn, as most people would do with a jack, but because of my remark, he feared I might not bet the turn, so he raised to get at least some extra money on the flop. I thought he held the jack, so I just called him down. Normally in this case a raise on the flop indicates either a bluff or a vulnerable hand like 10-10 that the player wants to protect. A raise on the turn would then be the logical play because, as I said, most players with quads would wait for the turn to raise. Anyway, my read was correct, as he showed me A-J.

You might be disappointed that I didn't follow my read and fold on the flop. That would have made a great story, but to tell the truth, my faith in my ability to interpret his situational tell was great enough not to raise the turn, but not enough to lay down the second nuts. Before that hand, I had never considered if it is possible to be drawing dead with a pair of aces on the flop if there is no straight flush possibile. But that's exactly what happened. There are 19,600 possible flops and only one of them contains three jacks (the only flop where I'm drawing dead). My opponent hit a 1-in-19,600 shot. Wow!

Here we had an honest situational tell, as my inexperienced opponent was simply overwhelmed when he flopped quads, and didn't know what to do. But like all tells, situational tells can easily be faked.

The game is $15-30 again. I raised under-the-gun with Q♠-Q♥.

Only Mike, a tough pro and a good friend of mine, called in the big blind. The flop looked favorable for my hand: 4♦-10♣-2♥.

Now, things got odd. Mike glanced at me several times and appeared unsure about what to do. Most middle-limit hold'em pros act very quickly, and Mike is no exception. When they face a tough decision, they usually act in just a couple of seconds. That Mike was stalling the action and acting extremely suspicious was out of the ordinary. I was sure that something fishy was going on. He finally bet. Losing no time, I raised with my overpair. Mike gave the impression of facing the toughest decision of his life. It was fun to watch. He thought for a long time and called reluctantly. The dealer flipped over the turn card, 6♠. Again Mike went into the tank. I watched his act in amusement. Surprisingly, after pondering a long time, he bet out.

Mike isn't going to play trash cards against me when I've raised under-the-gun, so the turn couldn't have changed anything, which made the bet strange. I figured Mike held a semi-strong hand like A-10s or 9-9, and he bet to deny me a free card in case I had two overcards. I interpreted his strange behavior as an attempt to prevent me from raising should I have an overpair; by acting weak, he tried to give the impression that he had a strong hand. I decided to disappoint him, and I raised. Mike called, of course not without another funny act.

The river brought the 8♥. Mike tapped the felt, indicating a check, and then looked at me. Feeling quite confident that I had the best hand, I bet. No more act by Mike this time; he raised me immediately. Now the scales fell from my eyes. Clearly, I should have folded here. Against my better judgment, I called, and he showed A-A.

This example is interesting for three reasons. First, Mike used a triple-faked tell. Anyone who has read Caro knows that acting weak means a player is strong, which by itself is a faked tell. Mike knew that I knew that, so he double-reversed the tell by acting weak when he actually had a strong hand, which is the original tell. Second, I'm no big fan of such a ploy, as it can easily backfire. I would have played the hand no differently had he just acted normally. By giving that Hollywood act, he ran the risk that I would respond differently than expected, therefore losing him money. Third, Mike played the hand expertly. No question, everybody would have won in this situation with A-A against my pocket queens, but there is no other way to extract that much money from me, and that's the difference between a very good player like Mike and an average one.

Most players in Mike's situation would either raise before the flop, raise on the flop or wait for the turn. If a player raises me pre-flop, I will definitively raise the flop. If he raises me back, I will simply call him down, and this way he wins five big bets from me. Should he be smarter, just calling my flop raise and raising on the turn makes him an additional small bet. If he waits for the flop to raise me, I will reraise with the same result. When he raises again, I will call him down, or by just calling, he can check-raise me on the turn. That way he makes the same amount of money as in the first case, 5 or 5½ big bets. Waiting for the turn is even less profitable, as you only make 4½ big bets. Now, compare that to the way Mike played. He got six big bets out of me. That's quite an achievement.

It's instructive to analyze how Mike played the hand. Before the flop he just called with pocket aces. Raising with the best possible hand is normally a reasonable play, but calling is superior here. By raising under-the-gun, I've defined my hand pretty well. He knows that, and I know that he knows that. Now, he is giving his hand away if he reraises out of position, knowing that his opponent has a strong hand. Calling conceals his strength. He sacrifices a small bet, knowing that it will pay big dividends later.

Mike bets out on the flop, fully aware that with this type of board I will raise no matter what I have. With an overpair I would raise, thinking I had the best hand, and with two overcards I would raise to regain the initiative. The sole purpose of his flop bet is to make the pot bigger without revealing the strength of his hand. Notice that the latter is the reason why reraising my bet is not a good play here.

The most interesting play is Mike's turn bet. So far he doesn't know if I have a big pair or a couple of high cards. If I have a hand like A-K, his bet denies me a free card and puts me in a difficult position. After his bet there is $320 in the pot. Adding another big bet I can expect to collect should I hit my hand at the river, the pot odds are 380-to-60, or about 6.3-to-1, just a little short for a six-outer that needs pot odds of 6.6-to-1. Taking into account that it looks like I have to beat a pair of tens, my outs are live[112] and Mike might be bluffing, a call would not be out of line.

From his standpoint, the situation will be really profitable if I have an overpair because I will raise for sure, and that's exactly what happened. Now, you can recognize his sophisticated turn play. By betting out, he gets the same amount of money into the pot as by check-raising but—and this is the crucial point—his hand is still undefined. That enables him to go for a check-raise on the river, whereas had he check-raised the turn, he could only bet out. Though I was the victim of that play, I think it was well worth discussing because it shows you how pros think.

When dealing with tells, the first player you should watch is you. While you observe the other players, they are observing you. Examine your own play for tells. It's often helpful to ask a friend to monitor you for this purpose.

There are two ways to play tell-free poker. One way is to always act in the same manner, regardless of the circumstances. Always take about the same amount of time before acting, put your chips in the pot with the same motion and speed and do the same thing when you have completed your action. For example, just look at the chips in the center of the table and don't say anything until all your opponents have acted. Howard Lederer uses this approach.

The other way is to act in a completely random fashion. Bet with the left hand, then with the right hand; use different betting motions; look at your opponent, then next time at your fingers; lean back, lean forward; tear your hair; and so on. The advantage of this approach is that it will absorb a

---

[112] That's somewhat dubious as he might have a hand like A-10 or K-10.

lot of energy from players who like to look for tells. The drawback is that it's easy to fall into the same behavioral patterns, and then your acting is no longer random. A proponent of this way to act is Daniel Negreanu, who tries to confuse his opponents[113].

I usually attach the highest value to tells when a player doesn't care if he gives away any information or not. You most often observe this when a player is done with the hand. He is ready to fold before it is his turn to act. Since he isn't going to play anyway, he thinks his behavior can't hurt him[114]. Amazingly, you can see such premature acting even after the flop. Some players look at the flop and if they don't like what they see, they grab their cards impatiently, waiting to fold. Needless to say, seeing such a tell can greatly influence your play. Of course, the folding tell can easily be faked, and I know some players who always employ it to fool their opponents, but you only fall into this trap once, and then you know about it.

Another tell that falls in this category is if someone who usually acts deliberately calls immediately in what seems to be a complex situation. In this case, he usually has a draw to what he thinks is the best hand. He doesn't care much what you read him for because he figures that without completing his draw he can't win anyway. His attention is only directed to his draw.

Exhibiting situational tells on purpose

When discussing tells, we usually talk about observing other players' tells and trying not to exhibit tells ourselves. On the other hand, you can actively employ tells to influence your opponents. Mike's strange behavior when holding the aces is an example. These are situational tells because they depend highly on the situation and are easy to recognize. I know just one middle-limit pro who is excellent at manipulating his opponents. It's an innate ability. As good as he is, his ploys are usually ineffective or even counterproductive against good to excellent players.

I've mentioned that I don't favor the use of situational tells to influence other players. I only use them if I think it will cost me nothing and I might

[113] See Daniel Negreanu, *Hold'em Wisdom for All Players. 50 Powerful Tips to Make You a Winning Player*, 2007, p. 29.
[114] That's incorrect reasoning. This way a player not only indicates when he isn't going to play but also when he is.

gain something. For instance, it's heads-up at the end and I bet what is, in all likelihood, the best hand. My opponent thinks for a while and then it becomes clear that he is going to fold. Of course, I want him to call, so I grab my cards as if I'm ready to toss them in. My opponent sees this and figures that because he pondered that long, I want to give him an incentive to fold. He gets suspicious and gives me a call. This tell actually works quite often.

Turning the tables, say you bet with nothing at the end and your sole opponent, after thinking quite a while, is considering a call. I might say, "If you call, it's your pot," or, "I thought my two pair were good." Your specific action is of no importance; you just try to make him question his decision. Admittedly, this tell doesn't work too often. If a player has decided to call, he will only rarely change his mind because he assumes correctly that you're trying to persuade him not to call. Nonetheless, should the tell work only one time in 20, that's a nice reward for your effort.

Notice two things. First, these tells cost you nothing. Your opponent has already made his decision. If you make him change his mind, you gain; if not, you lose nothing. Only use these tells if your opponent's intentions have become clear, not before, or it may backfire and cost you money. What you want is a free shot at winning some extra money. Second, only employ these tells against average or below-average opponents. Sharp players will quickly understand what you are doing and will take advantage of it. By stalling the action, they entice you to react, and then they know what to do.

I've stressed that there are often more important considerations than tells on which to base your decisions. Let's examine these factors. I already mentioned that in limit poker the pot odds become so high that you had better not rely on tells to make your decisions. High pot odds often make calling automatic if you can beat a bluff. Instead of being at the mercy of your ability to interpret tells, it's more promising to be able to read your opponent's hand.

Reading your opponents

You should consider three main factors when it's your turn to act: the pot odds, the strength of your hand and what you think your opponent might hold[115]. The absolute strength of your hand is not nearly as important as its strength relative to your opponent's hand. It's of utmost importance to have an idea of what you are up against. Poker players refer to that as "reading a player" or "putting a player on a hand".

Reading an opponent is a three-step process. In order of importance, these are:

- ♠ betting patterns and past actions
- ♠ your opponent's frame of mind
- ♠ tells

We've already discussed tells, so let's concentrate on the first two factors.

Betting patterns and past actions are by far the most important considerations when it comes to reading a player. Past action simply means how your opponent has played in the past. It's your task, even if you are not involved in a hand, to monitor the players at your table closely so you get a good idea of how they play.

For pre-flop play, that means keeping track of which hands a player limps or raises with; whether he adjusts his play to his position and, if so, in what way; whether he tries to steal the blinds; and how liberally he defends his blind.

Post-flop, you want to know if he bets his draws, if he gives up easily, whether he can be bluffed, if he bluffs himself, if he likes to raise for a free card, if he semi-bluffs, and what hands he'll bet for value at the end. That's not an exhaustive list, but it should give you the idea.

Betting patterns are equally important. How did an opponent play his hand so far? Did he bet, check, call, reraise, call a reraise cold before the flop, on the flop, on the turn? It's absolutely crucial that you can recon-

---

[115] There are actually several levels of thinking, depending on your opponent. The first level is to think about what your opponent has. The second is to think about what your opponent thinks you have. And the third is to think about what your opponent thinks you think he has. The key is to think one level above your opponent, but not beyond the third level. See David Sklansky, *The Theory of Poker*, 1992, p. 192.

struct your opponent's action at any time. If you don't pay attention to who raised before the flop—and many don't—you have missed an important piece of information. Your judgment becomes less precise. You may not be playing completely in the dark, but you certainly don't have all the available information.

Past actions and betting patterns can help you determine what a player might hold. Notice that you don't start with an assumption ("He raised in first position, so he must have A-K") and then try to confirm that. In that case you are just guessing. Instead, when a player enters the pot, past action dictates the range of hands he might have in that situation.

As the hand progresses, you try to narrow down his range of possible hands. It's often said that a good player is easier to read than a bad one. This is true for the simple reason that a good player plays tighter than his bad counterpart, so the range of his starting hands is smaller.

If a strong player opens the pot in first position for a raise, his hand is pretty much defined. He has something like a big pair; A-K, A-Q, maybe A-Js or K-Qs. There is not much room for variation because most hands are unprofitable in this position. An expert might occasionally raise with something like 8♥-7♥ just to throw you off, but that's about it. Even an expert can't play hands like that on a regular basis without losing money[116].

Optimally, when you narrow down the range of your opponents holdings, there is just one hand left at the end. However, this is the rare exception and not the rule. Normally, there are still a lot of hands possible, and you have to deal with that.

At the least, if you can beat a bluff you should look at the pot odds and connect that with the possibility that your opponent is bluffing. If your pot odds are 12-to-1 then you should call if you think your opponent will bluff more than 7.7% of the time. Another method is to work backwards and see if there are any hands your opponent could hold that you can beat.

Let's look back at an example we've already discussed. You have 10♥-9♥ and the board at the end is Q♥-6♣-2♥-2♠-10♦. The pre-flop raiser in first position had bet the flop and turn, and also bet the river after you checked. Since nobody played back at him and everyone else folded on the flop,

---

[116] Notice that I talk about typical middle-limit games. In a loose low-limit game, 8♥-7♥ in first position might be profitable, though you usually don't want to bring it in with a raise.

Since nobody played back at him and everyone else folded on the flop, you can't narrow down his range. What you can do now is to determine, based on the play of the hand, if there are any hands you can beat. He could hold A-K, A-J and maybe 9-9 or 8-8, hence you should call[117].

When you are heads-up at the end it's helpful to know what type of hands a typical player bets or checks with. The following table gives you the answer.

Player's possible action at the end when first to act		
Hand strength	Bet	Check
Very strong	✓	✓[2]
Good	✓	-
Mediocre	-	✓
Bad	✓[1]	✓

[1] As an attempt to bluff   [2] With the intention to check-raise

Notice that a bet at the end means as a rule that the player doesn't have a mediocre hand[118]. Even not-so-good players understand that mediocre hands are not good candidates to bet because when you get raised you can't call, and when you get called you usually have the worse hand. A player with a mediocre hand hopes for a free showdown.

On the other hand, when a player checks at the end, you can normally rule out a good hand. Your opponent will bet a good hand for value. He might

---

[117] It's actually a little bit more complicated than that. You should determine the likelihood of the hands you can beat and compare that to the pot odds. Let's say you think the raiser would play A-A down to 8-8, A-K, A-Q, A-Js and K-Qs in that spot. That sums up to 66 possible combinations, 29 of which you can beat. Thus you are only a 2.3-to-1 underdog to have the best hand while the pot odds are 8-to-1. Additional note: You should call against a typical player but probably not against an expert, because an expert would probably not bet a hand you could beat at the end.

[118] See David Sklansky/Mason Malmuth, *Hold 'em Poker for Advanced Players*, 1999, p. 226.

check-raise with a better hand; a good hand is strong enough to bet but not strong enough to check-raise.

When you try to narrow down a player's range, not all hands are equally likely. Bayes' theorem of probability is handy in this case. It shows how to calculate with conditional probabilities[119].

What I've said so far has been abstract and theoretical. Let's look at an example that puts it all together. The following occurred in a $30-60 game at the Bellagio. A middle-position player opened the pot for a raise, I made it three bets with K♣-K♠ and a tough lady in the cutoff seat raised again. Everyone folded to the original raiser, who called. Capping with pocket kings is not unreasonable. In the past I had seen her smooth-call three bets with A-K; that made pocket aces a distinct possibility. By capping I would just make the pot bigger, and the original raiser would go nowhere. Just calling would better conceal my hand, and I could take a cheaper look at the flop and see if the dreaded ace came. I called. The dealer spread the flop: 5♥-4♦-9♠.

The middle-position player checked and I bet, figuring the lady behind would make it two bets, hopefully eliminating the original raiser. It would be nearly impossible for him to call if he didn't have an overpair, because his call wouldn't close the action and he had to fear additional raises behind him. He was an average player, but skilled enough to understand that. No matter what he held, he was not drawing dead, so I wanted him to fold. The pot was already quite big, and eliminating this player would increase my chance to win it. My kings were vulnerable to any ace; making him lay down a hand like A-K or A-Q could very well save me the pot. The lady raised, the original raiser folded and I called. The turn was the A♠. I checked and the lady bet. What should I do? Think about it for a minute before you read on.

Now it's time to take a closer look at what she might hold. The crucial point is that in the past we had seen her call three bets cold with A-K. That eliminated all big-ace-hands like A-K and A-Q. Thus, only big pairs were left. A fair guess is that the lady had A-A, K-K or Q-Q[120]. Since the aces

---

[119] See David Sklansky, *Getting the Best of It!*, 1989, pp. 28-34.

[120] You can't rule out J-J and 10-10 completely. But for the analysis to be conservative we want to look at the worst case. Obviously, by adding J-J or T-T to the roster of possible hands things become more favorable for the pocket kings.

beat me, kings tied and the queens were behind, it appeared to be even money who had the best hand, so with a 50% shot and all that money in the pot I should have definitely played on. The conclusion was correct: folding would be a big blunder.

The intuitive assumption about the possibility of having the best hand is way off the mark; Bayes' theorem gives us the precise answer. Not all possible hands are equally likely. There are six possible combinations of Q-Q, one of K-K (remember I have pocket kings in my hand) and three of A-A (there is an ace on the board that reduces the number of possible combinations by half). There are ten possible two-card combinations; six are favorable for me, one is a tie and three are unfavorable. So, there is a 60% chance I'm ahead, a 10% chance we're tied and a 30% chance that I'm behind[121].

The interesting point here, and this is somewhat counter-intuitive, is that the ace on the turn actually helped me because it reduced the number of combinations that beat me. Had the turn card been a blank, I would have been even money to have the best hand. The ace made me a 2-to-1 favorite.

What would have been the worst turn card for me? After our analysis the answer should be obvious. Had a queen come, the lady would have had six possible combinations of aces, one of kings and three of queens. I would have been behind nine times and tied once, resulting in a pot equity of 5%!

This example shows nicely how to use past action and betting patterns to come to a conclusion, and demonstrates the usefulness of Bayes' theorem in some situations. By the way, if you are curious how the hand ended: The lady and I chopped the pot. When the original raiser saw that we both had pocket kings, he started lamenting that he had laid down A-Js on the flop.

Here is a second example. This one came up in a $40-80 game at the Mirage. It was folded to Andrew, an aggressive local pro, at the button. He raised and the small blind called. I called with 6♥-6♣ in the big blind.

The flop came K♦-K♥-6♠. The small blind checked, I checked my full house and, to my surprise, Andrew checked behind. The turn brought the 10♣. Again, the small blind checked.

---

[121] You might ask if I really did all these calculations at the table. Well, I did not because I already knew the answer. When the hand came up I remembered an article by David Sklansky in which he had discussed a similar problem. See David Sklansky, *Fighting Fuzzy Thinking in Poker, Gaming & Life*, 1997, p. 127ff.

Question: What should I do?

Answer: Most people think you should either bet and hope someone will call, or check again, giving Andrew a chance to make a move at the pot. Both answers are wrong. If you thing along these lines, your game needs a lot of improvement. To be successful in higher-limit games you have to ask the right questions, and the most important question here is: what do we know about Andrew's hand? The correct turn play depends on the answer to this question. We don't know much about the small blind's hand, but we can learn a lot about Andrew's hand.

Look at the situation so far. Andrew raised at the button. That means he can have a wide range of hands, not necessarily a premium hand. The flop is K-K-6. That's a perfect flop for a button raise. Assume Andrew has A♥-4♥. He would certainly bet that hand. If the blinds don't hold a king, a six or a pocket pair, it's hard for them to call because there is no draw out. The same is true if he holds A-Q, 10-8s or 10-10. No matter what he holds, a bet is pretty much automatic. Yet he doesn't bet. What does that tell you? His hand is too strong to bet! He doesn't just want to collect the blinds; he is hoping for some action later by giving a free card on the flop. That means he holds at least a king.

On the turn I have the fourth best hand. Only K-K, K-10 and K-6 beat me. If my analysis is correct, pocket sixes are a heavy favorite against Andrew's hand (6.5-to-1, to be precise, assuming that I'm not yet beaten[122]). Now the course of action becomes clear. I have to bet, knowing that Andrew will raise, and then I can reraise him. This gets the most money in the pot as a big favorite. That's exactly what happened. I bet, he raised, the small blinds went out and I reraised. Andrew called.

The river was the 10♥ (board: K♦-K♥-6♠-10♣-10♥).

Question: Now what?

Answer: Check, of course. Any king or ten beats me.

I checked and Andrew bet.

Question: Call or fold?

Answer: This promising hand had turned into a nightmare. It's hard to see

---

[122] If Andrew had a king in his hand (K-x) there were 45 unknown cards left. Six of them were winners for him (a king, two tens and three outs to hit his kicker); 39 were not.

how Andrew could not have a king or ten. A fold was probably in order. There were ten big bets in the pot, too many to risk an error. I called and Andrew showed K-Q. At least my analysis proved correct. But I would have rather been wrong and taken the $880 pot than be correct and lose it.

Andrew played the hand well. He flopped a monster. If he was ahead, giving a free card with that board wasn't too dangerous, and could win additional bets on the later streets.

When I bet the turn, he correctly raised me, assuming he had the best hand. I could have had a wide variety of hands he could beat: a ten, a king with a weaker kicker or a pocket pair. And I might have bet as a semi-bluff with a drawing hand (Q-J) or as a total bluff. Folding to my reraise was not an option. He could have still been ahead with his trips and the second-best kicker. I wouldn't have faulted him had he raised again. Even if he knew that I had sixes full, his call was still correct. He had six outs to make the best hand at the river (a king, two tens and three outs to hit his kicker) while the pot offered him 8-to-1 odds, and he could expect to collect one or two additional bets[123] if he hit his hand.

In addition to betting patterns and past action, you should consider your opponent's frame of mind before making decisions. By frame of mind, I mean all extraneous factors that influence a decision. For example, many people play differently depending on whether they are winning or losing.

Some years ago I played against a player on a regular basis. Every time I came into the poker room and saw him at the table, the first thing I would do was to take a glance at his stack. When he was winning, he was no pushover because he was a good and tough player. But when he was losing, you definitely wanted a seat at his table. He would chase with all sorts of hands in a desperate attempt to get even. His specialty was A-xs. When he was losing, he never laid that down pre-flop even to multiple raises. It was tough to bluff him, especially heads-up, which meant you could bet a lot of hands for value.

Always see if a player is distracted. Say a player talks intently to a nearby person, or he watches a football game on television. Chances are that if he is involved in a hand he won't fight hard for the pot and you can easily

---

[123] He gains two bets if he hits his kicker because with a board of K-K-6-10-Q I will bet again and he can raise me with the nuts.

run over him. His focus is not on the poker game. He gives up quickly and is happy to turn his attention back to the person he is talking to, or to the football game. If he doesn't give up, beware, as he probably has a stronger hand than usual.

Casinos usually offer alcoholic beverages for free. This is a good thing as long as you don't drink at the table, and other players do. I know some players that can drink and still play well, but most play looser than when they are sober, and that's exactly what you want. Always notice how the consumption of alcohol affects a player. Does he play more hands; does he call more; does he bluff more?

These are just three examples, and there are of course more things to look for. Take these external factors into consideration when judging an opponent, as they are mostly more valuable than tells. While I believe tells are overrated, that doesn't mean they're useless. I look for tells because I try to get any edge I can at the poker table, however small. But take care not to place too much emphasis on tells at the expense of other aspects of play.

Fundamentally, the most important element of winning is playing technically correct poker. Unfortunately, that ability alone only makes you a winner in low-limit games. Playing correctly won't help you much if you can't apply it because you don't know where you are at in a hand. To win in higher-limit games, the ability to read your opponents with a high degree of reliability is indispensable.

As Sklansky has stated, "reading hands is both an art and a science," [124] which means it cannot fully be taught. I've outlined how it's done, but the practical realization is up to you. It takes experience and practice—and some talent can't hurt either.

The conclusion is this: A good poker book can make you a winner in low-limit games if you have discipline and follow the advice, but no book alone, no matter what the author pretends, makes you a winner in higher-limit games. For that it takes hard work, dedication and to some extent, talent. The same holds true for tells. A book can point you in the right direction, but this won't make you proficient at spotting and taking advantage of tells. Maybe you are more talented than I am at spotting tells, in which case it will become a more important element of your game.

---

[124] David Sklansky, *The Theory of Poker*, 1992, p. 178.

Chapter 9

Two Inconvenient Truths

As a good and successful player, you have to deal with two unpleasant facts that seem counterintuitive at first glance:

- ♠ If someone wins really big at your table, it's not you
- ♠ You are more often the victim than the beneficiary of bad beats

Who scores the big wins at the table?

Let's say you hear that someone has shot a record round at a famous golf course. Who is most likely to have achieved this? a) Tiger Woods; b) John, a good and solid local player; or c) Wild Bill, who has no control over his shots? I guess you would say a), and that's by far the most likely answer.

Now, assume at your local card room you see somebody cash out with eight racks of chips. Who is most likely to win that big? a) Alan, a tough pro and the best player at that limit in the poker room; b) George, a tight and solid, but not very imaginative, local player; or c) Crazy Bob, a reckless player who likes to play and to raise with all sorts of hands? The natural choice is a) but the correct answer is nearly always c). The reason for this has something to do with the standard deviation.

For our discussion we will assume a $20-40 game. For a very good player the following assumptions are reasonable: He has a win rate of $50 and a standard deviation of $450 per hour. At three standard deviations from the mean this player can expect to make between -$1,300 and +$1,400 per hour[125]. For four hours of play the standard deviation is not four times as high, because the standard deviation increases only by the square root of the number of hours played. Therefore the result for four hours of play is between $-2,600 and $2,800 per hour.

I have no idea what the numbers are for a reckless player, so we will make an educated guess. Losing at a rate of two big bets per hour and having a standard deviation that's three times as high as the expert should not be an outlandish assumption. In this case our crazy player can expect to make between -$4,150 and +$3,950 per hour. For four hours, the results lie between losing $8,200 and winning $8,000 (see the table below).

Possible session results for two different player types				
	Very good player WR = $50/h σ = $450/h		Crazy player WR = -$100/h σ = $1,350/h	
	Min	Max	Min	Max
1 h	-$1,300	$1,400	-$4,150	$3,950
2 h	-$1,859	$1,959	-$5,828	$5,628
3 h	-$2,288	$2,388	-$7,115	$6,915
4 h	-$2,650	$2,750	-$8,200	$8,000

The results show clearly that a loose and crazy player can make much more money in a single session than an expert. Of course, the reverse statement is true as well. If somebody loses at an extremely fast rate, he is most likely a bad player. These findings are by no means hypothetical.

---

[125] $50 – (3 * $450) = -$1,300 and $50 + (3 * $450) = $1,400

Many times I have seen one of the worst players at the table win between $5,000 and $7,000 in the $20-40 game at the Mirage.

As a good player, you may ask why things like that never happen to you. At least you know the answer now. My biggest win in the $20-40 game was around $3,000, less than half what I have seen other players take home. Recently someone scored the biggest win I have ever heard of in a limit game. In a $100-200 game played at the Bellagio, a guy cashed out with 17 racks, winning about $44,000. It's equivalent to winning $4,400 in a $10-20 game or $440 in a $1-2 game. Having played against him, I have no doubt that it is true because he is the type of guy who goes berserk when he runs hot.

Conclusion: Don't be mad because a player wins excessively and it's not you. It's actually a good thing, because it happens to bad players more often than not. Winning big makes them think they are superior players and gives them an incentive to come back. That gives you the opportunity to win your share of their winnings and some more besides. Additional note: If you are proud that you often score big wins, you should reconsider.

Bad beats

A "bad beat" is a matter of definition. Many players think every time someone draws out on them they have suffered a bad beat. There are even a few players who think every hand they lose must be a bad beat—how could they possibly lose otherwise[126]?

I use the term in a more strict sense. "Bad beat" means a favorite hand lost against a long-shot where the lucky winner did not have the proper odds to draw. The latter qualification is important. If somebody hits a gutshot to crack your set and the pot was big enough to justify the call, that's not a bad beat but correct play. Had you been in your opponent's shoes, you would (hopefully) have played the hand the same way. Or take a more extreme example: Your opponent beats you with a one-outer at the end after you checked the turn. That's not a bad beat either. The only one you can blame is yourself because you gave your opponent infinite odds to

---

[126] Remember the famous Phil Hellmuth quote: "If there weren't luck involved, I would win every time."

draw at the one-outer. No matter what you hold before the flop, your opponent is never drawing dead. Even on the flop and turn this is only rarely the case. That's why bad beats happen; it shows you that your opponent was not drawing dead.

Now, why is it the good player that usually suffers from bad beats while the bad player is usually the beneficiary? There are two reasons: First, a good player plays fewer and better starting hands than a bad player. Since better starting hands tend to make stronger hands at the end, the looser player is dependent on help from the board. Second, bad players not only play too many hands, they go too far with them after the flop, often chasing draws with no consideration of the pot odds. That will lead to pulling bad beats on other bad players or on good players with legitimate hands that are often in the lead. Good players are the victims of bad beats because loose players, by drawing thin, sometimes get there. If several draws with insufficient pot odds are out, the chances to suffer a bad beat increase.

On the other hand, the good player only rarely benefits from a bad beat because he only draws when he thinks the pot odds warrant it, or there are other factors that make him think the play is profitable. When a good player benefits from a bad beat, it's because he couldn't know how strong his opponent really was.

Here is an example: In a $30-60 game a first-position player raises the pot, I reraise with A♦-A♥ and the cutoff calls. Three-handed, we see the flop: 9♦-9♠-4♥. This is an excellent flop for the aces. First, given the betting, it's very unlikely that one of the remaining players has a nine. Second, there are no possible draws to straights or flushes, which gives my opponents very few outs. Third, though there is no draw out, I can expect to get action as any pair and probably two overcards will call.

The original raiser checks, I bet and both players call. The turn is the A♣. The first-position player checks. I think briefly about slowplaying. But there is only one ace left and if nobody has it I probably wouldn't get much action anyway. Betting has the advantage that if the case ace is out, it's probably A-K or A-Q, and the holder of that hand might raise, giving me the opportunity to win three big bets instead of two by check-raising. I bet and to my delight the cutoff raises. The first position player folds and I reraise.

Now something unexpected happens. The player behind me raises again. I had put him on a big ace after he raised on the turn, but when he raises again it becomes clear that this couldn't be his hand. So I figure he must have 10-9, 9-8 or pocket fours. That's pretty loose by any standard, but I have seen worse three-bet calls.

I reraise. He shakes his head in disbelief, mumbles something about "running into aces" and calls. The river is a blank. I bet and he calls. I turn over my aces and he shows A♠-9♠. That comes as a big surprise. I never expected to see that holding, and I realize immediately that I had been drawing close to dead on the flop.

You may say that he had no business with A-9s in that pot and that it serves him right that he lost the hand. That's correct as far as pre-flop strategy is concerned, but that doesn't change the fact that I got extremely lucky on the turn by catching the only card that could help me, the case ace. My opponent didn't suffer a bad beat because I was playing badly. It was inevitable, as there was no way I could have known how far behind I was on the flop. Had he shown me his hand then, I would have laid down my pocket aces immediately.

Though it may be hard to accept, it's a good thing for you that the biggest winners at the table are bad players and that these players put bad beats on you. Were it not possible that loose players could score large wins, many of them would give up poker. They have seen in the past that they can score big, and they want to do it again. That's one of the main motivations that drives them on. Were it not possible for loose players with their sub-standard hands to beat players with tighter starting hand requirements, the better player would win nearly every time. Then the bad players would either become frustrated and stop playing, or they would quickly go broke. Then only the better players would continue to play, and the game would become very hard to beat. I don't know about you, but that's not what I want to see.

Poker is probably the only game where amateurs and professionals play against each other with their own money at stake. Would you play a tennis match against Roger Federer or a chess game against Gary Kasparov for money? If you say yes, you would do it because you think the money spent is worth the unique experience to compete against such a champion and not because you truly believe you have the slightest chance to win.

The reason you have no chance is that there is hardly any luck involved in these kinds of sports. Poker is different in this regard. Give a monkey two aces and he is a big favorite against the best hold'em players in the world.

The large short-term luck factor present in poker creates the illusion that most players think they could win if they were getting their fair share of good cards. Bad players assume that the cards break normally when they win and they are unlucky when they lose, while in reality they have winning sessions because of the large short-term luck factor in poker. The good player has to accept the fact that large swings and bad beats are actually his friends because otherwise there wouldn't be much of a game.

Where does the winners' money come from?

Success in poker is measured by money won. A successful player wins more money than he loses in the long run. A player is successful because he makes better decisions than worse players. However, poker is unique in that you can make the correct decision and lose, or you can make the wrong decision and win. From the preceding discussions we know that bad players have two things working for them: If they run good they can score a better session result than the good player would, and they benefit from bad beats while the good player suffers from them. So, the question remains: where does the winner's money actually come from? How can he overcome the two advantages the bad player has over him? We will try to settle this question by looking at two hands, one where I "undeservedly" lost and one where I "deservedly" won.

The first hand occurred in a $30-60 game. It was folded to me in the cutoff seat. I decided to raise with 7♥-7♣. Only the big blind, a loose Asian businessman, called. I knew beforehand that he would call because he hardly ever failed to defend his blind. We had played together for some time, and I knew he respected me. That meant he would proceed cautiously and not try to be fancy. The flop came K♠-7♦-4♥. He checked and I bet.

Most players, especially below-average players, would check here, thinking that giving a free card can't hurt, and may enable them to collect one or two bets when the stakes double in case the opponent catches something on the turn.

For this reasoning to be correct, two conditions must be met. First, your opponent doesn't have anything and wouldn't call your flop bet. But if he has flopped enough to call, you lose money. It's even worse if he intended to check-raise or if he has enough to call on the flop but not on the turn. For instance, should my opponent have pocket sixes, he will most likely call a flop bet, but when an ace comes on the turn he will probably fold because now there are few hands he can beat. Second, your action has to be consonant with your playing style so it does not look too suspicious. In the case where I raise and get called by a single opponent who checks to me on the flop, I bet close to 100% of the time. It's important to bet your strong and weak hands alike; otherwise you are too predictable and an astute opponent realizes quickly that you check your good hands. I sometimes might check in this situation, but only against bad players I haven't seen before.

The Asian businessman called. On the turn came Q♥. Again he checked, I bet and he called. I was sure I had the best hand. I was only behind K-K and Q-Q, and I knew my opponent couldn't have one of these monster hands since he wouldn't have slowplayed them on the turn. The river looked good for me: Q♠. The Asian gentleman checked and I bet. Surprisingly he shouted immediately, "I raise," completely excited.

Now, the tough question was: should I reraise or call? It depended on whether he had three queens or queens full. It was clear that he most likely had queens full. My opponent was loose but cautious, so what hand could he have called with on the flop that contained a queen without having hit a pair? The only hand that comes to mind is A-Q. It's much more likely that he had a pair on the flop and that the queens filled him up. I called. He showed Q♦-7♠ and joyfully grabbed the pot.

If you want, that's a bad beat story[127]. My opponent had to catch runner-runner to win that hand. Notice that a bad beat always signifies that your opponent was not drawing dead. He had some outs, and sometimes the underdog gets there. That means, mathematically speaking, that you didn't lose the whole pot because you were only entitled to win a fraction (okay, a large fraction in this case) of it. Take a look at the following table.

---

[127] If you call it a bad beat, it's because of the weak pre-flop call. Calling with middle pair on the flop is reasonable heads-up.

Pot equity							
		7♥7♣			Q♦7♠		
			Pot equity			Pot equity	
	Pot size[1]	Outs	%	$	Outs	%	$
Pre-flop	$140	-	69.4	97	-	30.6	43
Flop	$200	-	99.6	199	-	0.4	1
Turn	$320	42	95.5	305	2	4.5	15

[1] After the action is completed

To keep things simple and to ensure comparability with the next example, we will look only at the pot equity on the turn (notice that a different river card would have changed the action at the end). The size of the pot is $320. The trailing hand has two outs, therefore a winning probability of 4.5%, which translates into a pot equity of $15. That's way below the 60 bucks the Asian gentleman had to invest to chase his draw[128]. The other side of the coin is that I didn't lose the whole pot, because I wasn't entitled to win it all. Put another way, mathematically I lost $305, not $320.

Let's look now at the second example, again from a $30-60 game at the Bellagio. The under-the-gun player raised and there were six callers. Being in the big blind, I would have been content in this spot with any remotely playable hand. So, clearly I was happy to call with 8♦-8♣.

The flop was also to my liking: J♥-8♠-3♥.

With a big pot and several players, there is no sense in slowplaying, even with the second nuts. You want to eliminate players quickly, or at least make them pay as much as possible to draw. I bet out, hoping the original raiser would raise. He didn't disappoint me. Three players called, I made

---

[128] Of course, that doesn't mean the call was incorrect because the Asian businessman couldn't know how far behind he was. That he only called with two pair on the turn showed how cautiously he played. I would have check-raised.

it three bets and everybody called. Five players still contested the pot.

The turn was the A♠, a good card for me. It was no heart, and judging by the action, it was doubtful that anyone held pocket aces. I was confident that I still had the best hand. I bet. The under-the-gun player, a young, somewhat loose and aggressive player, raised, and only Joe, a tough local pro, called. I reraised and both players called.

To throw in a little hand-reading exercise, what are the young guy's and Joe's hands?

Let's start with the original raiser. He was a bit loose, but his under-the-gun raise indicated a quality hand. I put him on something like a pocket pair down to 7-7, a big ace, K-Q or two suited pictures like Q-Js. He raised the flop. You can rule out A-K and A-Q. He wouldn't raise two overcards with several players to act behind him. That leaves a split pair of jacks, pocket jacks or an overpair. The next clue is that he just called my reraise. That eliminates pocket jacks; with a large pot and a possible flush draw, you are not going to slowplay. An overpair (A-A, K-K, Q-Q) is unlikely for the same reason (remember, he was an aggressive player and would try to protect his hand). It is reasonable to assume he had a jack with an un-known kicker. He raised me again on the turn. The only logical deduction is that an ace had hit him. Hence, I read him for A-J.

Joe called two bets cold on the flop and turn, a clear indication that he held a draw. Joe was attracted by the big pot that was developing, and had called with two hearts before the flop. His exact holdings are unclear, but a tough player like Joe doesn't call two bets pre-flop with a trash hand. I was sure that he had two big hearts, hence he could have an open-ended straight draw, double belly-buster or gutshot as well as a flush draw[129].

My opponents looked to have plenty of outs. I definitely didn't want to see an ace, jack or any heart on the river, and a king, queen, ten, nine or eight could also be disastrous. The dealer burnt the top card and turned over 6♦. On the outside I remained emotionless, on the inside I breathed a sign of relief. I mean, to win or lose such a large pot makes a big difference not only for the session but even for the month. I bet, the young guy called and Joe threw his cards in the muck angrily. The original raiser indeed

---

[129] Open-ended straight draw: 10-9; double belly buster: Q-10; gutshot: K-Q, K-10, Q-9, 10-7, 9-7, 7-6 (the last three hands are unlikely for a player of Joe's caliber)

showed A-J and Joe had, as he told me later, Q♥-10♥.

It's interesting to take a look at the pot equity of all three hands.

		A♣-J♠	Pot equity		Q♥-T♥	Pot equity		8♦-8♣	Pot equity	
Pot equity										
	Pot size[1]	Outs	%	$	Outs	%	$	Outs	%	$
Pre-flop[2]	$480	-	32.8	157	-	35.5	170	-	31.7	153
Flop[2]	$930	-	1.8	17	-	35.7	332	-	62.6	582
Turn	$1,470	4	9.5	140	13	31.0	455	25	59.5	875

[1] After the action is completed [2] Ignoring the other present hands

I used this hand as an example of the best hand holding up. Anybody with pocket eights on this flop would think he deserved to win. Indeed, the eights are a big favorite. But note that my pot equity on the turn was just $875, though I won the whole pot. In other words, since the winner takes it all, I was overpaid.

Now things become much clearer. When you suffer a bad beat, mathematically you lose less than you think while in reality you lose more than you should. When your hand holds up (and your opponent is not drawing dead) it's just the opposite. Mathematically your fair share of the pot is less than the whole pot, but in reality you win more than you should. The conclusion is this: The times you lose because someone draws out on you are balanced by the times when your hand holds up. We can now understand where the winner's money comes from. The losses are overcompensated in the long run by the wins when his hands hold up. That includes the times when he gives up on unprofitable draws while a bad player keeps chasing, and when he draws with the right pot odds and gets there.

These findings are by no means academic. It helps to put things in perspective to understand that bad beats are unavoidable against bad players and that you are more than compensated when your hand holds up or you hit your draw. Handling bad beats is tough, but understanding the underlying mechanism may help you keep your cool. You should strive to not go on tilt, no matter what happens at the table. I know that's easier said than done. Limit hold'em is a game of small edges. When your game deteriorates, it can quickly cross the line and you no longer have the best of it. Don't let that happen. Take a break or stop playing. Then try to analyze what made you mad, so you can learn to deal with it. Bad beats are an indication that the game is good because somebody makes mistakes. Be the one who takes advantage of these errors and not the one who goes on tilt.

Chapter 10

Stepping Up

When you start playing poker and you have never played cards before in a casino, you should begin at the smallest limit possible. For limit hold'em in Las Vegas this usually means $3-6 or $4-8; at other places you may find lower limits such as $1-2, $1-3 or $2-4[130]. The reason is simple: If you have studied some good books about limit hold'em and are disciplined enough to follow the advice, you can be an immediate winner at low limits.

I have often seen new players jump directly into a middle-limit game and never develop into winning players. If you can't win, playing at the lowest limit still has two advantages: it limits your losses and it is much easier to improve your play to the point where you can win. Don't think about stepping up before you can beat the lowest limit in your local card room.

---

[130] If you intend to play online, there are even lower limits, such as $0.05-0.10. However, starting at about $1-2 seems a good choice to me. If you play lower, you (and your opponents) may have trouble taking things seriously because there is hardly any money involved, and if you plan to build a bankroll by playing poker, it takes you a long time to reach a level where you can really make some money. Hence, start low but not so low that the money you play for is insignificant.

Preconditions

For a serious player, stepping up becomes a sensible option when two conditions are met:

- ♠ You are a winner at the level you are currently playing
- ♠ You have a big enough bankroll for the higher game

Of course, if you are playing for fun and don't care about the money, you can play at any level you can afford. But, if your goal is to make money playing poker, you should start at the lowest limit and then try to work your way up. Every successful player I know has done this.

Suppose you do as I suggest. When should you think about stepping up? It's imperative that you first put in a reasonable amount of time at the table and have a solid win rate. What do "reasonable" and "solid" mean in this context? Before moving up you should play at least 500 hours at low limits and at least 1,000 hours (2,000 hours would be better) at the higher limits ($10-20 and up).

That looks like an awful lot of time, but because the win rate converges slowly, it's not even enough to guarantee you are a winning player. After just 500 hours of play your actual win rate can vary more than a big bet per hour in either direction from your calculated win rate. If you play less time, you can easily be fooled by a nice win rate that in fact is the result of pure luck. Proceeding based on a bad estimate of your ability may result in a rude awakening at the higher limit.

Nevertheless, I believe you can give the higher limit a shot after 500 hours of low-limit play[131]. Lower-limit games are easy to beat and the financial consequences of failure are not too severe. This becomes less true at higher levels, and it becomes more important to log a reasonable amount of time to obtain a reliable estimate of your win rate.

The main qualification in stepping up is a solid win rate, I would say greater than 0.5 big bet per hour. Don't assume that as you move up, your winnings will be proportional to the limit. The opposition will be tougher at the higher game and your relative win rate will shrink, at least at first.

---

[131] This implies, of course, that you are winning and adequately bankrolled; see below.

It is likely you won't be able to beat the higher game if your win rate is lower than 0.5 big bet per hour at a low-limit game. In that case you should remain at the lower limit and work on your game. It's better to be a winner at a lower game than a loser at a higher game.

There is a limit at which most players can win, and where they should settle. Don't fall into the trap of playing higher-stakes games and staying at a level where you aren't a winner while attempting to learn[132]. That's an expensive strategy.

There are always some losing players who say they can't beat low-limit games because the players are too bad, and that higher-limit games are easier to beat. That's complete nonsense. People who say that are looking for excuses. If you have some basic knowledge about limit hold'em, winning in low-limit games is like taking candy from a baby.

If you can't beat the limit you are currently playing, thinking that you may be more successful at a higher limit is just wishful thinking. Of course, if you look at the tables in your local card room you will often see a higher-limit table that is easier to beat than a nearby lower-limit table. But this is not the rule. In general, the higher the game, the tougher the players. This is easy to understand, as the better players move up in limits. Here is an admittedly extreme example.

In the late nineties, when I was in Las Vegas on a poker trip, I played daily in the $10-20 limit hold'em game at the Mirage. One of the regulars in that game, for a time, was a young guy who liked to be the center of attention. He was very talkative, convinced that he was by far the best player at the table, and certain that every hand he lost was due to incredible bad luck. As it turned out, he was a former dealer who was tired of dealing to all these "idiots that have absolutely no clue what they are doing," and so he decided to become a pro.

In his imagination the $10-20 game was just to warm up; he already considered himself in the same league as Doyle Brunson and Chip Reese. Though he was out of touch with reality, people generally liked him because he was not a bad guy, he was very entertaining and he contributed

---

[132] In business this is called the Peter Principle. It states that in a hierarchy every employee is promoted until he rises to his level of incompetence and stays there. See Laurence J. Peter/Raymond Hull, *The Peter Principle*, 1970.

to the game. Unfortunately, his playing abilities were not as big as his ego, and one day the inevitable occurred. He put his last chip in the pot, announcing, "If I lose this pot I'm broke." Well, he lost the hand and left the poker room with his head bowed. Though he talked a lot, he wasn't lying. He no longer showed up in the $10-20 game.

Several months later, back in Vegas for another poker trip, I was again playing in the $10-20 game when I saw the same guy that couldn't beat our $10-20 game, heading to the high-limit section with a rack of black chips[133] in his hand. I assumed he was making the chip run for one of the high-limit players, trying to hustle a toke. I couldn't believe my eyes when I saw him take a seat in a $200-400 mixed game and start stacking his chips in front of him. I knew that one of the regulars at my table had played with this guy before, and I asked him what was going on. He told me that our young friend had won a World Series of Poker event in a game that he had never played before. In fact, a friend of his had taught him the rules a few moments before the event started.

Now, instead of taking the money he won in the tournament and trying to work his way up in limits, he had jumped right into high-limit games. Can someone who is unable to beat a $10-20 game be successful in a high-limit mixed game? Of course not! Our friend lost all his tournament winnings, and a lot more, in cash games.

Today he is one of the biggest names on the tournament circuit. After he won a million bucks at the WSOP main event, an interviewer asked him what he was going to do with the winnings. He had kept his honesty. With disarming candor, he said, "That's just enough to pay some markers back."

There is a lesson to be learned here: Don't let your ego decide your level of play. The only objective guiding principle is your win rate.

Another factor you shouldn't overlook when you intend to step up is your bankroll. This is the amount of money you have put aside exclusively for gambling. Most poker theorists agree that you should have a bankroll of at least 300 big bets to play regularly at a particular limit. If you follow my advice of putting in the required hours before stepping up, your bankroll will take care of itself.

---

[133] If you don't know, a black chip is a $100 denomination chip and 100 chips fit into a rack.

Let's look at an example. You start playing in the $3-6 game. For that you need a bankroll of 300×$6 = $1,800. You play for 500 hours in that game and your win rate is 0.75 big bets per hour. Consequently, your bankroll has increased to $4,050, which is enough to play in the $6-12 game. This assumes that you don't withdraw money from your bankroll.

If, as I suggest, you play even longer at your new limit before moving up again, you may be able to reward yourself while also building the necessary bankroll. Assume you play for 1,500 hours in the $10-20 game and achieve a win rate of $15. Your bankroll has increased to $28,500. You can spend $16,500 and still have a sufficient bankroll to play $20-40.

Of course, you don't have to wait until you have the full 300-big-bet bankroll to play in the bigger game. There is nothing wrong with occasionally taking a shot at a higher limit if you think the game is good. The key is never to jeopardize your bankroll for the lower game. In other words, never play in a higher game if your bankroll could drop below the 300 big bets you need to play the lower game.

There is one last consideration: Only step up if you are emotionally and psychologically prepared. You should have the desire to play higher and the confidence that you can be successful. If that's not the case, stay at your chosen limit and enjoy yourself. There is nothing wrong with that. I know several players that could probably be successful at a higher limit, but they don't move up because they don't like the hassle that comes with it, such as bigger swings, tougher opponents and less fun at the table. If you can't handle a $2,000 loss, don't play at the $20-40 limit.

One thing I found extremely helpful before actually stepping up was observing the higher games. I watched the $20-40 game for countless hours before playing it. When I went into a card room and there was no seat in the $10-20 game, I would watch the action at the $20-40 table. When I took a break from my game, I studied the $20-40 game. I began to get a better feel for the higher game. Sometimes just by watching, I could see more than a player at the table could. Standing behind a certain player, I was often able to see his hole cards. I could get information on how he played his hand even if there was no showdown. There's an enormous advantage to identifying the good players and how they play before entering a new game. I always found the time I watched a game was well spent.

An experience report

In theory, stepping up is easy. You log in the required hours, build up your bankroll and move to the higher limit. Unfortunately, in practice, it's anything but easy. The game becomes tougher as you move up. What worked at one limit doesn't work at the higher limit, and you have to change your game. The fluctuations get bigger and bigger, and the inevitable downswings drive you crazy. Dropping a couple of hundred bucks costs a weary smile, but losing thousands and thousands of dollars is tough to swallow.

Maybe you will find it worthwhile to see how I worked my way up.

The first few times I came to Las Vegas, I did so exclusively to play blackjack. I had learned to count cards and wanted to see if I really could win in a casino. I started at the smallest levels I could find, the $1 and $2 tables. Then I moved up to $5 and $10 tables. It wasn't difficult to win. But it soon became clear to me that the difficulty wasn't winning, but getting away with it. This was not an issue at the small limits, but it would be at the higher limits—because the house doesn't want you to win.

Blackjack is different than poker because if you can win at a $5 table you can, at least theoretically, win at a $500 table as well. It's just the color of the chips that's different; the dealer plays exactly the same way, no matter if you have a $5 chip or a $500 chip on the felt. On the contrary, in poker, beating a $3-6 game in no way means you can beat a $300-600 game.

Of course, every blackjack pit boss knows that the game can be beaten by counting cards, so they are always on the lookout for card counters[134]. The casinos have an arsenal of weapons to deal with card counters. They can shuffle up on you, reduce the penetration, only allow you to flat bet, ask you to leave or, as a last resort, bar you.

The ten bucks or so I was making in an hour at blackjack didn't even cover my expenses. I knew I couldn't play much higher without getting into trouble. To succeed at blackjack at a higher level requires a good act, and I had none. I fit exactly in the category pit bosses were looking for: I was young, male, white and didn't look like a dummy.

---

[134] Today many casinos have continuous shuffling machines. These games cannot be beaten by counting cards.

These were the thoughts that went through my head one day when I was standing at the Mirage poker room rail. At home we had a draw poker game for a while, but that was my entire poker experience. I watched the stud game a little bit. Since I knew the hand rankings from playing draw poker, I was able to understand the game.

Realizing that it would be difficult to make more money from blackjack, I thought I might as well play a little poker. My natural choice was stud since I already knew the rules—although I had never really played. Now, you probably assume that I took some money out of my wallet and sat down at the stud table. Wrong! I had studied intensely before I ever played a single hand of blackjack. I didn't change my method after I had made up my mind to play poker. I study—that's what I do. So, I went to the Gambler's Book Shop and bought all the books they had on stud. Back home, I read the two sources I thought to be the best[135] about ten times.

My first poker session in a card room was my most memorable; that's why I still remember it so vividly. Prepared to play some stud poker, on my next gambling trip I flew to San Francisco, rented a car and drove to Reno, Nevada, the Biggest Little City in the World. I ended up standing at the rail of the poker room at Harrah's, watching a stud game for about 15 minutes. Though I had never played a single hand of stud in my life, I had the impression these guys had no idea what they were doing. I definitively wanted to play in that game. But how to get a seat? I noticed a front podium, behind which was a man who was obviously running the poker room. People talked to him, and from time to time he was calling names.

I went to him and said, "I want to play at that table", pointing to the stud game I had observed.

"That's a $1-5-10 seven card stud game," he said. Noticing my confused face, he added, "You can bet between one and five dollars on any street, and between one and ten dollars at the end."

Ten bucks seemed a bit much to me, as I was only prepared to play $1-4 and $1-5. But I figured the double bet at the end would give the better player an extra edge and, since I already considered myself a good player,

---

[135] Doyle Brunson, *Super/System. A Course In Power Poker*, 1989, pp. 129-168; David Sklansky/Mason Malmuth/Ray Zee, *Seven Card Stud For Advanced Players*, 1992 (expanded version 1999).

I let the floorman put my name on the list.

After about 10 minutes my name was called. The floorman pointed at a table at the other end of the poker room. I protested and told him that was not the table I wanted to play at. In a friendly voice, he explained that I had to take the first open seat, but that he could put my name on the transfer list. That sounded fair to me.

He asked, "How much do you want to buy in for?" I had already made up my mind that I would buy in for $100 in the $1-4 and $1-5 I had planned to play. I bought in for $150 because of the double bet at the end. Holding one-and-a-half racks, I headed to the directed table and sat down in the 3 seat. Things went well, and after about an hour I was more then 50 bucks ahead when the following hand came up.

I had a split pair of kings and bet all the way. At the end I had K♠-A♠-K♦-Q♣-A♣-T♠-A♦. Having made aces full, I bet $10 at the end. The only remaining opponent was the 2 seat, who showed X-X-Q♥-3♥-K♣-4♦-X. He was very loose, liked to chase and was slightly drunk. You couldn't tell from his behavior, as he didn't talk much, but since I sat down he had already ordered three bottles of beer.

So far he had just check-called me all the way. Now he said "Raise", counted out 20 dollar chips and put them in the pot. I couldn't believe how lucky I was, and I raised him back. He promptly said "Raise" again and put another 20 bucks in the middle. I quickly glanced at his board to make sure I hadn't misread anything. Still convinced he had a flush, I reraised. Without hesitation he raised again. How could he be that confident with just a flush? Getting nervous, I tried to look methodically at the hand. What can beat my aces full? A straight flush! That wasn't possible, as he only had the queen and trey of hearts. The only other hand that could beat my full house was quads.

Suddenly I realized that you can make quads in stud without having a pair on the board. I had never thought about that before. Cold shivers ran down my spine. How could I have overlooked that? I tried to stay calm and determine if quads were a possibility. I had a king and a queen in my hand, and I was pretty sure someone had folded a trey. Hence, only quad fours were possible, and that was the only hand that could beat me. I felt relieved. If he really had that hand, so be it. I decided I had to take the risk.

We raised each other about ten times. Since he had me covered, I went all-in. The whole table was covered with chips, about 500 $1 chips in total. The huge pile of chips attracted players from the other tables, who came over to see what was happening. Now the moment of truth came. Being first to act, I slowly turned over my hole cards. The player in the 2 seat leaned forward, nodded and said, "I thought you had a straight"! That was all.

He might have been drunk, but he was a class act. He knew how to lose with style. He had lost an enormous amount of money for that limit, but he didn't bat an eyelid. Since that day, this guy has been a great example of losing with decency and grace. I don't know how I would have reacted if I had lost that pot. Maybe my first poker session would have been my last.

A little later another player at my table made a seven-card, queen-high straight flush. A dealer who came over to look at the hand said to me, "I'm dealing for 30 years but I have never seen that before"[136].

Starting as a stud player was nothing unusual then. Seven-card stud was the predominant low-limit game at the time. In Las Vegas, most of the small poker rooms with four or fewer tables rarely even had a hold'em table. At the beginning I usually played $1-4 7-card stud at the Stardust or the Circus Circus because it seemed to me that the players at those places were worse than at the more upscale casinos. I beat that game for $4.86 per hour. Then I moved up to the $5-10 game, and finally to the $10-20 game at the Mirage.

Even while I was playing stud, I always thought that Texas hold'em was the "real" game. I had the impression there was more action and more fun at the hold'em tables. One day I took a seat at the $3-6 hold'em game at the Mirage. I knew the rules of the game but hadn't studied it. I figured hold'em can't be too different from stud, and being a successful $10-20 stud player should be enough to have an edge in a low-limit hold'em game. I played for three hours and managed to lose $243, one of the biggest losses I ever had in terms of big bets.

Feeling completely lost, I had no idea what to do and where I stood in a hand. If I remember correctly, I won one tiny pot and even that was split. There was no question that I didn't understand anything about the game. I

---

[136] To give you an idea how unlikely it is to make a seven-card straight flush let's take a look at the math. Of 133,784,560 possible seven-card combinations, 36 are seven-card straight flushes, thus you are a 3,716,238-to-1 underdog to be dealt such a hand. Assuming you play 40 hours per week and are dealt 30 hands per hour, on average you make a seven-card straight flush about once in 60 years.

had broken my own cardinal rule—"Understand what the hell I need to do and get prepared." So I did what I had done before: I went to the Gambler's Book Shop and bought all the hold'em books available. Luckily, at that time, there weren't that many hold'em books on the market. I found three sources to be excellent[137], and studied them obsessively over the next few months back home.

Finally, feeling well prepared, I headed back to Vegas. I had stopped playing blackjack so I could concentrate fully on hold'em. Though I was already playing middle-limit stud, I didn't jump into a $10-20 hold'em game. Quite the contrary, I looked for the lowest game I could find to gain some experience. That was the $1-3 game at Circus Circus. But that low-level game had some disadvantages.

The first time I tried to check-raise, the dealer informed me that it wasn't allowed. When the hand was over, I went to the floorperson and asked about this strange rule. "It's meant to be a friendly game; nobody should be hurt too badly," was his response. That was the only time I saw a poker game in a casino where check-raising wasn't allowed. Clearly, without that option, the early-position player is at a severe disadvantage, losing the only weapon he has to compensate for the positional advantage of the players behind him. With the no-check-raise rule and a stiff $3 rake, the game was not interesting, so I went next door to the Stardust[138].

I always liked the Stardust low-limit games. The dealers were okay, the staff friendly and, best of all, the players among the worst you could find. Besides some $10-20 stud action at the Mirage, I played mostly $3-6 hold'em at the Stardust. On my next trip I continued playing $3-6 and took occasional shots at the $6-12 game. On my third trip after taking up hold'em, I played $6-12 at the Mirage exclusively.

Things had gone well so far. I won at the $3-6 game right from the beginning. Though I had some tough times, I managed to win over one big bet per hour. The players in the $6-12 game were more selective about the hands they played, and they didn't chase that much with hopeless hands, but otherwise the game was very similar to $3-6. I had little difficulty beat-

---

[137] Doyle Brunson, *Super/System. A Course In Power Poker*, 1989, pp. 353-415; David Sklansky, *Hold'em Poker*, 1989; David Sklansky/Mason Malmuth, *Hold'em Poker For Advanced Players*, 1994 (expanded version 1999).

[138] The Stardust was demolished on March 13, 2007, to make room for a new mega-resort.

ing that game either, but due to some tough downswings, I didn't make one big bet per hour in the short time I played that game.

I wasn't satisfied with beating the low-limit games. I wanted to play the middle limits. It wasn't just an ego thing; I wanted to win enough to cover my expenses: the flight from Europe, the rental car, my hotel room, food and beverages. I couldn't do this by playing blackjack for nickels or low-limit poker, but my success in the $10-20 stud game had proven that it was possible. Now I wanted to do it in the limit hold'em game.

By my fourth trip I knew that sooner or later I would try my luck at the $10-20 hold'em game. After some good results at $6-12, I took a shot. On the first round I picked up pocket kings, made kings full and won a huge pot. Up $650 with my seat barely warm, I smiled from ear to ear. I thought, boy, it's as easy winning here as at the low limits, not realizing that a monkey can win with kings full. At the end of the session I was down $100. No big deal, I thought. But I kept losing. I scored a few small winning sessions, but overall I lost.

Every time I dropped back to the lower-level games, I started winning immediately. After winning a grand or so at the lower limit, I headed back to the $10-20 game, but the winnings from $6-12 never lasted long. For a while I thought I had just hit a bad streak and things would turn around. But I kept losing.

I felt quite comfortable in the $6-12 game, but felt no such comfort at $10-20. This was partly because if you don't win, you lose confidence and always expect the worst. But there was something else. I felt deep in my heart that there was something wrong with my game. I had no idea what it was, and it was driving me nuts. How can you win regularly in the $6-12 game but have absolutely no chance at $10-20?

When I was back at home and had distanced myself from the game, I tried to analyze the situation. It was clear that I had to make a decision. I had three options: stay in the $6-12 game and make money, play the $10-20 game and lose, or try to elevate my play so that I could win at $10-20. I chose the third option, but how could I achieve this? It was clear that studying wouldn't do it. I knew the better references nearly by heart. My problem was not a lack of knowledge, but the inability to put my knowledge into practice. The only thing that could help was savage analysis of my play.

One day I sat down at my desk, took an empty white sheet of paper and tried to write down my shortcomings compared to the successful players. I started with my pre-flop game. I knew what hands to play, adjusted correctly for position and didn't go on tilt by playing substandard hands. Not tilting was always one of my greatest strengths.

The only problems I saw were that I didn't attack the blinds enough when it was folded to me in late position, and that I folded too much to late-position raises. For instance, when the cutoff brought it in for a raise, I routinely folded hands like K-Js and A-10 on the button. That's correct against an early- or middle-position raise, but a late-position raiser can have a wide variety of hands. By three-betting, you'll most likely be heads-up, and you have position and probably the best hand.

These are typical problems for low-limit players who play higher, because these situations rarely come up in low-limit. Multiway pots are the norm. Trying to steal the blinds is pointless, as at least one or even both blinds will call just because the cost isn't great and the players aren't good.

I concluded that my pre-flop play in middle-limit was as good as or better than that of a typical $10-20 opponent. Hence, pre-flop strategy could not be the problem, though there was always room for improvement.

In low-limit hold'em the pot is generally contested by multiple opponents, and consequently, post-flop strategy becomes easy. You bet if you think you have the best hand or have pot odds to justify a draw. This strategy is not completely optimal, but if you follow it, beating low-limit games becomes easy. That's why I always liked to play in low-limit games and generally succeeded at them. I'm good at figuring out the odds, and hardly make any mistakes when drawing.

The main difference between low- and middle-limit is that the latter usually has fewer players after the flop. Two-, three- and four-handed pots are the norm. Sure, volume pots do come up, but not as frequently as in low-limit. With fewer players battling for the pot, the likelihood increases that nobody hits anything, in which case the one who bets first has the best chance to pick up the pot—and that was never me.

When I looked at my post-flop play, I started to realize that I was using a multiple-player strategy while most pots were shorthanded. I bet when I likely had the best hand, drew when the odds were favorable and folded otherwise. In other words, I played showdown poker. What works like a charm in low-limit doesn't take the money down in middle-limit. You simply don't win often enough to compensate for the times you give up or are beaten up by a better player when you perhaps have a better hand.

That's one of the main reasons why successful low-limit players fail when they move up to the middle-limit games. In the beginning, I was no exception. Successful low-limit players have learned to play tighter pre-flop than the typical player, and then they patiently wait to make their hand. In middle-limit, that strategy is doomed to failure. The pots are mostly short-handed and the players are more aggressive. People run over a tight, non-aggressive player when s/he doesn't have much of a hand. When the tight, non-aggressive player really has a hand, the opponents become cautious and don't give much action. So, what's the remedy?

You have to make sure that you win your fair share of shorthanded pots. You have to fight hard—you often want to be the aggressor. With a flop of 8-3-3, you can't routinely fold a hand like A-Q, thinking that the pot is not big enough for a six-outer. By putting pressure on your opponents, you can pick up pots when you don't have the best hand. For instance, if you bet that 8-3-3 flop, a player might fold pocket sixes. If not, and the turn brings an overcard, another bet will likely accomplish the mission.

Of course, plays like that are risky. You can easily bet or raise into a much better hand, costing you money. But that's the point. You have to take risks; otherwise you can't win in middle-limit. The risk-free play that takes down the money in low-limit is not going to work here. You have to bet or raise, even if you don't know where you stand, and you must have the courage to do this if you don't have the best hand but think you can make the other player lay down his hand. If this goes against your nature, then you should stay at the lower limits.

I was quite confident that I had identified the biggest leak in my play, and resolved to be much more aggressive in shorthanded pots. I would no longer automatically check should the flop miss me. Instead, I would look for reasons to bet, and if someone bet in front of me I would always first consider raising.

I thought this aggressive play would ensure that I won my fair share of pots, and that my opponents could no longer fold confidently when I bet my legitimate hands. But only practice could tell if I was right. I knew I could beat the low-limit games, but playing in those games wouldn't win enough to cover my expenses. It would cost less to stay home and solve crossword puzzles. All I wanted was a free vacation. Only by winning in the $10-20 game could I achieve this. The next trip was decisive. I would either beat the $10-20 game or it was all over.

My poker trips usually lasted between one and two months. That looks like a lot of poker, given that I play full-time, seven days a week, but it's not enough to get reliable results. It was possible that my losing was due to pure chance. Losing one or two months straight is not uncommon even for the best players. But I had faith in my ability to recognize whether my losses were due to luck or the competition.

With great hopes, I took a plane to Las Vegas for a six-week stay. I didn't bother with $6-12 anymore; I jumped right into the $10-20 game. I was about even after a week. That wasn't what I was hoping for, but I wasn't disappointed. At least I'd halted the negative trend, and I felt much better playing at that limit than before. Playing more aggressively pre-flop in late position and in shorthanded pots after the flop had raised my game to a new level. And I realized that my game was rusty from not having played for six months. I'd made a couple of judgment errors such as calling a player who hadn't bluffed since World War II, and trying to run over a calling station. That's a routine problem I have because I don't play on a regular basis.

Things started to turn around in the second week, and I was able to employ my new tactics successfully. I had estimated that a very good player could make about a grand per week, but after six weeks I had won $7,800. That was more than expected. Fortune had smiled on me, but it wasn't just luck. By playing tight pre-flop and very aggressively later, I could pick up a lot of pots without the best hand. This combination of tightness and aggressiveness made the other players at the table fear me. One player said that I was the most aggressive player he'd ever seen. He may have exaggerated, but the truth was that I played tighter and more aggressively than the regulars, and that was the key to my success.

I said earlier that you should play at least 500 hours in a low-limit game before thinking about stepping up, but I didn't follow that advice. Because I didn't play regularly, this would have taken too long and in any case it became clear that I could beat that limit. I had played about 250 hours in the $3-6 games and about the same time at $6-12 when I moved up. That changed when I advanced to the $10-20 game. I played for about two years exclusively at that limit.

I stayed at that limit because, for the time being, I was satisfied with my accomplishment. I no longer had the desire to step up in limits. I could finally make enough money to cover my expenses. And I liked the $10-20 game. I averaged $28.67 per hour, my highest win rate, in terms of big blinds, of any limit I'd played. It's my conviction that of all the levels I had played, my edge was the greatest in the $10-20 game.

Though I had the occasional brutal downswing, I was a consistent winner in the $10-20 game. So it was just a matter of time until thoughts about stepping up to the $20-40 crossed my mind. The longer I played, the more concrete these thoughts became. I wasn't so naïve as to think that my win rate would double at the higher limit, but the prospect of making $40 instead of $28 was seductive. I started to watch the $20-40 game intensely.

On the surface it looked like a very good game. It was pretty loose and had a lot of action. All the action junkies played in that game and stayed away from $10-20. When regulars at the $20-40 game played $10-20, usually while waiting for a seat to open in the higher game, they always moaned about how tough the game was compared to $20-40. Indeed, it was my observation that most players who were accustomed to playing the bigger game usually did poorly in the $10-20 game. They played their typical power game and it rarely worked. You may ask why playing aggressively didn't work for them when it was the key to my success at $10-20. Well, there was a big difference. They played loose and aggressively; I played tight and aggressively.

As I said, most regulars in the $10-20 game were on the tight side. Tight players understand when they see a loose player that their big advantage, starting with the better hand, works for them regardless of what the loose player is trying to do after the flop. The loose player might move the tight player off of a pot once in a while, but in the long run, loose players, aggressive or not, are slaughtered by tight players. Of course, not everyone from the $20-40 game falls into this trap.

I still remember the first time I played with Roy Cooke in the $10-20 game. I liked Roy the first time I saw him, as a human being and as a player. He is a nice guy and has a great personality. His game is rock-solid, he has excellent instincts and superior judgment, and he never falters when things are going badly. I always like the way he plays a hand.

He was waiting for the $20-40 game and didn't mind playing at a lower limit. I was immediately impressed by his play, and at how effortlessly he adjusted to different playing conditions. He wasn't just trying to over-power his opponents, as many of the $20-40 players did (generally in vain); he played tightly and aggressively, using his knowledge, experience and instinctive card sense to outplay his opponents after the flop.

Another point that sticks in my mind is how serious he was when in-volved in a hand. Most people take it easy when playing at a lower limit while waiting for their regular game. There is less money involved than they are used to, so they become less attentive. When they lose they don't care much, because they think they'll easily make it up in the bigger game. Not so Roy Cooke. At every level, he plays the best he can.

Flattering myself a bit, I think his game resembles mine. Over the years, I've played at various levels from $10-20 to $60-120 with Roy, and he is one of the few players I've never seen make a mistake. I don't mean a judg-ment error (e.g., you call with a weak hand and your opponent holds the nuts, or you bet a strong hand and you're raised by an even better hand) but a play that you can, in retrospect, rationally understand was wrong. Sure, everybody makes mistakes and Roy is no exception, but he never showed it when I was at the table, or I wasn't able to recognize it.

Back to the $20-40 game, many people held the opinion that the $20-40 game was the better and the $10-20 the tougher game. If you think in terms of ac-tion, and many people do, that was true. But $20-40 was often the highest hold'em game spread at the Mirage. That meant there were a lot of not only good, but excellent players like David Sklansky, Roy Cooke, Ed Hill and players that became famous later, such as Daniel Negreanu. All in all, the best limit hold'em players in town were assembled in that game.

When my desire to play in the $20-40 game got stronger I had to realize that there was a problem: I lacked the bankroll to do so. I'd made some money at $10-20, but I spent the winnings. I always came to town with $3,000. I used my winnings to pay my expenses, and if there was some-thing left, I bought myself something. The next time I returned to Las Ve-gas with $3,000 again. You can't think about playing $20-40 on a $3,000 bankroll; it's just too small. Two bad sessions and you find yourself on the way to the ATM. Of course, I could have come up with more money, but I didn't want to risk my own money. I played exclusively with money I had won, and I didn't want to change that.

After I had watched the $20-40 games for quite a while, I decided that I would try to play at that level. But how could I do that with my $3,000 bankroll? The safe route would have been to run my bankroll up to $12,000 and then start playing $20-40. It would take at least two or three trips—well over a year—to build my roll to that size. But I wanted to play immediately. I decided to play in the $10-20 game until I had $6,000, and then take a shot at $20-40.

On my next trip I started playing $10-20, and after I had won $3,000 I played in the $20-40 game for the first time. My beginning in that game was neither a Cinderella nor a horror story. I lost and I won, with no obvious tendency. But two things quickly became clear: $20-40 was a different animal and I had to learn a lot. I correctly decided not to force anything. I played mostly $10-20, and only jumped into the higher game when I thought it was good.

Similar to my previous jump in stakes, at first I didn't feel confident in the $20-40 game. There was a lot of money involved, and I couldn't suppress feelings about that. If things went badly I could easily lose two grand or more in a single session. It would take about two weeks at $10-20 just to win that back. If you play regularly it's not really a big deal, but if you're leaving town in two or three weeks, it's worrisome to contemplate playing the remainder of your trip just to make up what you lost in a single session.

There was another factor concerning the money involved. Don't make the mistake of assuming that, because the blinds double, it costs you only twice as much to play. Capped pots were extremely rare before the flop at $10-20, but quite common in the $20-40 game. Usually there were a couple of players who craved action. Not only does it cost you more to play, but many hands that rely on implied odds are no longer playable.

At $10-20 there was often no raise, or just a single raise and several callers before the flop, making it correct to play hands such as A-5s or 8-7s in late position. With three or four bets pre-flop, these hands are no longer worth playing, and don't forget that the action didn't stop before the flop. These action players do a lot of betting and raising after the flop, meaning that even if you hit something, drawing becomes expensive. You don't get the implied odds you need for these types of hands.

This didn't come as a surprise, as I had studied the game intensely before playing. What really was unexpected, however, was how the players responded to my game. I was the tightest and most aggressive player in the $10-20 game. At $20-40 I was still the tightest, but by no means the most aggressive, player. I had assumed that I could dominate the post-flop play as I had in the $10-20 game. I thought that people would fear me because I played few hands, and that they would give up quickly after the flop if they didn't hit big. In reality, exactly the opposite occurred.

Of course, the action guys noticed that I played tight. But their thinking was not that this player has a better hand, so we have to be careful. Instead they thought a tight player would give up easily if you hammered on him enough. I said earlier that I was once check-raised twice in a row as a bluff (see p. 244). That was just one example of how some of these loose-aggressive players tried to make a tight player like me lay down his hand.

Facing just one of these action players is no problem; you just let him bet and call him down. The math is on your side. But if you face two or three of these guys and they start a raising war, you are in deep trouble. You don't know where you stand as these players raise with nothing, over-cards, draws, bottom pair, top pair, sets or the nuts. You assume that not all of them have what they represent. You can beat one or two of these guys, but can you beat all of them? It costs a lot to find out.

I had difficulties at first adapting to that style. I laid down good hands, only to find out later that nobody had much. Next time I went all the way and sure enough, one of my opponents had flopped a set. As I gained experience, I learned that I had to protect my hand better and that good hand-reading abilities were required. These guys played loose-aggressively but not randomly. They played certain hands in certain positions in a certain way. My task was to determine their playing patterns.

Hand-reading is a useful but nonessential skill in low-limit. At $10-20 it becomes important and in $20-40 it's crucial. After some time, I became proficient at it and my results improved noticeably.

When I first tried $20-40, I stuck to the lower game most of the time and only occasionally played at the higher limit. On my second trip I played more in the $20-40 game. Fortunately, I always won immediately when I stepped down after a losing session at $20-40. That was a big relief financially, and it rebuilt my confidence. I was clearly improving in the $20-40 game, but my hourly rate was still better at the smaller game. It would still take a lot of effort to achieve real success at $20-40.

By watching my spending, I had doubled my bankroll to over $6,000, so on my third trip I could start playing $20-40 immediately. I knew that $6,000 is just about half of what you should have to play in the $20-40 game regularly, but I was ready to quickly step down if I ran into trouble.

That third trip marked my transition from $10-20 to the $20-40 game. From that point I only played at the lower game when there was a long waiting list for $20-40, or when the game didn't look good.

The longer I played at the new level, the better I felt. Having the opportunity to play with all the excellent players at $20-40, my game improved considerably, and my win rate rose slowly but steadily. But I was never able to make one big bet per hour, although my rate continued to increase. It's always my goal to win 1 BB/h at whatever level I play because if you can achieve this, you know you are one of the top players at that limit. I believe the reason why I didn't reach my goal was that I didn't play long enough at that limit. I had no intention to switch levels again, but something happened that I hadn't foreseen, and that marked a watershed in the Las Vegas poker life of middle and high-limit players.

The Bellagio opened its doors on October 15, 1998, and overnight, everything changed. I arrived in Las Vegas in late October, two weeks after the opening of the Bellagio. I was curious to see this new poker room, but as usual, I first went to the Mirage. I couldn't believe my eyes. Though it was Friday night, the poker room was half-empty. Usually at this time there were three or four $10-20 games and four or five $20-40 games in progress. Now they had just one $10-20 and one $20-40 game.

I went over to the Bellagio. The poker room was jam packed. I recognized most of the dealers, the shift managers and even the chip runners. All the common faces from the Mirage $10-20 and $20-40 game were now here. It was like the Mirage poker room had been transported to the Bellagio.

At three-and-a-half weeks, this was one of my shorter trips. Though I occasionally played at the Bellagio, I stuck to the Mirage for two (probably not very good) reasons. First, I didn't felt as comfortable in the Bellagio poker room as in the Mirage. I always liked the Mirage poker room best. To me it was, at least before the remodeling of the casino, the most beautiful poker room in the world. Second, things were finally looking good for me in the

$20-40 game, and the Mirage was the only place that offered it. The result was that I played in a game that mostly was not very good, as I desperately hoped that the players would come back. I believed that it was the appeal of something new that attracted players to the Bellagio poker room, and that most of them would eventually come back. That was a misconception.

The whole trip was not a complete disaster, but it only yielded a modest profit. The reason was obvious. Before the Bellagio opened you could play at the Mirage $20-40 game around the clock. Now the game started sometime in the afternoon and broke down at 1:00 or 2:00 a.m. With only one or two games going, there was little selection. When the games were bad, I often went to eat, watched a show, went shopping or returned to my room to work on the computer, thus losing a lot of playing time.

It became clear that if things didn't change, I had to play at the Bellagio. Things didn't change, hence I had to decide what limit I wanted to play in the future, since the Bellagio spread different limits than the Mirage.

The Mirage and the Bellagio belong to the same company, the MGM Mirage. So as not to compete directly, the Mirage spreads the even limits ($10-20, $20-40, $40-80) and the Bellagio the odd limits ($15-30, $30-60 and up). I made what proved to be the right decision by taking the safe route and opting for the $15-30 game. I didn't feel ready for $30-60, and taking uncalculated risks was never my thing. And there was another, oft-overlooked factor. Moving from even to odd limits, the ratio between small and big blind changes[139]. The smaller limit was the better choice to get accustomed to the new structure.

For about three years I played nearly exclusively in the $15-30 game. My trips varied from not-so-good to excellent. I averaged about $36 per hour during this time, always trending up. After this long period of time, I felt confident stepping up to the $30-60 game and, to my surprise, the transition went smoothly. I started winning right from the beginning. The $15-30 and $30-60 games at the Bellagio share similar characteristics. The difference is that you will find a lot of good players, usually regulars, but no great players at $15-30, while the excellent players and tough pros sit in the $30-60 game. The $30-60 game is more aggressive, but the difference is not nearly as great as between $10-20 and $20-40 back at the Mirage.

---

[139] To understand how the blind structure affects the game see p. 324

The story of how I worked my way up is pretty typical, and most successful middle-limit players I know have a similar story to tell. There is no player I'm aware of who jumped right into a $20-40 game and started winning immediately. Don't have any illusions, though. Winning in low-limit games is easy. Winning in middle-limit games is not.

First and foremost, you must realize that the qualities that make you a winning low-limit player are not enough to beat middle-limit games. If you stubbornly stick to what worked at the lower games, you will inevitably fail. You must be willing to constantly improve your game and to adjust to changing playing conditions. It's not easy, but it can be done, and you don't have to be a poker Houdini.

Several lessons can be learned from my story:

- ♠ If you study hard and are disciplined, you can win in low-limit games right away even with no playing experience.

- ♠ This isn't true for middle-limit games. So – start low.

- ♠ Never step up in limits before you can beat your current game for at least 0.5 big bet per hour.

- ♠ Higher-limit games are almost always tougher to beat than lower-limit games. Have no illusions about this.

- ♠ The qualities that make you a winning low-limit player are not enough to beat middle-limit games. Particularly, being aggressive and being proficient at reading hands is essential to succeed in middle-limit games.

- ♠ You must have an adequate bankroll to play at a higher-limit game on a regular basis. Having 300 BB at your disposal is a good rule of thumb. It's okay to take occasional shots at a higher limit with a smaller bankroll.

- ♠ Most people think the bigger the pots at a table, the better the game is. This is not so. Big pots mean a lot of betting and raising. If you have a choice, always opt for a table where people play passively rather than aggressively[140].

- ♠ Always look at where the games are the most profitable for you. If that means changing the casino, by all means do so.

---

[140] For a more thorough discussion see Mason Malmuth, *Poker Essays*, 1991, p. 114f.

Chapter 11

Professional Play

You have studied hard, and you have worked your way up from low- to middle-limit hold'em games. After having some troubles with the transition, you now finally make money in the middle-limit games. If that happens, it's usually just a matter of time until some thoughts about making a living as a poker pro cross your mind. Thoughts like that are natural, since you can make some serious money in middle-limit games.

The idea of being a pro seems seductive to many because there are some undeniable advantages: within certain limits you have control over your income (the more you play, the more you make), you have no fixed working time, you are your own boss, nobody tells you what to do and you can go on vacation whenever you want. If you play online, you don't even have to leave your apartment.

Of course, there are some drawbacks, such as an unsteady income, no pension fund, an unsure future and having to reconcile playing poker with a family life. And if you want to switch professions later, it's probably no asset when you have to explain to a potential employer that all you were doing in the past was playing poker.

What makes playing poker for a living so attractive is that many people see it as mixing business with pleasure. What can be better than being paid for doing what you like best? But I can assure you that playing poker loses a lot of its fun and charm if you do it full-time. Nonetheless, wherever there is a middle-limit game you will usually find some pros, though not as many as you would guess. Playing as a pro is no fantasy. It can be done, but it's a tough job and—whether you're a winning player or not—it's not for everybody.

What it takes to be a professional player

Let's first define what a poker pro is. A poker pro is someone who derives a large part of his income from playing poker. In other words, he is dependent on making money by playing poker. Consequently, most winning players are not pros because they depend on another source of income. In the Las Vegas card rooms you find a lot of retired persons who have settled down in town and play regularly. Though a lot of them are quite good and some are excellent players, they are no pros. They live from their savings or have a pension check coming every month. If these regulars make money from poker, it's a nice bonus, but they don't rely on it.

One day before Christmas I was talking to Mike, a middle-limit pro from Canada and a good friend of mine. He complained that he had had an unsatisfying year, that he had made a lot less than expected and that the last two months had been especially tough for him. To tease him a little bit I said, "Come on, Mike. Beating these games is easy. I've come to Vegas for years and I nearly always win."

"I know," he said, "but you're not a pro." His response hit the nail on the head and made me think a lot. It is a lot easier for me because I have no financial pressure to win. It makes a big difference whether I have to win or if it is just nice.

Another friend of mine, Trevor, was a geologist who worked in the country near Las Vegas. Being single, he spent a lot of his leisure time in the card rooms playing $15-30 and $20-40 limit hold'em. Then he met a nice girl, they got married and two years later had a child. Understandably, Trevor wanted to spend more time with his family, but nobody in the city of Las Vegas needed a geologist. Being an excellent middle-limit player, he decided to give up his job and try to make a living from poker. He started playing full-time in June, one of the slowest months in Vegas, and lost. Then he played the whole month of July and lost as well. Losing two months in a row is not that unusual but, with a family to support, his life as a poker pro was over.

He took a job in the post-office and only played poker casually. Several months later, we sat at a poker table next to each other and talked about how things were going. He suddenly grabbed some chips from his stack, showed them to me and said, "That's what I'm now making a day at the post office." Though it was just the equivalent of what he might make playing two hours in a $20-40 game, he seemed happy, and I have no doubt that he made the right decision to work a regular job.

If anyone had what it takes to be a successful pro, it was Trevor. What went wrong? I don't know. Maybe it was just bad luck. Maybe he could no longer play his best game because he was confronted with a situation he never had dealt with before: the fact that he now had to win.

As you can see, being a winning player and having an adequate bankroll are not enough to become a successful pro. To make it as a professional requires a quality you can't train for or simulate, namely the ability to handle the pressure to win that comes with playing for a living. You will only know if you have that quality when you have played as a pro.

I have been playing and winning for more than fifteen years in middle-limit poker games. Could I make it as a pro? I have no idea.

How much can you make?

It's commonly accepted that a very good player can win about one big bet per hour at limit hold'em[141]. Say a player with a win rate of 1 BB/h is willing to put in 2,000 hours a year, which is about the number of hours a person works as an employee in the Western countries. Then that player can expect to make $80,000 per year by playing $20-40, or $120,000 at $30-60. Not all pros achieve 1 BB/h. On the other hand, the very best pros make around 1.5 BB/h in middle-limit games. I have occasionally heard of larger, even much larger figures. Much is possible over a period of time, but in the long run about 1.5 BB/h is the maximum, and only a few players can achieve this.

---

[141] For a realistic estimate of what you can make at the different limits and games, see Mason Malmuth, *Poker Essays*, 1991, pp. 52-54.

You can make a decent living even if you are not in the very good or excellent category. A pro that makes 0.5 BB/h at $30-60 can still expect to make $60,000 on average annually. That's more than the median income of an American household.

This is true for low and middle-limit games. The win rate in terms of big bets per hour goes down in high-limit games ($100-200 and up). Nevertheless, it is advantageous to play in these games if you can be successful. Playing in a $200-400 game with a win rate of 0.5 BB/h nets you a lot more than 1.5 BB/h at $30-60.

Many people don't understand that potential winnings in terms of big bets per hour are about the same at all low and middle-limit games. Shouldn't you make more big bets per hour in low-limit games, since they're easier to beat than middle-limit games? Therefore, shouldn't a very good low-limit player have a much higher win rate in terms of big bets per hour than a very good middle-limit player?

Yes and no. Yes, an excellent low-limit player wins more big bets per hour, and no, his net win rate in BB/h is not higher. This is because playing in a casino is not free. The casino either shortens the pot (called taking a rake) or charges a time fee for the privilege to play. To understand what I mean, let's compare two very good players, a low-limit $3-6 player and a middle-limit $30-60 player.

The calculation is easy for the $30-60 player. He has to win $74/hr to net 1 BB/h. The Bellagio charges each player $6 each half-hour to play in the $30-60 game. That's $12 an hour. This player tips the dealer $1 per pot won, and as a very good player, he wins two to three pots per hour, so let's say he spends $2/hr on tips. So, with $14/hr in expenses, our player needs to win $74/hr to net $60, or 1 BB. Put another way, this player has to win 1.23 BB/h to net 1 BB/h.

Low-limit pots are raked, making the calculation more difficult for the $3-6 player. We will make the following assumptions: 1) Since low-limit games are typically looser than middle-limit games, our very good player (correctly) plays more hands and wins on average three pots per hour that are fully raked. The maximum rake at the Bellagio for low-limit games is $4, and of course our player tips $1 for every pot won. His average expenses for one hour are $15 ($12 for the rake and $3 for the tips). Consequently, to make 1 BB/h this player has to win $21 from his opponents. In other words, to net 1 BB/h the very good player in a low-limit game has to win 3.5 BB/h.

The lower the limit, the higher the relative cost of play. The statement, which you even can find in print[142], that you can make several BB/h in low-limit games is not true; the cost of play is simply too high[143]. Of course, this is only true for brick-and-mortar casinos. Online, your win rate can be significantly higher, since the game is usually faster and you can multi-table.

Bankroll

As I said, you should have a 300-big bet bankroll to absorb the inevitable downswings that are part of the game. That's fine as long as playing poker is just additional income, but the bankroll should be considerably larger for a full-time professional player. Johnny Chan suggests a bankroll of more than 500 BB[144]. The size of the bankroll depends on the risk you are willing to take, but if your future is at stake, you can't be too risk-adverse. To me a 1,000-BB bankroll seems about right.

Of course, Johnny Chan prefers an unusually large bankroll because he is a high-limit player. In high-limit games the win rates are lower, hence you need a larger bankroll. Nonetheless, I think a 1,000-BB bankroll makes sense for middle-limit games as well. Let's see why.

The bad news is that, at least theoretically, your chance of going broke in poker is always greater than zero, no matter how large your bankroll. If a negative outcome for any single event is possible (which is the case in poker) the risk of going broke cannot be zero[145]. So, what is the chance of going broke? We will use the Chen-Sileo formula[146]:

---

[142] See, e.g., Angel Largay, *No-Limit Texas Hold'em. A Complete Course*, 2006, p. 9.

[143] Just to set the record straight: I'm not saying that the experts at all low- and middle-limit games win exactly the same amount in terms of BB/h. There might be some extremely juicy low-limit games where an expert can make more. What I say is this: excellent players in low- and middle-limit games win about the same amount of BB/h. The claim that you can net several BB/h in low-limit games on a long-term basis is a fallacy.

[144] See Johnny Chan/Mark Karowe, *Million Dollar Limit Cash Games*, 2006, pp. 26-29.

[145] See Bill Chen/Jerrod Ankenman, *The Mathematics of Poker*, 2006, p. 282.

[146] See Patrick W. Sileo, *The Evaluation of Blackjack Games Using a Combined Expectation and Risk Measure*, in William R. Eadington/Judy A. Cornelius (ed.), *Gambling and Commercial Gambling: Essays in Business, Economics, Philosophy and Science*, 1992, pp. 551-563.

$$p(R) = e^{\frac{-2BW}{\sigma^2}}$$

where:

p(R) = probability of going broke (risk of ruin)

B = bankroll

W = win rate

σ = hourly standard deviation

For a typical middle-limit pro with a win rate of 1 BB/h, a standard deviation of 10 BB and a bankroll of 300 BB, we get a probability of going broke of 0.22%. This doesn't look like much, and it's a fairly reasonable approximation for a recreational player, but for a pro it's way off the mark.

The formula assumes that you play forever and don't take money out of your bankroll. This last assumption is not true for a pro, since he must cover his basic needs with poker winnings. It's practically impossible to come up with a reliable risk-of-ruin percentage for a pro, since his living expenses impact his bankroll, and his game may deteriorate when things go badly. I would assume that a pro is much more affected by a run of bad cards when his bankroll is in jeopardy than a non-pro; this is yet another reason why a pro's bankroll should be larger.

When his bankroll dwindles, a pro comes under a lot of pressure because he has to face the possibility of going broke. I once had a $4,500 downswing, 225 BB, at $10-20, despite having a win rate of over 1 BB/h to that point. This is solid proof that a significant downswing is definitely possible. I was annoyed, but it didn't threaten the basis of my existence, and I was able to keep calm and maintain my confidence. Luckily, things turned for the better and at the end of my trip I still had booked a sizable win.

Now, consider a pro that makes his living playing $10-20 with a $6,000 bankroll (300 BB). A $4,500 loss would leave him with just $1,500, and the bills are filling the mailbox. He has lost three-quarters of his bankroll. Do you think that makes him play better? Athletes in certain sports often play better under pressure (John McEnroe in tennis, for instance), but I doubt this is the case in poker[147].

I think that most poker players couldn't withstand such pressure and their game would take a turn for the worse. You may say someone shouldn't be a pro if he can't handle the pressure. I disagree. The point is not to get into such a situation in the first place. A larger bankroll minimizes that risk.

Say our $10-20 pro has 1,000 BB instead of 300 BB. Then, after a $4,500 downswing he still has $15,500. He needn't worry that he'll soon go broke. He can remain calm, maintain his confidence and wait until his luck changes. Having 1,000 BB instead of 300 BB makes all the difference.

The last example, losing $4,500 with a 300-BB bankroll in a $10-20 game, should never happen to a pro who knows what he is doing. After losing half his bankroll, he no longer has the funds for his regular $10-20 game and should step down in level. Specifically, that means after losing $3,000 at $10-20, you have a 300-BB bankroll for $5-10, which should now become your regular game. If again you lose half your bankroll, you have to step down once more, or if you double your bankroll, you can return to the $10-20 table. Stepping down is the sensible move in this situation, but I've seen pros who stubbornly play on at their regular level and go broke.

Stepping back is annoying because it takes you on average more than twice as long to recoup your loss (due to the higher cost to play at lower levels) than by playing at your regular game. This is another advantage of a larger bankroll; it reduces greatly the need to step back. Stepping down in limits is humiliating for many pros. It feels like having a sign on your head that reads, "I'm running badly and I no longer have the money to play in my regular game."

To summarize: a pro should have a larger bankroll than a non-pro for two reasons. First, the pro has to earn his keep by playing poker. He relies on his winnings to pay his bills and has to cover his expenses by taking money out of his bankroll, thus increasing his risk-of-ruin percentage. Second, having a larger bankroll reduces the pressure when a big downswing kicks in, and frees him from stepping down.

---

[147] Tournament poker may be different in that regard as there are some players that always play better when it counts. However, don't confuse this 'pressure' with the pressure when things are going bad for a cash game pro and his bankroll is in jeopardy. In tournament poker your buy-in is already gone before you have played your first hand, thus you can only win by playing.

What pros are doing wrong

There is no question that poker pros must do many things right, especially when it comes to playing. Otherwise, they would quickly become ex-professional poker players. But that doesn't mean they're doing everything right. In fact, many pros do a lot of things wrong, but play well enough to compensate for these shortcomings.

Let's look at a pro like Alan, one of the best middle-limit hold'em players in Las Vegas.

When Alan comes into the card room he immediately puts his name on the $30-60 list, glances quickly at the $30-60 tables in progress, then takes a seat at an empty table and waits patiently until his name is called. If the card room is busy and it takes two hours to get a seat, so be it. He is pre-pared for that; he takes a book out of his bag and starts reading. It would never cross his mind to play in a lower game. A player of Alan's caliber can expect to win more than $40/hr in the $15-30 game. To not play in a lower-limit game definitely costs him money.

Most pros are also good at table selection, and are quick to change tables when they spot a more lucrative opportunity. Alan is the exception. He always seems to be happy with the table he gets. In the years we've played together, I hardly remember an occasion when he switched tables. A player with Alan's skill is going to do well regardless of the table, but no matter how good you are, a better table means more profit.

Changing seats at the table can be productive, especially with bad players in the game. Alan does change seats, though less often than other players.

I usually take a break every two hours or so to relax my mind, which helps me maintain my focus at the table. Alan never takes a break. I have seen him play twelve hours straight. As soon as he gets a seat, he plays without interruption. He goes to the restroom when he's in middle position, so he doesn't miss the blinds. He has excellent stamina and can stay focused for a long time, therefore playing without a break doesn't seem to hurt him. However, you often see pros play straight through long sessions when taking a break would be beneficial.

I play on all shifts regularly, and I'm certain that the day shift (11:00 a.m.-7:00 p.m.) is the toughest. You have the most regulars and the fewest tourists, especially on weekdays. Night shift (7:00 p.m.-3:00 a.m.) is usually better because there are more tables in progress, making it easier to find a good game, and more tourists are playing. Graveyard shift (3:00 a.m.-11:00 a.m.) is often the best time to play, especially if you can find some over-tired tourists desperately trying to recoup their losses.

Alan has a regular schedule. He usually comes to the poker room around noon and plays for a couple of hours. He almost exclusively plays during the day shift. I suppose he does this to maintain a regular life style. Not everyone wants to play all night and sleep during the day, so I don't blame him, but clearly this habit costs him money.

Alan has another characteristic that is the downfall of many not-so-good players. If he has made a grand or so, he often quickly hits the door even if he has just played an hour or two. And if he is losing, he may play longer than usual in an attempt to recoup his losses. This is usually a bad strategy.

First, if you are winning, that often means the game is good, and if you're behind, that indicates that the game might be bad. So, Alan's strategy tends to reduce his playing time in good games and extend it in bad games.

Second, most players play worse when they are losing, hence they should employ the opposite strategy. With Alan it's different. He is always the favorite, no matter if the game is good or not, and being behind doesn't affect his game. Therefore, playing longer is always +EV for Alan. I just wonder if he wouldn't do better if he based his playing time on the game condition and not on how he was doing.

Another key for the professionals is social skills at the table. Ridiculing a weak player for a bad play is stupid. The humiliated player will either leave the table or play tighter, which means that he will play better. All pros I know understand this. Only wannabe pros chastise others for their weak plays.

When it comes to social skills, Alan has none. He's not rude; he just lives in his own universe when he is at the table.

Let me give an example. I was sitting in the 7 seat, a tourist was in the 8 seat and Alan was behind him in the 9 seat. Alan took a tiny scrap of paper and wrote his session result on it. I knew his playing session was now over and he would leave the table. He took off his sunglasses, unplugged his earphones and got into a conversation with the guy in the 8 seat. They talked for about ten minutes while Alan told him that he was responsible for the introduction of Omaha poker in Las Vegas late in the eighties. After Alan had left the table the tourist turned to me and said, "Incredible, I have been playing for over three hours next to this guy and he never said a word. Now he starts talking!" I could have answered that I have played for over ten years with Alan and that we have never exchanged more than a few words.

Tourists like the guy in the 8 seat come to have fun. They don't want to just play poker. They want to chat with the other players, to have a good time. For someone like Alan who plays day-in, day-out, playing poker is no longer fun, it's the job he has to do to earn his income. His sunglasses and his earphones form some sort of protective shield, signaling to the other players, "Don't talk to me. I'm not here to have fun. I'm working."

This approach makes other players feel unwelcome. One such player is not much of a problem. But imagine that a tourist sits down at a table and five or six mirror sunglasses stare at him. He would probably quickly say to himself, "I don't feel comfortable here. Let's go to the blackjack pit, where I can make some noise and have some fun." Sunglasses should be banned at the poker tables; they scare the fish away.

Being friendly to the contributors not only makes them happy. I often pick up valuable information I would have missed if I was listening to music while playing. These players are often happy to discuss their hands with you, giving you a good idea of how they play. If you are nice to them, they let you see their hands when you are not involved in the pot, which gives you an even better idea.

Sometimes it's better yet. Here is an example.

In a $30-60 game at the Bellagio I raised with K♣-Q♣ from middle position in what turned out to be a multiway pot.

The flop came Q♥-4♦-8♥. I bet my top pair and three players called.

Turn: K♠. I bet again and only Nadine, who had limped pre-flop under the gun, called.

The river brought the 10♣ (board: Q♥-4♦-8♥-K♠-10♣). Since the flush card didn't come, I was absolutely sure I had the best hand. Now, interestingly,

Nadine bet out. Immediately I got a bad feeling about the hand. For that you have to understand that we had played together quite often. I knew Nadine had a lot of respect for my game. After I showed that much strength in a multiway pot, I was quite sure she wouldn't bluff with a busted flush draw. I doubted that she would bet a hand like K-10, since I could easily have a set or a better two pair. You see why I no longer liked my hand. However, with pot odds of over 10-to-1, folding was not an option. In limit hold'em this is an automatic call.

Since I knew I was going to call and that my prospects to win were slim, I tried something. I said to Nadine, "I think you have me beat." She looked briefly at me and said, "Then throw your hand away." That wasn't what I wanted to hear. So I continued: "I have the top two pair." She showed no reaction. I turned over my hole cards. She glanced at my hand and said, "I have a straight," showing J♥-9♥. That little move saved me sixty bucks.

Alan plays with Nadine nearly every day. Would it have worked for him, too? Not in a thousand years! You have to be friendly to your opponents to make a ploy like this work. I have pulled this one off successfully many times. Usually it works only with recreational players. These players are usually at the table to have some fun. They are satisfied with winning the pot; their goal is not to squeeze out every possible penny with their winning hands. It can only work if you are on good terms with your opponent and if you show your hand. The latter part is important, as most players otherwise assume you're trying to make a move on them.

As I said, this ploy doesn't work with pros or regulars. As a regular player, Nadine was an exception. She is an elderly lady who plays nearly every afternoon at the Bellagio. She obviously has enough money, so a bet more or less doesn't mean much to her. Her pride is that she can hold her own in this tough game, and she does this pretty well.

As you can see, you can do many things wrong and still be a big winner. I have no doubt that a smart guy like Alan knows what he is doing and why he is doing it. The points mentioned may influence your win rate, but they alone will not make you a winner. Your table-selection skills may be excellent and you may know how to make other people feel comfortable at the table, but if you can't play, you won't win. The most important factor is still your playing ability, and that's where someone like Alan really excels.

What impresses me most about Alan is his ability to adjust to any playing situation. In a full-ring game he looks like any other tight-aggressive player. The shorter the game gets, the more he opens up his game. Every good player does this, but his play is always totally balanced, his level of aggression completely in tune with the playing conditions. I have played with him shorthanded, and he completely dominated the table. He knows what's exactly right in a certain situation. Therefore, he plays under all circumstances. If five players are walking, the game often comes to a halt because some players refuse to play. Alan is never one of them. If there are three players on the waiting list, Alan being one of them, and the other two want to play, Alan will gladly start a three-handed game.

This total flexibility, the ability to take advantage of every possibility, is what distinguishes Alan from most middle-limit pros. High-limit pros are different. These games are often shorthanded, so you have to be an expert at this form of poker or you will not survive for long, but middle-limit pros are mostly ring-game players. They will play shorthanded when they think the game is favorable, but most of them don't feel as comfortable as when the game is full.

Okay, I know what you're thinking: If this player is really that good, how comes he only plays $30-60 and not $400-800? Only Alan can answer that question. But I think he is just satisfied with what he has achieved, and with the money he is earning. The $30-60 game is the highest limit hold'em game that is spread around the clock at the Bellagio. If there is no big tournament in town, the higher-limit hold'em games like $60-120 or $100-200 start in the evening. Since Alan mostly plays in the afternoon, this may be a factor. Playing higher would mean changing his habits.

I don't want to get into the old debate about who's the best poker player. Is it someone like Doyle Brunson, who plays in the highest-limit games, or could the best player be one of the top middle-limit pros like Alan? It's all a matter of definition and opinion. Of course, Doyle is the better player in the sense that he is an expert at all forms of poker, while Alan only plays limit hold'em. Alan has no chance against a player like Doyle in a mixed game. But if the question is who would make more money in a $30-60 limit hold'em game, I would put my money on Alan.

Why pros fail

Playing poker for a living is a tough business, and not all who try it succeed. In fact, having played for over fifteen years with pros and aspiring pros, in my experience most of them fail sooner or later, usually sooner. There are diverse factors that lead to disaster. I have tried to categorize them:

- ♠ Overestimating one's own playing strength
- ♠ Ego problems
- ♠ Bankroll
- ♠ Handling swings
- ♠ Bad beats
- ♠ Flexibility
- ♠ Bad habits
- ♠ Lacking discipline

This list is by no means exhaustive, but it covers the most important aspects. Of course, most of the reasons are valid for non-pros as well. These factors help to explain why players lose, or don't win enough.

1) Overestimating one's own playing strength

This is probably the top reason why pros fail. If someone who can beat the $10-20 game for 0.6 BB/h stubbornly plays $30-60 to make a living, then this is a sure way to go broke. People tend to advance in limits until they reach a limit they can no longer beat, and then stay at that limit. You see it all the time.

When I say someone is a weak player in a game like $30-60, this is relative to the limit. Most of these so-called weak players could in fact be winners if they played lower. I know a Korean woman that has played in the $15-30 and $30-60 games for years. She is just too predictable to have a shot in these games, but she knows enough about hand selection and post-flop play to be successful in a $4-8 or maybe an $8-16 game. It is beyond me why a player would lose hundred of thousands of dollars in games she simply cannot beat, when she could make some money at smaller limits.

2) Ego problems

All the good players I know are confident and have trust in their game. Having confidence in one's own game is a vital quality of every successful player. However, there is a fine line between confidence and overconfidence. If you think you are invincible and all the other players at the table are idiots, you probably have lost touch with reality.

In poker it's imperative that you are realistic about your own and your opponents' playing abilities. Otherwise, the quality of your decisions will suffer and you will be doomed to fail. You needn't fear your opponents, but you must respect them, and you must assess their playing abilities realistically. Overconfidence is always a shaky basis for a decision.

Some years ago a young player from the Bay area, Gary, came to town to make it as a pro. We played poker together nearly every day and were on friendly terms. In my opinion he lacked some basic poker knowledge and played much too loose-aggressive to make it as a pro in Vegas. Of course, that was not his own appraisal. He dreamed of playing in high-limit games in two or three months. I thought we were close enough friends that I could tell him what I thought. So, one day when we were chatting, I said, "Gary, you are not going to make it here, the way you play."

He came unglued, yelling all sorts of insults at me. Finally, he challenged me to a heads-up game, saying I could choose the limit and the game. Though I didn't want to escalate the situation, I couldn't resist the temptation to reply that I would always be around and that he would be gone the next time I came to Vegas. My prediction proved true; I never saw him again. If Alan or Roy Cooke would come to me and say, "In my opinion, there is something wrong with your game," you can bet I would listen.

Here is a short list of indications of an ego problem:

- ♠ You try to impress the other players at the table
- ♠ You want to prove that you are by far the best player

- ♠ You take losing against any player personally
- ♠ You stubbornly play in games you cannot beat
- ♠ You refuse to step down in limits when your bankroll is insufficient for your regular game

Always remember that as a pro, or a serious player for that matter, your goal is to make money at the table, as much as you can, nothing else.

3) Bankroll

There is no question that many pros are under-bankrolled. Some know it and take the risk; others believe they don't need a bankroll as big as most poker theorists think, because they are superior players. This is mathematically sound, as the size of the required bankroll depends upon one's playing strength. The higher your edge in terms of BB/h won, the smaller the bankroll required. But this is just one factor. A pro has to win to make a living, and he takes money from his bankroll to cover his living expenses. This increases the required bankroll substantially.

A pro comes under more pressure when things don't go well and the bankroll shrinks. The threat of being out of action quickly becomes real when someone plays on a short bankroll and a downswing sets in. A lot of pros go broke because they don't understand bankroll management.

4) Handling swings

If you play long enough, it's just a matter of time until you experience a devastating downswing, no matter how good you are. It will come as sure as the sun comes up tomorrow. I've experienced two serious downswings in about 15 years of poker playing. In the $10-20 game I lost $4,500 (225 BB) and at $30-60 I dropped $11,500 (192 BB).

Don't jump to any quick conclusions that a big downswing comes about every seven years or so. First, I don't play as much as a pro or most regulars. I only play about two to three months full-time a year. Second, I play tighter than most people, which makes me less susceptible to downswings. Third, because I have a pretty steady temperament, I can handle losing streaks fairly well. Many people start to lose confidence when things go poorly for a while, and as a result their play deteriorates. Fourth, the two downswings mentioned are just the tip of the iceberg. Steady losing streaks lasting for weeks or months occur all the time for full-time players of all skill levels.

For a seasoned pro with a big enough bankroll, a downswing is not a big deal. He has the experience to handle it and knows that it is unavoidable. He just plays his normal game and waits for his luck to change. A large downswing is often devastating for a novice pro because he isn't prepared for it. What worked before seems to work no more. Consequently, he thinks there is something wrong with his game and he tries to make adjustments. But changes made under pressure when losing are only rarely beneficial. He sees that players are taking down pots with all sorts of hands. He waits a long time for a premium hand and then gets beat by a lesser hand. He figures that he plays too tight and has to loosen up. E.g., he may decide that because most players play any ace, he will play any suited ace and any unsuited ace down to A-8; this way he figures he still has an edge. Such a player usually plays looser and less aggressively.

It's understandable that a player who experiences a losing streak plays less aggressively. He has lost confidence, always expects the worst and thus tries to save money. The cumulative effect of these two factors, playing looser and less aggressively, is often that such a player no longer plays a winning game. If that is the case, his fate is sealed.

Interestingly upswings can also lead to disaster. Players are much more likely to go pro when they are running good than when they are losing. Thus, a novice pro often overestimates his own playing strength and how much he can make. Let's say a winning $20-40 player decides to make a living as a poker pro. In the first three months everything goes well. He makes about $7,000 a month. Now, he plans a budget that looks like this: He spends $5,000 for his living expenses and puts $2,000 aside to grow his bankroll. This all sounds very reasonable and solid. But the budget is based on a $7,000 income while his true earning is just $3,500. That means this player has a $5,000 lifestyle but a true earn of only $3,500. He must either cut back on his lifestyle (which is hard to do after you get used to it) or improve his game if he doesn't want to go broke.

Upswings are dangerous for inexperienced pros because they don't recognize that they are the counterpart to downswings. Instead, they erroneously believe that their game has improved so much that the higher win rate has become their true earn. Consequently, they become sloppy and overconfident and, thinking they are that much better than the rest of the table, they quickly move up to a higher game or start spending too much money.

I once saw a pro watching movies while playing. I asked him if he didn't think that he was losing a lot of information about the other players by doing this. His response was, "I know how all the players play at the table. I could probably beat them without even looking at the cards!" A typical case of overconfidence and a lost sense of reality. (By the way, he wasn't watching movies for long.)

5) Bad beats

Players react to downswings and bad beats in different ways. The common reaction is to start to play looser. When a player is running bad for a while and sees his premium hands losing to weaker holdings, he figures he has to play more hands to give him a better chance to win. The victim of a couple of bad beats usually plays looser because he wants to win his money back. He also tends to play more aggressively—he wants to quickly win back what he lost.

When I started playing poker, all the books I read said that bad beats are part of the game and that you shouldn't let them affect your play. No big deal, I thought. In the long run, the money will come my way. Unfortunately, theory and practice are two different things. If you see, hand after hand, some clown drawing out on you with ridiculous holdings, that's tough to swallow. And when you lose a good-sized pot in a $30-60 game due to a bad beat, that means that the miracle card your opponent caught cost you a grand or so. And that's just one hand!

One day when I was playing $6-12 at the Mirage, there was a drunk to my left. He was so drunk he could no longer read the board. At the end he simply turned over his cards and let the dealer read his hand. He handled the cards so clumsily that I could see one or both of his hole cards most of the time. Well, he beat me every hand, and not only did he beat me, he was the biggest winner at the table. I guess when he woke up the next morning he had no idea where all the money in his pocket came from.

Several years ago I was playing in one of the best $30-60 games I had ever seen. My nine opponents were throwing a party, not caring about the money they were splashing around. The pots were usually eight-, nine- or ten-handed. Everybody had a good time—except me. I was the biggest loser at the table, though I was the only one who had some idea what he was doing.

One last example. On a weekend I went to the Bellagio poker room at midnight. When I got a seat in the $30-60 game I noticed that Alan was at the table. That told me two things. He was losing heavily (he was playing past his usual quitting time) and the game was exceptionally good.

I posted behind the button and was dealt 10-8 offsuit. There was a raise with a couple of callers. That's not much of a hand, but since I was already halfway in, had position and there was a volume pot, I called. I flopped two pair that held up.

The very next hand I picked up A-Js, made a flush at the end and picked up another nice pot. On the third hand I looked at pocket fives. Since the table was loose, I called. I flopped a set and picked up my third big pot in a row.

In less then ten minutes I had won about $2,500. At the same time, by far the best player at the table, Alan, had been playing for twelve hours straight and was about as much down as I had won in ten minutes. That's poker. In the short run anything can happen. That's what makes poker attractive to so many people. The other side of the coin is that it can be very frustrating for the good players.

In any chess match, if the difference in skill between players is large enough, the better player will nearly always win. This is not so in poker. Even if you are the best player at the table, there is no guarantee that you will win any given session, because the short-term luck factor is huge in poker.

If bad beats cause you to play a lot looser (and more aggressively) than usual in a desperate attempt to get even, then you are steaming or going on tilt. Players with big egos are especially prone to steaming. For them, it's not just the money that counts. They view losing due to a lucky suck-out or against what they think is a weaker player as an insult. Then, they play more hands in an attempt not only to win back what they lost, but to show the other players that they are the best player at the table. This is plain silly. You have to accept the fact that in poker you can't prove anything in a single session. If the cards are not falling your way, there is nothing you can do about it.

A player who is on tilt is no longer playing a winning game. He is just burning money. When you watch poker on TV and see a player fall off his chair and roll on the floor after a bad beat, you can be sure this player (if he is not doing it for show) couldn't beat a $10-20 game if his life depended on it. This is one of the reasons why so many successful tournament players can't beat cash games: they are steamers. In tournament play the tendency to steam doesn't hurt you as much as in cash games, since you can't go to your wallet and put more money on the table.

All the successful pros I know handle bad beats well. One day I was playing with Paul, a $30-60 pro. He had come to the table with two racks of chips ($2,000) and was running really badly. After a while he put in his last chip—and lost the hand. He stood up, said smilingly, "Tomorrow is another day," and left the table. That's the attitude you should strive for.

Generally, I'm not a friend of fixed stop-loss limits but for most players there is a limit to how much they can lose before it affects their game. Find out what your limit is and leave the table if your loss exceeds it. I guess Paul knew that he could handle a loss of $2,000 without problems, thus he left the table when he lost that amount.

Being outdrawn hurts. People are not robots; they have feelings. This is especially true for pros. They play for a living and the money involved is significant. Let's say a pro loses a $1,000 pot because a weak opponent hits a two-outer at the end. He just lost his rent. I have seen pros crack at the table after a series of bad beats. I remember a young guy who came to Vegas to make his fortune as a poker pro. He appeared to be a good to very good player, definitively well versed enough to win at $30-60. Unfortunately, after a while things were not going well for him.

Then the following hand came up. He held A-K and flopped two pair. At the end somebody hit a gutshot with 5-3. He looked at his opponent's hand in disbelief and threw his cards in the air. "How can I always lose against the most ridiculous hands? This is unreal. I lost $7,500 the last two days. I can no longer stand it!" He began to sob, grabbed his remaining chips and left the table. Most people watching this incident found it funny to see a young man cry. For him it was anything but funny. His hopes and dreams were shattered. Having experienced similar situations, I knew how he felt and he had my sympathy. He never showed up again.

Even a seasoned pro like Alan, who has more than thirty years of playing experience, feels the pain of losing. If you watched him after he took a bad beat, you'd notice nothing but perhaps a quiet sigh.

Once the following hand came up. Alan raised and got a couple of callers. The flop came A-x-x. Alan bet and one fellow called. The turn was a Q. Again Alan bet and his opponent called. On the river a 10 fell (board: A-x-x-Q-10). Alan bet and his opponent raised.

The raise came completely unexpected. I mean, what could Alan's opponent hold that enabled him to raise at the end? A-10 seemed the only logical hand, though it was odd that he didn't raise on the flop to protect his hand when the pot was still multiway. Alan studied the board and then called reluctantly. I guess he had a bad feeling. His opponent turned over K-J! Alan looked at the hand, then turned over to me and said, "That's kind of bizarre." That was the biggest stirring of emotions I ever saw in him. He has seen it all, but bad beats still hurt.

The key to handling bad beats is not to suppress your emotions, but not to let it affect your play. When you look at the next hand, all your bad feelings should be gone and you should fully concentrate on the hand in progress. If this is tough for you, take a walk to cool off. Don't play when you are overwhelmed by bad emotions.

The conclusion is simple: Don't even think about playing for a living if you can't handle bad beats, because you won't make it.

6) Flexibility

A pro has to adjust to varying playing conditions. That sounds easier than it is.

First, even if a pro only plays one limit, the conditions at the table change all the time. Sometimes the game is shorthanded, then the table turns from loose/aggressive to tight/passive or you have to deal with a maniac. A pro has to maximize his profits by constantly adjusting his game to what's going on at the table.

Second, middle-limit games tend to get tougher over time. A pro has to react to these slow changes so he can still be ahead of the competition. When I was playing $10-20 at the Mirage, from time to time there were new players that had dropped down from the $20-40 game.

I remember a middle-aged woman that played every day in the $20-40 game. One day she appeared in the $10-20 game. I talked to her a little bit and she told me, "When the Mirage opened, the $20-40 was like a candy store. Now I can no longer beat it." After I played with her for a while, her problem became clear. She did a lot of things right. She knew what hands to play, understood the importance of position and never drew on short pot odds, but she didn't protect her hands enough. When she raised, your alarm bells went off, since she never did that without a big hand.

The lady is a classic example of an inflexible player. What once worked now didn't work, and she refused to change her game. The competition got tougher until it reached a point where she no longer had an edge. I have seen that many times. Today there are many good books on the market, you can get extensive experience in a short time playing online, and there is a lot of poker on television. All this makes the games tougher to beat than in the past. A pro has to observe developments and make the necessary adjustments.

Third, different limits have different structures, and a pro who makes the transition has to take that into account. Before the Bellagio opened, the $10-20 and $20-40 games were stable for years; you would always encounter the same faces day-in, day-out. When the Bellagio opened, these players left the Mirage for the new card room. The $10-20 player now played $15-30 and the $20-40 player $30-60. Then something interesting happened. Within a short time, most of these players were gone.

I believe this is related to the structure of the Bellagio games. At the Bellagio, the ratio between the small and big blinds in middle-limit games is 2-to-3, whereas at the Mirage it is 1-to-2. For instance, $10-20 is played with a $5 small blind and a $10 big blind. Had the $15-30 the same structure, the blinds would be $7.50 and $15; instead they are $10 and $15. Can a one-third increase in the small blind really have a considerable effect? There is no doubt in my mind that this is the case.

Most middle-limit players would like to play at a higher limit. They don't do it because they don't have the money, they can't beat the higher limit, they are afraid of the stakes or they can't handle the bigger swings. Making the transition from one level to the next is a big step, emotionally and financially.

When the Bellagio offered $15-30 and $30-60 games, most $10-20 and $20-40 players took the opportunity to play higher, since it looked like the stakes increased just by half and they thought they could handle that. Notice that in the $10-20 game it costs you $15 ($5 + $10) in blinds for every round, at $15-30 it's $25 ($10 + $15) and at $20-40 it's $30 ($10 + $20). The $15-30 game is actually much closer to $20-40 than to the $10-20 limit, and $30-60 is closer to $40-80 than to $20-40. In my opinion, most players that failed at the transition underestimated the consequences of the higher limit. They didn't have the money and/or couldn't handle the swings.

Then there is another point. The different structure demanded some adjustments that many players failed to see. Shortly after the Bellagio opened its doors, I played in a $15-30 game with Ginger, a very good $10-20 pro from the Mirage. Three players had limped, I folded at the button and Ginger threw her hand away in the small blind.

Normally I don't give advice at the table, but I had played with Ginger many times and she was a really nice lady. So I said to her, "Ginger, you should have called." She whispered, "I had an ugly hand, 5-3 offsuit." I responded: "It doesn't matter. You had pot odds of 14-to-1. No hand is that much of an underdog." She looked at me and said, "I will think about it".

The next time I played with her she made the same mistake again and again. She failed to understand that what was correct at $10-20 was no longer right at $15-30[148]. In the $15-30 game she was just a shadow of the player she had been at $10-20. She had lost her confidence and seemed to be scared by the limit. As a consequence, she quickly dropped back to $8-16, and today she plays $4-8. What a pity; she was one of the best $10-20 players. She wasn't prepared for the higher limit and wasn't able to make the necessarily adjustments.

The 2-to-3 blind structure not only affects the way to play the small blind, but several other aspects of play. Take, for example, blind stealing. In the $10-20 game you risk $20 to win $15, while at $15-30 you risk $30 to win

---

[148] For a more detailed explanation of why you should call from the small blind in a limit hold'em game with a 2-to-3 structure, see hand 1/6.

$25. Since at $15-30 it costs you less in relation to the reward, you should usually raise more liberally. On the other hand, the big blind gets better pot odds[149], thus he should call slightly more often.

Every good stud player understands that the higher the antes in relation to the bring-in, the looser he should play. This is true for hold'em as well, though the differences are not as significant. In a 2-to-3 structured limit hold'em game there is initially more money in the pot than in a game with a 1-to-2 structure, therefore the 2-to-3 game should play somewhat looser than a 1-to-2 game. It doesn't matter much for early-position play, but it makes a difference for late-position players and the blinds.

I prefer the 1-to-2 structure because it favors good players, while weak players have an advantage with a 2-to-3 structure. Most weak players call too often, especially from the small blind. This is often a serious blunder in the $10-20 game, whereas it is often correct at $15-30.

Playing conditions change all the time. A pro should be able to make the correct adjustments. Inflexibility is a serious sign of a lack of understanding.

7) Bad habits

Have you ever noticed that in a casino, the poker room is usually next to the sports book? Most poker players are gamblers that like all sort of action, sports betting being a favorite (and of course the casinos know this).

As a poker pro, you have to realize two things about gambling. First, what you do is not gambling. A typical gambler relies on luck, while a poker pro uses skill to win. Second, being a winning poker player doesn't make you an expert at all forms of games that a casino (or online card room) offers. There are games that can't (legally) be beaten, such as roulette, craps and keno, because the house always has the best of it. Sports betting and blackjack can be beaten, but it requires much time and effort to be successful (especially at sports betting). Rash gambling activities have been the downfall of many poker pros. There is a highly successful tournament player who is famous for always gambling his winnings away at the craps

---

[149] If a late-position player raises and the small blind folds, the big blind gets pot odds of 3.5-to-1 in the $10-20 and 3.7-to-1 in the $15-30 game.

tables. As a poker pro, you have to stay away from –EV situations.

Another bad habit is superstition. Most of the time this doesn't hurt a player. If you don't change your clothes after a winning session, or if you always bring a specific lucky charm to the table, that will have no bad effect on your outcome. However, there are superstitions that will influence your game.

For instance, if you insist that the 4 seat is your lucky seat, it can have a negative impact. First, when you are not in the 4 seat, you are not fully focused on the game. You hope that the 4 seat will open quickly. Second, the 4 seat may not objectively be the best seat, e.g., when the two players who give the most action sit in the 5 and 6 seats.

When I was playing $6-12 and $10-20 at the Mirage, I met a professional player whose name was Elton, and we quickly became good friends. Once I was standing behind him and watched a hand he was playing. Several days later I asked him about the hand. To my surprise, he remembered the hand immediately. It soon became obvious that he had a photographic memory. He not only remembered the hand, but all the players at the table, in which seat they were, what they were wearing, how much money they had in front of them, every single detail. It was unbelievable. I thought, wow, if I had that ability. Amazingly, his photographic memory, coupled with his superstition, was the reason for his downfall.

When we were playing together in the $10-20 game I noticed that he often took extensive breaks. Usually he was standing at the rail, smoking cigarettes and observing the action. Since he was a heavy smoker, I first assumed he just took a cigarette break because he didn't want to bother the other players at the table[150], but then I noticed that he always left the table when certain dealers sat down and returned immediately after they had left.

I asked him about this strange behavior. He told me that these dealers never dealt him good cards, hence he waited until a "good" dealer sat down. I was baffled. His photographic memory enabled him to know which dealers (seemingly) made him money and which cost him money. To refuse to play with certain dealers seemed completely rational—not because there was any real underlying process but because he was convinced he would do badly, and this hurt his game.

---

[150] At that time smoking was still allowed in the Mirage poker room.

Not playing with those dealers cost Elton money because it reduced his playing time. At least it didn't affect his win rate, but it got worse.

One day there was a long waiting list for the $10-20 game and Elton was already playing. I took a chair and sat behind him to watch him play. Except for his superstitions, he was a great player, and I could learn a lot from him. Then the following hand came up. A very loose and weak player raised under the gun. Everyone folded to Elton at the button. He held A-Ks and threw the hand away immediately. I nearly fell out of my chair. "How could you fold that hand? The guy who raised is very weak; he could have nearly anything," I whispered. He turned back to me and said, "He always beats me." Again, his photographic memory played tricks on him. To give up a clearly +EV situation is insane. You can probably guess the end of the story. The last time I saw Elton, he was dealing at a tournament.

Gambling on games that cannot be beat, and yielding to superstition are just two examples of bad habits some poker pros develop. Others are drinking at the table, taking drugs, playing without proper rest and spending too much money on women, just to mention a few.

8) Lacking discipline

A pro must have discipline in order to win in the long run. A poker pro is independent, he has no boss and can organize his life the way he wants, but he can't do whatever he wants and expect to be successful.

I have seen pros that after a while only came into the card room when they needed money. They played until they had won a fixed amount of money. If that took two hours, they were gone after two hours; if it took twelve hours, they played for twelve hours; then they disappeared until their money was gone. For them, going to the card room was like withdrawing money from their bank account. This often works for a while, until their luck changes, and then the roof falls in and their bankroll disappears.

Playing as a middle-limit pro means that you have to put in a fair number of hours to ensure that you have earned a reasonable income at the end of the year. This demands discipline. If you only want to play sporadically, or if you are not willing to play more than 20 hours a month, then playing poker for a living is not for you. Nearly all the successful pros I know are very disciplined when it comes to playing poker—and they have to be. It's their business.

What makes successful pros so damned good?

In an interesting essay, Mason Malmuth treats the question of what separates excellent players from average players. Mason believes that, since a player has only a limited amount of time at his disposal to come to a decision, a quick-thinking player has a significant edge over those who think at more normal speeds[151]. I agree that this makes a difference, but I don't think it is the sole factor, or even the most important one.

Chess is comparable to poker in that a player has a limited time in which to make a move, and that more time leads to better decisions, which are often non-trivial. Given this time limitation, it was first assumed that the ability to consider more moves would be a significant advantage, and that the best players would think more rapidly than their weaker opponents.

Surprisingly, research showed that a world champion like Dr. Max Euwe didn't think faster, nor did he consider more moves. It turned out that world-class chess players are able to more quickly identify potentially good moves[152]. In other words, superior players better understand position and focus quickly on the more promising moves.

I think these results also apply to poker. The very best poker players, and these are mostly pros in middle- and high-limit games, just have a better understanding of situations and thus come up with the best play more often than their lesser opponents in complex situations. Let's look at three examples.

Example 1

This hand took place many years ago in a $10-20 game at the Mirage. A middle-position player limped and I called at the button with Q♠-9♠.

Kenny raised in the big blind, the middle-position player called and I called as well.

---

[151] See Mason Malmuth, *Poker Essays*, 1991, p. 102.
[152] See Adrianus Dingeman de Groot, *Thought and Choice in Chess*, 1978.

That Kenny, a tough pro, had raised out-of-position was bad news for me. I knew I needed help from the flop, and help I got: A♠-Q♥-9♦. Kenny bet out as expected, the middle-position player called and I raised. Kenny made it three bets, the middle-position player, facing a double bet, folded, and I raised again. Now it took Kenny a couple of seconds before he called.

The turn was the 10♣. Kenny checked, I bet and he called. On the river the dealer revealed the K♣ (board: A♠-Q♥-9♦-10♣-K♣). Kenny bet out immediately. I couldn't believe my bad luck. The pot was too big to take any chances, so I called. Before you read on, try to identify Kenny's hand.

Most readers will come up with A-J, and that was exactly the hand I put Kenny on. Well, if it was A-J, the story would have no point. No, Kenny turned over A-K! I hadn't expected to see that hand. I was completely stunned, not because he bet that hand on the end but because he was absolutely sure his hand was best. When he showed that A-K, you could see that he hadn't the slightest doubt that he had turned over the winner. How could he know that I didn't have a jack for the straight or a set?

This hand has been imprinted in my memory because I thought for the first time, wow, this is a great play, this guy knows something I don't know. Having mostly played low-limit, I hadn't felt that way before. When I later analyzed the hand in my room, it wasn't too difficult to see why Kenny did what he did. Let's look at the hand from Kenny's point of view.

His pre-flop play was pretty standard. Two players had just limped, hence he had no reason to believe his hand was not best. Most players would correctly raise here. The key to understanding Kenny's river bet is the flop.

Having flopped top pair, top kicker, Kenny led with a bet. My raise didn't give him much information. I could have a better hand than his, a semi-strong hand like A-x, trying to find out where I stood by raising, or I could be making a free-card play with J-10. Kenny made it three bets for two reasons. First, he thought he very likely had the best hand. Second, by raising, he could probably knock out the middle-position player, adding dead money to the pot. I raised again because I wanted to find out if I had the best hand. Having played with Kenny before, I knew that he would reraise with a better hand (A-A, Q-Q, 9-9, A-Q) but just call otherwise. That's exactly what happened. I got the information I was looking for, but I didn't realize that in doing so, I gave my hand away.

Recall that Kenny briefly paused before acting. He realized immediately that I wouldn't make it four bets if I couldn't beat top pair, top kicker. Then he figured out my hand. Unfortunately for me, that was very easy. I couldn't have a set. I would have raised before the flop with A-A, Q-Q or 9-9. He could rule out A-Q for the same reason. Consequently, the only possible hands I could have were A-9 and Q-9[153]. It was now a simple matter of comparing the pot odds to his chances of winning. The pot odds were 11-to-1, meaning that, excluding future bets, he only had to win more than 8.3% of the time to make the call profitable. Against A-9 he had six outs and a backdoor straight draw; against Q-9 he had five outs on the flop, eight outs on the turn (if I didn't fill up) and a backdoor straight draw. All in all, it was an easy call[154].

The turn brought him some help. The 10♣ gave Kenny seven more outs (4 jacks and 3 tens). With 7-to-1 pot odds, he had nothing to think about; his call was automatic. Before the river card came, Kenny already knew what cards would give him the winning hand. Any king, jack or 10 would do it. With an ace, queen or 9, he might or might not have the best hand. Thus, when the king fell on the end, Kenny knew he was best and bet at once.

Example 2

This is a hand Roy Cooke played in the $20-40 game at the Mirage.

> A very loose woman player—a Vegas local who has lost hundreds of thousands of dollars over the years—raised the pot up front in our $20-$40 hold'em game. The field mucked to me, two to the right of the button. I peeked at my cards and saw two 10s.[155]

From playing before with the lady, Roy knew she would only raise with a big pair (jacks or higher) or A-K. And she played very predictably: she would bet all the way with a big pair, she would not bet the turn if she had A-K and no ace or king had shown up, but she would call with A-K no

---

[153] By the way, the analysis of the hand showed me that it was wrong to just call. I should have raised. That would have made it a lot harder for Kenny to put me on a hand.

[154] The stats are as follows: A-K wins against A-9/Q-9 26.6%, loses 73.0% and ties 0.3%.

[155] Roy Cooke, *Real Poker: The Cooke Collection*, 1999, pp. 78-81; reprinted in Roy Cooke, *Real Poker II: The Play of Hands*, 2001, pp. 85-87.

matter what. And the last important point: the lady never bluffed. Because the turn would define her hand, Roy called with the pocket tens. As the hand played out, the lady had A-K and failed to improve, so Roy won the pot with the pocket tens.

Here is his conclusion:

> While I was lucky that she did in fact hold the A-K and also that she did not make a pair, the pot laid me 170-60 that this event would happen. While this by itself does not make the play correct, if you add up the richness of the scenarios where I sucked out on her when I was beat before the flop, then the combination of all possible outcomes tilted the scales into a bet where I had the best of it.

Without question, if you have a predictable opponent or a player over whom you have good control, then your starting hand can be a little worse because you play better after the flop. The question in the above scenario is: how inferior can your starting hand be and still show a profit? When I read that article for the first time in *Card Player* magazine, I thought Roy had the worst of it. There are 24 combination that give the lady an overpair and only 16 combinations for A-K. It's obvious that Roy is either a big dog or a small favorite, a situation you usually want to avoid.

Rereading the column in his book *Real Poker*, I decided to take a closer look at the problem. A hot-and-cold simulation shows that two tens win about one-third of the time[156]. That means Roy is about a 2-to-1 underdog. If they play the hand three times, Roy will lose on average two times, costing him $60 each time ($40 pre-flop and $20 on the flop; he will fold on the turn). So his total loss is 2×$60 = $120. Now, will Roy win more than $120 in the one time he wins? Yes, indeed he will.

When he wins, the the pot is $170 ($30 from the small and big blind, $40 + $20 + $40 + $40 from the lady, not counting his own investment) for a win of 50 bucks. You might argue that the analysis is not complete; Roy can make a set on the flop or turn, in which case he will collect more money. This is correct. But there are also some bad scenarios. She can suck out on the river (with A-K she has six outs) and if it's set-over-set, Roy always has the worst of it. But all in all, this shows that calling with the tens is clearly

---

[156] The precise results are as follows: 10-10 wins 33.45%, loses 66.14% and ties 0.40%.

correct. At least for me, this was a big surprise. It demonstrates Roy Cooke's playing experience and deep understanding of the game.

Example 3

I observed the following hand in a $30-60 game at the Bellagio. There were three limpers, then the small blind raised, the big blind folded and the limpers all called.

The flop came 2♥-7♥-K♥. The small blind bet, the first limper (middle-position) called, one of the late-position limpers called and the other folded.

Three active players saw the turn: 5♦. The small blind bet, the middle-position player called and the late-position player folded. The small blind and the first limper were now heads-up.

River: A♠ (board: 2♥-7♥-K♥-5♦-A♠). The small blind bet and the middle-position player called. Without delay, the small blind turned over Q♣-Q♠ and the middle position player took the pot with A♥-6♣.

You're probably thinking that the small blind made a bad bet at the end. He can't beat the flush, he can't beat the ace and he can't beat the king. Looks like a –EV play. I would have thought the same thing, but the player in the small blind was Alan. So I did what I always do in such a case: I memorized the hand and analyzed it later in my room.

Until the turn, Alan's play can't be rebuked, though some players would have been more cautious given the dangerous looking board, but that's not Alan's style. Pre-flop, he raised the pot with his pocket queens out of the small blind. With three limpers that had shown no sign of strength, this is clearly the correct play. I sometimes like to just call in this situation for deception reasons (see, e.g., 1/188), but raising is the better play. None of the limpers was a regular or a very good player, another reason to make the straightforward play.

The flop was a mixed bag for Alan. It didn't contain an ace, the most dangerous card for him, but a king and a three-flush were on board. Until you have reason to believe otherwise, you have to assume you have the best hand. Notice that Alan didn't have the queen of hearts. Betting serves two purposes: protecting the hand in case he is ahead and trying to eliminate flush draws. Clearly, no one with a high heart (A♥, Q♥, maybe J♥) would fold, but the last thing you want is to lose to a hand like A♣-4♥ that would

333

have folded to a bet. Alan's flop bet may seem risky, but it was far superior to a check.

The 5♦ on the turn change nothing. There was no reason for Alan to believe he didn't have the best hand. His bet was mandatory. One player called and the other folded. Things looked good so far for Alan. He had eliminated all but one player and very likely had the best hand. If he could avoid an ace or a heart on the end, the pot would likely be his.

The river brought the dreaded ace, but not a heart for Alan. Interestingly he bet out immediately. Seeing his play, I put him on A-A, K-K, A-K, A-Q or a made flush with a hand like A♥-J♥. Alan's bet here was the interesting part of the hand. It looks dubious, but was it really? Let's see.

At the end Alan had just one opponent, a young, loose-aggressive player. What do we know about his hand? Unfortunately, not much. Since he was aggressive but didn't raise pre-flop, it was probably not very good. As a loose player limping from middle position, he could have a wide range of hands. On the flop and turn he just called, which doesn't help us to reduce his range. But we can break down his possible holdings into categories. He could have:

a) a made flush

b) a busted flush

c) a set

d) two pair

e) an ace

f) a king

g) a split pair other than aces or kings

h) a pocket pair

We can rule out cases a), c), d) and f). An aggressive player would have raised along the way with a made flush, case a). The same is true for case c). A set is a very strong hand even with this dangerous looking board. You have either the best hand or a very good draw in case somebody has made a flush. Every aggressive player would raise here with a set. There is no way Alan's opponent could have flopped two pair, case d). This player was loose, but not so loose as to play K-7, K-2 or 7-2. The turn could have made him two pair, but that's very unlikely (7-5 probably being the only possible hand). I think he would have raised in this case. Therefore aces up at the end is the only real threat. But I doubt he would have played the hand differently from case e), a single pair of aces. We can rule out case f) because with a pair of kings our young friend would have raised on the flop to see if his hand was good.

If Alan's opponent had an ace, case e), it would make no difference if Alan bet or checked. If Alan bet, he would call and Alan would lose that bet (and the pot). That's what actually happened. If Alan had decided to check, his opponent would instantly realize that the ace kept him from betting. The logical conclusion would be that Alan couldn't beat a pair of aces, thus his opponent would bet his ace. With 9-to-1 pot odds, Alan couldn't risk being bluffed out of the pot. His call was automatic.

Now, let's look at case b). What should Alan do if his opponent holds a busted flush draw like Q♥-J♦? He should check, of course! Betting is pointless since his opponent cannot call. By checking, there is a chance that Alan can induce a bluff.

We can treat cases g) and h) as one. In each case Alan's opponent has flopped a pair with a hand like 8♠-7♠, or has a pocket pair like 8-8 or 6-6. With just one big card on the flop (K♥) he decided that his hand might be best, since he could beat some legitimate hands Alan would have raised with, such as A-Q or A-Js. Maybe he had a small heart with his pair (for instance, 8♥-8♣) that made him think he could have additional outs in case he was beat. Because the turn didn't change anything, he had to call again. The ace at the end posed a problem. There were hardly any hands left that Alan could have that he could beat—maybe Q♦-J♦. Nonetheless, the pot was large, so it's not unrealistic that Alan might get a call if he bet. What did that all mean for Alan? If he checked, his opponent would gladly check behind. If he bet, his opponent could give him a crying call due to the size of the pot. Therefore, Alan should have bet in cases g) and h) because checking didn't achieve anything.

Let's now summarize our findings. It made a difference if Alan checked or bet in three cases: b), g) and h). One time a check was better; two times it was better to bet. It's now a matter of weighing up which was more likely, that he lost or that he won an additional bet. In my opinion, Alan was slightly more likely to get a desperation call in cases g) and h) than to lose a bet in case b). Although Alan's opponent was aggressive, most players intuitively understand that it's not a good situation in which to bluff with a busted flush. Alan showed a lot of strength before the river, hence he must have had something. The ace on the river might have restrained him from betting, but not from calling, because the pot was simply too big.

Admittedly, the difference between checking and calling is miniscule. But these small differences in the quality of play add up, and the sum is what separates a good to very good player from an excellent player like Alan.

Let's see what these three examples tell us about the difference between excellent pros and lesser players:

♠ Time indeed plays a role. Given enough time, a good player will usually come up with the right play and understand the reason behind it. At the table, such a player often lacks the time to see through complex situations. But this does not mean that he is not thinking fast enough.

♠ What distinguishes excellent players from their weaker opponents is not that they think faster. They understand complex situations better, enabling them to quickly steer their thinking in the right direction.

♠ Excellent players are far more likely to bet when a scare card falls (see examples 1 and 3). Weaker players nearly always check in these situations and hope that their hand is best.

♠ Excellent players push small edges even if it increases their standard deviation (see example 3). They often find slightly better alternatives to the obvious play.

♠ Excellent players think one level above their lesser opponents (see example 1), enabling them to make seemingly surprising plays.